A REBELLIOUS PEOPLE

A Book of the Basques
by Rodney Gallop
In A Hundred Graves:
A Basque Portrait
by Robert Laxalt
Basque Nationalism
by Stanley G. Payne
Amerikanuak:
Basques in the New World
*by William A. Douglass
and Jon Bilbao*
Beltran: Basque Sheepman of
the American West
*by Beltran Paris, as told to
William A. Douglass*
The Basques: The Franco Years
and Beyond
by Robert P. Clark
The Witches' Advocate:
Basque Witchcraft and the
Spanish Inquisition
(1609–1614)
by Gustav Henningsen
Navarra: The Durable Kingdom
by Rachel Bard

THE BASQUE SERIES

CYRUS ERNESTO ZIRAKZADEH

A Rebellious

UNIVERSITY OF NEVADA PRESS

BASQUES, PROTESTS, AND POLITICS

RENO AND LAS VEGAS

Basque Series Editor: William A. Douglass

Jacket artwork is by Qijano, from *ihabla tú Gernika!*
(copyright 1977 La Gran Enciclopedia Vasca, Bilbao).

The paper used in this book meets the requirements of American
National Standard for Information Sciences—Permanence of
Paper for Printed Library Materials, ANSI Z39.48-1984. Binding
materials were chosen for strength and durability.

Library of Congress Cataloging-in-Publication Data

Zirakzadeh, Cyrus Ernesto. 1951–
  A rebellious people : Basques, protests, and politics / by Cyrus
Ernesto Zirakzadeh.
      p.   cm. — (The Basque series)
  Includes bibliographical references and index.
  ISBN 0-87417-173-3 (cloth : alk. paper)
  1. País Vasco (Spain)—Politics and government—20th century.
2. Violence—Spain—País Vasco—History—20th century.   3. País
Vasco (Spain)—Economic conditions.   4. País Vasco (Spain)—
Social conditions.   5. Euzko-Alderdi Jeltzalia.   6. ETA
(Organization)
I. Title.   II. Series.
DP302.B53Z57   1991
946'.608—dc20   91-2185
                                                                      CIP

University of Nevada Press, Reno, Nevada 89557 USA
Copyright © University of Nevada Press 1991.
All Rights Reserved
Designed by Kaelin Chappell
Printed in the United States of America

9   8   7   6   5   4   3   2   1

FOR BARBARA

CONTENTS

ACKNOWLEDGMENTS

Many friends, teachers, and colleagues thoughtfully read and commented on this manuscript, which began several years ago as a prospectus for a doctoral thesis. I am especially grateful to Giuseppe Di Palma (my dissertation advisor), Ernst Haas, Hanna Pitkin, Michael Rogin, Michael McCann, George Shulman, Joseph White, John Kautsky, William Caspery, William A. Douglass, J. Garry Clifford, Betty Seaver, everyone in the Berkeley chapter of the Caucus for a New Political Science, and the editors and anonymous reviewers for the University of Nevada Press. The late Margaret Shedd, a novelist and dear friend, played a key role in stimulating my interest in Basque politics and society. Fellowships from the Danforth Foundation, the University of California at Berkeley, and the University of Connecticut helped finance research and writing.

Debts to my family must be acknowledged. I could not have completed this project without the encouragement and support of my mother and late father, Refugio Flores and Aboulghassem Zirakzadeh. Barbara Louise Macy Zirakzadeh spent many hours listening to my ideas, reading drafts, and helping me clarify my arguments. She also somehow found time to work outside our house and support the family during those bleak graduate-student years. Our energetic children, Vanessa and Daniel, provided me with *many* healthy distractions from writing. Sometimes during their own early adventures in writing, they discussed with me the disappointments and exhilarations and frustrations of being an author, and their comments were very insightful. I am lucky to have them as friends.

INTRODUCTION

Much of what has been written about Basque politics in English-speaking countries during the past two decades is very limited in scope. It focuses narrowly on armed struggle and says little about interest groups, unions, or nonviolent social movements. Certainly reports in the *New York Times*, the *Christian Science Monitor*, and the *Los Angeles Times* emphasize terrorism of one kind or another.[1] And when describing politics in the Basque region, even respected scholars in the United States and Great Britain often implicitly condense their descriptions to acts of violence.

Gordon Smith, in his introductory textbook about contemporary European politics, writes that Basque politics "conforms exactly to the extremist model" of "a swift progression from protest and disruption to violence and fervent terrorism," and says little else about the nature of Basque politics.[2] Stanley Payne declares that Basque politics involves an unusually high amount of "shrillness and extremism" in addition to "the most lethal terrorist offensive in the Western world."[3] He fails to comment at any length on nonshrill, nonextreme, and nonlethal political activity by Basque residents. Juan Linz writes:

> The Basque situation is unique in the sense that consociational arrangements had to be worked out in the face of continuous terrorist activity, attacks on the legitimacy of the participants in the political process, and domination of the street by activist groups and violent youth.[4]

He further generalizes that the Basque region is "a society in crisis," and that it suffers from a "downward spiral of frustration, polarization, conflict, and violence."[5] For all three scholars, violence seems to be the sine qua non of politics in the Basque region.

Viewing violence as a central element of Basque politics, journalists and scholars usually rely on an implicit social theory to explain the phenomenon. The theory is a variant on a paradigm in the social sciences about the inevitable breakdown of traditional and preindustrial societies, and the emotional disturbances that tend to surface in its wake. The logic of this paradigm, as it is applied to the Basque case, runs roughly as follows. During the Francoist decades, the rural characteristics of the Basque region, in which small property holders and neighborliness had been common, rapidly disappeared. Large cities, scientifically run businesses, enormous and impersonal worksites, and geographically and socially mobile populations proliferated. Many Basques came to feel socially isolated, disoriented, culturally odd and quaint, and unfairly disrespected by workers immigrating from other parts of Spain. Such unsettling anxieties and emotions are alleged to have prompted those with small-town backgrounds to lash out physically at the symbols of modern society, police officers and industrialists among them, and to harm innocent persons for no obvious reason. By narrowly utilitarian criteria—such as profit maximization or overcoming immediate economic hardships—the acts certainly are irrational. But in terms of reducing levels of personal frustration and resolving an acute sense of shame, they are sociologically and psychologically understandable.[6]

Further, many scholars and journalists maintain that the political violence in the Basque region is the work of only a small minority, primarily those who in addition to being socially frustrated believe fervently in a loosely coherent ideology that is articulated frequently by leaders of the Basque Nationalist party. This ideology, in the opinion of most scholars, is fundamentally antimodern and pastoralist. It rejects modern industry and urban living, and urges restoration of preindustrial forms of production and prebureaucratic values and life-styles. According to Linz, the formal ideology of the Basque Nationalist party typifies "the puritanism of communal protest we find in some of the teetotaler movements of rural liberalism in northern Europe."[7] It is substantively a so-called populist ideology that celebrates the security of the small, stable community and the intimacy of the petite bourgeois family, and is said to evoke in its followers "a moralistic fervor, an opposition to cosmopolitan corrupting influences, not too different from some prohibitionist ruralist movements against bourgeois-urban society."[8] It is, in short, a highly nostalgic ideology that can attract the socially displaced and easily reinforce their natural hostilities to modern, industrial society.

Most scholars and journalists who write for English-speaking audiences also generally avoid attributing political violence in the Basque region to either economic grievances or concrete class interest. They usually note that the levels of economic production and of per capita consumption are measurably higher there than in other parts of Spain. So material deprivation seems an unlikely explanation for the unusually high level of violence in the Basque region in comparison to other regions of Spain. They also often assert that recent political violence in the region has demonstrably disrupted, not enhanced, local economic activity. Given these consequences, economic grievances and concerns cannot plausibly be at the root of the political violence. If one must identify a single set of factors as "the cause" of recent political violence, the process of rapid social change, the sudden disappearance of small-town and preindustrial society, and the subsequent, widespread feelings of social dislocation offer a more satisfactory explanation.[9]

Scholars and journalists not infrequently couple this hypothesis about rapid social change and intense frustration with another line of reasoning that relates to the responsiveness of the Spanish political system. It is a variant of a well-known perspective in contemporary social science, commonly known as pluralism. Of course, pluralism is a protean term that can refer to a variety of political and analytic perspectives.[10] For purposes of this study, pluralism refers to a belief in the existence of "pluralist" political systems in which (1) no cohesive group monopolizes political power within a society, (2) political resources are so widely distributed among the major groups that any group intensely concerned about the outcome of a particular policy decision can be assured that its interests will be considered by government officials, and (3) government elites respond neutrally to the demands of all groups and do not consistently favor a particular interest or group.[11] When discussing the political significance of political violence in the Basque region, most journalists and scholars in English-speaking countries adopt a pluralistic interpretation of the Spanish political system. That is, they assert (but usually without systematic presentation of evidence) that the system, at least since

1977, has been generally responsive to policy demands made by all major groups in the society.[12]

The pluralist interpretation of Spanish politics contributes to a negative characterization of Basque political violence. Because of the supposed openness of the system, the violence appears not only morally repugnant and economically irrational but also politically irresponsible. After all, how can it be reasonable or responsible to harm people or property when government officials respond without bias to peaceful forms of political dissent, petition, and consultation? Moreover, might not constant acts of violence ultimately destabilize Spain's pluralist system—for example, by arousing citizens' and government officials' fears for their safety, thereby encouraging backlashes in kind, states of emergency, and even preemptive coups?

Here I will call the foregoing cluster of ideas and themes—about political violence, the passing of traditional society, historically nostalgic ideologies, the threats to Spanish pluralism, and economic and political irrationality—the modernization interpretation of Basque politics. This interpretation seems to be the currently dominant mode of analyzing Basque politics. It also seems to be an intellectually powerful interpretation, for it identifies what is judged to be a worldwide trend toward mechanized production, large cities, and bureaucratically organized workplaces as the root cause of political violence in the Basque region, and thereby enables a comparison of political events in the Basque Country with political conflicts in other rapidly modernizing regions and/or countries. Finally, the modernization interpretation is in many ways a partisan view of Basque politics: it tends indiscriminately to represent participants in all disruptive actions (and not just incidents of violence) as economically irrational, politically irresponsible, and socially reactionist, while portraying established political institutions and government officials in a much more favorable light.[13]

THE CLASSICAL MODEL OF
SOCIAL MOVEMENTS AND ITS CRITICS

The use of the modernization interpretation in scholarly studies of Basque politics is not entirely fortuitous. The interpretation draws upon a number of theoretical conventions commonly found in social science. In addition, its general logic is compatible with a method of analyzing social movements that, from the 1940s through the 1970s, has enjoyed hegemony within U.S. political science and political sociology.

Doug McAdam has designated this highly influential analytic tradition "the classical model of social movements."[14] The model, he declares, combines two causal hypotheses. The first involves a relationship between an individual's psychological experiences and large-scale social changes such as secularization, industrialization, commercialization of the economy, and urbanization. McAdam notes that scholars who have developed different versions of the classical model, such as Kornhauser's Mass Society theory of social movements or Davies's J-Curve theory of revolution, differ in the types of large-scale social change that they emphasize. But the various theoretical formulations share the proposition that there is some type of large-scale social change—say, rapid urbanization—that creates unusually intense psychological discomfort within individuals. The discomfort has been variously described as "heightened anxiety," "frustration," "alienation," "anomie," "stress," and/or "tension."

The second hypothesis is that once a person's psychological discomfort rises to a certain level, he or she is internally pushed into extrainstitutional forms of political participation that may involve confrontationalist tactics and unruly behavior toward other groups in the polity. Groups that engage in such extrainstitutional activities are often called social movements. It is held that people join social movements not because of reasoned decisions about how best to effect long-term change, but because the movements' extrainstitutional activities give promise of ameliorating their discomfort. In the words of one theorist, "Mass movements are not looking for pragmatic solutions to economic or any other kind of problem. If they were so oriented, their emotional fervor and chiliastic zeal . . . would not characterize the psychological tone of these movements. In order to account for this tone, we must look beyond economic interest to deep seated psychological tendencies."[15]

The classical model, as described by McAdam and others (see figure 1.1), has been criticized by growing numbers of scholars on several grounds. One apparent problem involves the hypothesis that the acute psychological pain, which is induced by macrosociological change, leads directly to movement activity. Critics maintain that the

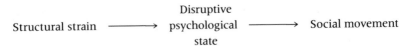

Figure 1.1. Classical Model.
Source: Doug McAdam, *Political Process and the Development of Black Insurgency, 1930–1970* (Chicago: University of Chicago Press, 1982), p. 7.

vast majority of scientific attempts to measure and correlate levels of social change and pain with levels of movement activism show no statistically significant relationship. Movements sometimes appear during periods of rapid social change, but often do not. Aldon Morris and Cedric Herring are typical of critics when declaring, "There is little empirical support for the claim that movements emerge from conditions of structural breakdown and social or psychological strain accompanying rapid change and catastrophe."[16]

A second common criticism involves the proposition that people who engage in movements are unconcerned with effecting social change and achieving tangible goals; their primary purpose is simply to reduce psychological strain. Critics contend, again, that the evidence is not there. Interviews, memoirs, and declarations of purpose suggest that participants in movement activities such as sit-down strikes and the civil rights movement's "jail-ins" are no less concerned about tangible goals than people who engage in institutionalized forms of politics, such as serving on school boards or campaigning for parties. Michael Rogin, for example, concedes that cranks and narrow-minded people sometimes participate in social movements, but he emphasizes that it is unwise to generalize about the psychology of movements on the basis of a few individuals, given the amount of information suggesting instrumental reasoning.[17]

Finally, several political sociologists have decried the classical model for its silence about the institutional context of political action. According to Doug McAdam, Maurice Pinard, Charles Tilly, and Sandor Halebsky, people are embedded in a wide array of formal and informal institutions—churches, schools, unions, professional associations, neighborhoods, friendship networks—that greatly influence perceptions and actions. Hence, any satisfactory explanation for the emergence of a social movement must take into account institutional influences on expressions of grievance. To try to explain political behavior independent of the intermediate social context is self-evidently preposterous.[18]

The modernization interpretation of Basque political violence, which emphasizes the psychological pain created by rapid modernization and explains violence in terms of the political channeling of that pain, appears to be an heir of the classical model of social movements. Like the classical model, the modernization view emphasizes macrosociological change and personal feelings, and neglects the local institutionalized settings.[19] Furthermore, it interprets the psychological condition that leads to violence as largely nonrational in terms of the systematic pursuit of tangible goals.

To the extent that the modernization interpretation of Basque politics implicitly borrows and relies upon the causal logic of the classical model, it seems to be open to the common criticisms of that model: (1) it asserts rather than demonstrates that social strain and the emotional strain it is said to produce were the primary causes of political violence, (2) it ignores the social-institutional context of the political violence, and (3) it asserts rather than demonstrates the non-rationality of movement participants. Indeed, a reading of essays by Linz, Payne, Juan Pablo Fusi, and other prominent writers on Basque politics suggests that these shortcomings are prevalent in current academic research on Basque politics. For example, the literature reveals a striking lack of appropriate documentation about the alleged "extreme" and anomic psychologies of Basque guerrillas.[20] And there are surprisingly few words about the local institutional contexts.

DIFFERENT QUESTIONS, DIFFERENT THEORIES?

Although I am generally sympathetic to the critiques of the classical model advanced by McAdam, Halebsky, Rogin, and others, and although I think their critiques are relevant to how Basque politics is currently being depicted in English-speaking countries, I believe that the modernization interpretation has utility in accounting for specific aspects of Basque political violence. For example, the modernization interpretation is useful in accounting for why the violence has largely been the work of self-defined nationalist organizations (in contrast to, say, groups with social-democratic or liberal-democratic ideologies). The interpretation also offers an initially plausible explanation of why those who engage in violent actions come disproportionately from small towns and semirural areas.

The modernization interpretation, however, seems less useful in explaining other characteristics of Basque political violence. For example, although the modernization interpretation helps one understand how some regionwide, macrosociological sources of intense stress may have provoked violence, it does not explain why relatively few self-defined nationalists and nationalist organizations engaged in violence while most nationalists and nationalist organizations did not. If the macrosociological sources of stress were almost everywhere and not in a few atypical towns and/or villages, why did only a few hundred of the region's tens of thousands of nationalist activists and sympathizers directly engage in violence?

Nor does the modernization interpretation greatly help one understand the temporality of Basque armed actions. As Robert Clark has noted, killings and kidnappings by Basque nationalist groups were almost nonexistent before 1970, were modest between 1970 and 1975, escalated sharply between 1975 and 1980, and then significantly declined.[21] If the rapid rate of modernization was presumably steady during this time, why did the yearly levels of violence fluctuate? Exploration of additional factors seems necessary to answer the question.

Finally, the modernization interpretation, unless supplemented by additional causal factors, seems unable to account for certain characteristics of the victims of violence. Allegedly, antimodern anger, caused both by rapid rates of social change and by local nationalist-populist doctrines, led in the Basque region to privately motivated attacks on available representatives of modern society. Not all possible representatives of modern society became targets, however. Military and law-enforcement officers and government officials accounted for 76 percent of the fatalities. Owners of large businesses accounted for 71 percent of all kidnap victims. Other residents with distinctively modern social roles (social scientists, medical technicians, and computer scientists, for example) were largely ignored.[22] Why the skewed selection of targets?

The analyst of Basque political violence apparently needs to consider more factors than those put forward by the modernization interpretation. This does not mean that the modernization interpretation should be discarded. An explanatory theory's adequacy is largely dependent on which of the innumerable aspects of reality interests a particular analyst.[23] No single theory can explain *every* aspect of

Basque armed attacks—for example, the time of day of attacks, the organizational division of labor by sex, the age of the attackers, the press interpretations, and the government's response. There are some aspects—such as the relatively small size of the communities whence the attackers hail—that the modernization interpretation renders understandable. But there are other aspects that seem to demand additional perspectives.

TOWARD A NEW INTERPRETATION OF BASQUE POLITICS

This book is a reinterpretation of the evolution of Basque political violence since the late 1960s. It is inspired in part by the growing criticisms of the classical model of social movements. It is also inspired by curiosity over certain aspects of Basque political violence—say, its temporality—that the modernization interpretation seems unable to explain satisfactorily. And on an "existential" level, it is inspired by my fieldwork in the region, where I discovered forms of popular politics, such as neighborhood activism, not mentioned in the conventional accounts; and public issues, such as economic displacement, not seriously discussed as possible motivations for political violence.

The book views Basque political violence as not solely a consequence of intense nostalgia generated by rapid social change. It was also a consequence of strategic choices by a set of political activists enduring economic crises who believed they could launch a spontaneous social revolution from below through the calculated use of violence. The hope of ending (or at least greatly reducing) economic suffering, of course, does not absolve the activists of moral responsibility for their acts. Murder and kidnapping, even when undertaken for purportedly humanitarian ends, are still murder and kidnapping. But this book modifies the current modernization interpretation by emphasizing the purposefulness and intended effectiveness behind violent acts, and raising questions about the material interests, local social institutions, and theoretical reasoning that led to the violence.

This book expands upon most accounts informed by the current modernization interpretation in three ways. First, unlike the modernization interpretation, it denies that the economic backdrop of the violence was primarily prosperity. It argues, instead, that particular classes and economic sectors were suffering greatly during the late 1950s, 1960s, and 1970s, and that alleviation thereof had motivated some radicals to armed action. Granted, there were some radical nationalists who solely wanted to protect, and if possible revive, older cultural practices, such as the use of indigenous dialects in everyday life, but they seldom endorsed armed action and organizationally separated themselves from its advocates once it became clear that the latter intended to act on their beliefs.

Stated differently, whereas most current writings in English on Basque politics view political violence primarily in terms of cultural disruption and anxiety, this book places considerably more emphasis on local economic disruption and dislocation. It adopts what might be called an *economic view of modernization,* in which capitalist development creates new problems (job obsolescence, business cycles, impersonal relations at work) that producers and consumers must cope with.

Even these explicitly economic motivations, however, did not lead directly to armed action. Local and short-term political circumstances—including the rise of nonviolent rural protest, the militancy of labor unions, and the infighting and alliance building within the Basque Nationalist party—affected the decisions of local political activists. Local social and political struggles, some of which arose in response to rapid capitalist development, facilitated the use of violence in three analytically distinguishable ways: by providing the organizational resources, such as publicity, that the advocates of violence needed to implement their strategy; by inducing optimism among many younger nationalists about the potential for an uprising by the entire people against capitalism and the Spanish state; and by providing innovative social arrangements that some younger nationalists enthusiastically perceived as models for a new postcapitalist society.

Finally, this book argues that the decision by groups of political activists to resort to violence resulted not only from economic grievances and concerns and a conducive set of grass-roots struggles but from influential formal ideologies, often developed abroad, that suggested how best to achieve a social and political revolution. Although one might want (perhaps with good reason) to characterize ideologically derived actions as simplistic, misinformed, and/or immoral, it seems that strategic calculations were made and that they fused with strong emotions. The decision to engage in armed action cannot be understood by looking at passions and grievances alone.

In these three ways, then—by emphasizing (1) the existence of economic problems, (2) the indirect effects of other, largely nonviolent local political and social struggles, and (3) the informing role of formal ideologies—the present study complements current thinking about political conflict in the Basque region. It is worth stressing again that this book does not attribute the violence of Basque politics to economic disruption and dislocation alone. Not one but a combination of *three* sets of factors—economic, political, and ideological—contributed to the emergence (and later decline) of political violence between 1965 and 1980.

INTELLECTUAL INFLUENCES

No study is ever developed in intellectual isolation. Certainly, many writers, books, and schools of theorizing have influenced the argument presented here.

One strong influence is the vast historical literature on the interplay between political conflict and rapid capitalist and industrial development. Karl Polanyi, E. P. Thompson, Eric Hobsbawm, Hannah Arendt, Charles Maier, Lawrence Goodwyn, and Adam Ulam, among others, have shown how economic and political history can intertwine in subtle, complex, yet significant ways.[24] None of the above authors is an economic reductionist, saying that economic change explains all facets of politics. But all the aforementioned authors are partially economic determinists, arguing that how goods are produced and consumed profoundly influences political behavior and conduct, and vice versa.

A second influence is a tradition in U.S. political sociology commonly known as "collective-action" theorizing, which began to achieve prominence in the late 1970s.[25] This approach involved seeing public acts of disruption—for example, sit-ins, food riots, and sit-down strikes—not simply as direct expressions of discontent, but also as calculated and imitative behavior. It is argued that disruptive acts are never totally novel but are extensions and adaptations of known ways of protecting interests. Collective-action theorists maintain that any act of resistance is part of a long chain of calculated imitations, what is sometimes called the local protesters' "repertoire of actions." "Like inventions in the usual sense, items of repertoire may remain in use simply because no one can think of something better."[26] The researcher's task is, in part, to uncover the precedents.

In addition, collective-action theorists argue that disruptive groups often first receive resources—material and ideological—from less militant social groups in the vicinity.[27] These resources include meeting places, communication networks, potential recruits, symbols and slogans, and even lists of grievances. The substance of what is given influences not only what the disrupters can materially attempt but also, on a more cognitive level, what they desire and expect. Even highly militant groups are thus indirectly imprinted by their often far less militant predecessors.

A third feature of collective-action theorizing involves the broader political system.[28] Collective-action theorists lean toward a utilitarian viewpoint when thinking about tactics and strategies. They hold that people becoming politically active for the sake of a particular goal tend to travel the path of least resistance: activists do not violently challenge elites unless it appears to be the only feasible course. Violence is chosen only if other known, more legalistic methods have been proved unsuccessful and if there are known models of armed action successfully influencing elites. Further, once armed action has been chosen as a tactic, it will be jettisoned either if nonviolent action suddenly appears more effective or if the current armed action appears ineffective and counterproductive (for example, because of the effectiveness of the state's police forces). Violence is seldom purely an expression of hatred or purely a vent for private frustration; it has an instrumental dimension, tied to the workings of the broader political system.

Many collective-action theorists further argue that observation of spirited protest by contemporary groups can embolden and energize observers who are normally politically timid and quiescent despite deeply felt grievances. This seems especially true during periods of generalized protest, in which there is "heightened conflict across the social system: not only in industrial relations, but in the streets; not only there but in the villages or in the schools."[29] If disruption of "normal" peaceful political dealings is not limited to one or two issue areas but involves numerous and disparate social groups, hope and militancy spontaneously spread. Frequently, aggrieved but despairing populations come to believe that their situations can be changed, and they act accordingly—a process one collective-action theorist terms "cognitive liberation."[30]

This book uses the above-mentioned ideas and logic of collective-action theorists to understand characteristics of ETA (an acronym for Euzkadi ta Askatasuna, or Basque Homeland and Freedom), the Basque revolutionary movement whose followers perpetuated most of the killings and kidnappings by nongovernmental groups in the Basque region from the late 1960s through the late 1980s. In some ways ETA resembled the U.S. "New Left" of the 1960s and early 1970s, which eventually contained some groups oriented toward armed action but originally was composed almost entirely of nonviolent groups. Because ETA can be used in at least two ways—as a shorthand for a very loose coalition of revolutionary groups desiring political independence and social revolution for the Basque region, and as shorthand for only those groups that engaged in armed struggle[31]—establishment of a standardized definition seems wise. Therefore, as used in this study, *ETA* and *the ETA movement* will refer to all Basque political groups whose existence was inspired largely by some or all of the ideals articulated during the early 1960s by a small clandestine Basque nationalist study group known as ETA. Specific groups that engaged in armed action will not be called ETA but will be given more specific names, for example, the Berezi commandos.

Drawing upon the theoretical framework of collective-action scholars, this study considers how contemporary traditions of non-elite protest and political opportunities to contest the regime affected the goals, timing, and targets of political violence and the strategic evolution of the ETA movement. The book argues that ongoing struggles between the government and dissatisfied social groups provided members of ETA with issues to address, real and imagined proletarian allies, organizational resources, and a sense of revolutionary possibility. It also argues (a slight departure from the collective-action approach) that international events and intellectual developments, such as the appearance of national liberation movements in Third World countries and the development of New Left theories of proletarian resistance in Western Europe, shaped how activists in ETA assessed their own political situation and strategic options. Last, it argues that the changing status of political liberties in Spain, such as the legalization of neighborhood associations in the 1960s and the legalization of trade unions and political parties in the 1970s, had great bearing on the tactics and strategies that participants in the ETA movement adopted in any year.

A final intellectual influence to be discussed is the work of Robert P. Clark.[32] His writings since 1979 have emphasized the purposeful dimension of Basque politics, the constant reevaluation of goals and strategies by nationalists and nationalist groups, and how changes in legal rights and government antiterrorist policies have led to tactical and strategic adjustments among etarras. Broad generalizations about abnormal psychological stress are seldom made in his work. Instead, he tries to represent the instrumental, pragmatic, and calculated nature of Basque politics. Although Clark does not publicly discuss his theoretical framework and perhaps does not interpret the relationship between social science theory and social science research the way I do, his empirical findings are generally compatible with the type of research attempted by collective-action theorists. Helping me see Basque politics in a new light, Clark's writings provided a springboard for the current study.

ORGANIZATION OF THE BOOK

This book is organized into three parts. The first, which has four chapters, examines economic change and social protest in the Basque region. Chapter 1 describes some of the economic conditions and concerns that gave rise to local social movements during the 1960s and 1970s. Chapter 2 describes various incidents of rural protest during the late Francoist and early post-Francoist years. Chapter 3 sketches the complex history of proletarian politics in the Basque region—especially the evolution of factory juries and factory assemblies during the late 1960s and early 1970s. Chapter 4 focuses on the novel urban-neighborhood association movement that flourished during the final decade of the Francoist regime, and then languished.

The book's second part, which has two chapters, deals with ideological and political currents within the Basque Nationalist party. Chapter 5 asks "were the Nationalists antimodern?" by noting the multiple social bases of support during the 1970s for the party's program of regional autonomy. Chapter 6 describes the historical evolution of two very different social and political ideological traditions—one pro-rapid capitalist industrialization and one anti-rapid industrialization—within the party.

The final part, which again has two chapters, treats the ideological evolution and organizational fragmentation of ETA during the 1960s and 1970s. The chapters focus on etarras' diverse and changing views about armed struggle and on the frequent overt struggles within the movement, partly over violence as a political method. Chapter 7 looks at the evolution of social goals and political strategies within ETA prior to the first widespread public demonstrations of support for ETA, the Burgos trial of 1970. Three broad ideological-political traditions are delineated: a cultural nonviolent tradition inspired largely by aspects of the Basque Nationalist party; a militant but largely nonviolent industrial-struggle tradition informed by contemporary Basque labor politics and inspired by New Left ideas in Western Europe; and a tradition of violence, inspired in part by contemporary National Liberation movements and theories in Cuba and Algeria. Chapter 8 looks at the dualistic change in ETA's strategies and activities since the Burgos trial: the sharp escalation in armed attacks between 1975 and 1980, and the simultaneously increasing use of electoral and trade-union opportunities by former etarras.

The book's eight chapters substantiate that there is much more to Basque politics than acts of violence fueled by feelings of anomie and by an antimodern populist ideology. There are also numerous economic problems and concerns, a context of nonviolent political struggles and social movements, and diverse social and political ideologies informing deliberations about (and reconsiderations of) strategy. These specific dimensions of Basque politics, generally ignored by current writings in English,[33] are the study's foci.

EVIDENCE

The information presented in this study comes from three general sources: (1) the primary literature about Basque politics, such as speeches, manifestos, election platforms, and memoirs, written and spoken by political actors themselves; (2) the secondary literature about Basque politics written principally by scholars, journalists, and novelists that is available in the United States; and (3) three months of field research that included open-ended interviews with more than seventy local party activists, neighborhood officers, and labor leaders.[34]

The Basque Studies Program at the University of Nevada, Reno, provided me with an abundance of primary and secondary literature, including the major newsletters and periodicals published by components of ETA. I located additional secondary literature at the University of California, Berkeley, which has an extensive collection of Spanish books, newspapers, and newsmagazines.

Field research occurred in the summer of 1980. The late novelist Margaret Shedd wrote letters of introduction for me to a half dozen political activists in the Basque region, and suggested hotels, bars, and restaurants where I might meet other activists. Largely by means of these initial contacts, the number of my acquaintances in the region quickly multiplied, ranging from a dues-paying but largely nonactive member of the Basque Nationalist party to its president, Xabier Arzallus. I interviewed representatives and members of the Spanish Workers' Socialist party (PSOE), the Spanish Communist party (PCE), the Communist party of Euskadi (PCE-EKP), the International Communist League (LKI), the Basque Left (EE), the Popular Revolutionary Socialist party (HASI), the Basque Nationalist party (PNV), the Union of the Democratic Center (UCD), the Union of the People of Navarre (UPN), the Workers' Commissions (CCOO), the General Workers' Union (UGT), the Basque Workers' Solidarity (ELA-STV), and the National Confederation of Labor (CNT). I also met and talked with activists in the neighborhood associations and several former members of ETA, who had belonged to the movement before some of its subgroups had fully engaged in armed action.

I have used the interviews largely as checks on my interpretive readings of written material. Almost all the arguments in this book are based on sources (books, magazines, library holdings of pamphlets, and so on) in the public domain. Only in the chapter on neighborhood associations (chapter 4) do I extensively cite interviews; this is because published scholarly studies on the subject are few, and hence interviews must serve as one of the primary sources of data.

CHAPTER ONE

THE ECONOMIC CONTEXT OF
BASQUE POLITICS

To understand Basque politics during the 1960s, 1970s, and early 1980s, it is useful to become familiar with local economic conditions, which may have shaped political issues and concerns. At first glance this appears an easy task, for in comparison with other parts of Spain, the Basque region seems a place of few economic worries. During the past forty years the annual per capita gross product and per capita disposable income have consistently been among the highest in Spain.[1] And if one looks at consumer indices—say, percentages of homes with indoor plumbing or with television sets—the region again seems well set.[2]

Some observers—among them, Stanley Payne, Juan Linz, Vernon Bogdanor, Walter Laqueur, and Walker Connor—minimize the role of economic concerns in fueling Basque politics.[3] Life is comfortable in the region, at least by Iberian standards. Noting relatively high income levels, Linz writes, "in the Basque case, Marxist theories of 'internal colonialism' and non-Marxist theories of relative deprivation are inapplicable."[4] Laqueur similarly declares that economic grievances probably are not significant motivators of political unrest in the Basque provinces because they "have traditionally been among the richest and most developed parts of Spain."[5]

Comparisons of average income and average levels of spending cannot tell us everything about the economic conditions of a people, however. Inequalities in the distribution of scarce resources remain hidden. So, too, do displacements of particular products and methods

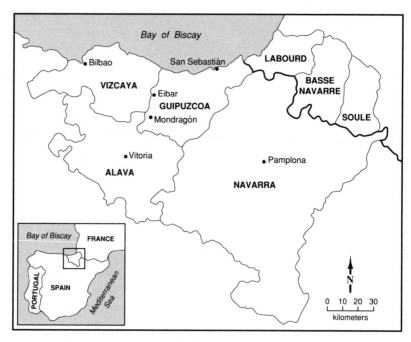

Map 1.1. The Basque region (Euskadi).

of production, and corresponding job loss. When such phenomena are considered, economic pressures on local political life become more evident.

ECONOMIC GEOGRAPHY

The Spanish Basque region lies in northern Spain, where the Pyrenees meet the Bay of Biscay. Nationalists call their country *Euskadi* and see its borders extending into France. According to most Basque nationalists, three provinces in France and four in Spain compose Euskadi. Its area is roughly equal to that of New Jersey.

On a political map, the Spanish Basque region is triangularly shaped, its base a sixty-mile-long coastline on the Bay of Biscay (see map 1.1). The predominant commercial centers are the coastal cities of Bilbao and San Sebastián and the inland cities of Pamplona and Vitoria. Bilbao and San Sebastián are also the capitals of the region's two most populous and heavily industrialized provinces, Vizcaya and Guipúzcoa. Pamplona and Vitoria are the capitals of Navarra and Alava, two inland, largely rural provinces that underwent rapid industrialization during the late 1950s and 1960s. The Bilbao metropolitan area has about 800,000 inhabitants. San Sebastián, Pamplona, and Vitoria each has between 100,000 and 200,000 inhabitants.[6]

The coast is quite hilly and has several natural harbors. The Cantabrian Mountains lie less than ten miles inland, parallel to the coast, and abut the Pyrenees. Here, the land is extremely uneven, with steep, narrow valleys and fast-flowing rivers. South of the mountains are arid plains and a few meandering rivers. The plains account for over half the region's total area, but about two-thirds of the region's 2.5 million people live on the coast.[7]

With regard to communication and transportation, the area is not unified. The rivers do not connect its different parts: those of the plains flow southeast, away from the mountains and the coast; those in the mountains and on the coast are far too shallow, rocky, and swift to permit easy and safe movement of goods and persons. The steepness of the mountains also has discouraged construction of paved roads and railroads between the coast and the plains.

Partly as a result of the physical problems that the mountains pose to intraregional travel, parochial languages have evolved in the mountain valleys, often mutually unintelligible.[8] For example, in the mountains of Vizcaya the common indigenous words for "work" and "to fall" are "bear" and "jausi"; and in Guipúzcoa they are "lan" and "erori."[9] The diversity has led linguists to disagree throughout the twentieth century about whether there was a single early Basque language from which all the dialects descend, or more than one.[10] On the plains of Navarra and in most coastal cities, the indigenous dialects of the mountains are seldom heard, and the vast majority of residents speak and read only Spanish (or what Basques call "Castilian").

Besides directly and indirectly obstructing transportation and communication, the Cantabrian Mountains interact with the winds and moisture over the Bay of Biscay to produce two climates and two types of natural vegetation. The ocean's clouds drop rain and snow primarily on the northern slopes, which in effect shield the plains. The plains receive less than twenty inches of precipitation a year, while the coastal area receives about forty inches. The consequences for the landscape are evident: the south is largely treeless, with dry, brown grasses, whereas the coastal lands have abundant oak and chestnut trees, ferns, and lush grasses.

The differences in climate, vegetation, and transportation services between the north and south have made for two strikingly dissimilar types of agriculture: large-scale, mechanized, commercial agriculture in the southern plains; and small-scale, partly subsistence farming in the mountains and coastal hills. Extensive lines of communication with other provinces in Spain, flat land, and mild weather all have contributed to make large-scale commercial farming with seasonal wage laborers a profitable activity in the south. Farmers in the Cantabrian Mountains and the coastal hills, however, must deal with inhospitable winters, frequent floods, and land that is uneven and stony—conditions that make it difficult to utilize heavy farm machinery effectively and to produce bountiful crops.

Alongside differences in agricultural production, there are subregional differences in the evolution of industrial production and manufacturing. Industrialization only recently has occurred on the plains, contributing to the emergence of two overcrowded provincial capitals, filled with former farmhands, tenant farmers, and small-farm owners who lost their previous means of livelihood because of mechanization and rigorous market competition in the countryside. While the populations of the smaller towns and villages on the plains have dwindled since 1960, Vitoria and Pamplona have burst with new immigrants, many of whom are poor, untrained for urban jobs, and suffer under the constant threat of unemployment.

Light manufacturing occurs in many of the Cantabrian Mountain valleys. Because of shortages of capital, cooperatives are a common form of business enterprise, with each worker purchasing shares of the firm. During the international economic boom of the 1960s, manufacturers enjoyed high sales and expanded product lines. Since the middle 1970s, however, stagnation has been the norm, and even the cooperatives have been forced into temporary closings and layoffs.

On the coast lies the metropolis of Bilbao—one of the largest centers of mining and metallurgy in Western Europe and the home of almost one-third of the region's population. Great wealth and great poverty lie side by side. On the east bank of the city's large river are university campuses, mansions, and high-priced shops. On the west bank are tenement houses, docks, steel mills, and mines. In the center of the metropolis are blocks of tall banks, flashy hotels, large department stores, and exclusive business clubs.

Having briefly distinguished the region's three economic subregions, let us study the economic life of each in more detail.

COASTAL MINES AND METALLURGY

Partly because of the immigration of Basque ranchers and farm workers to California, Idaho, and Nevada, many North Americans today automatically associate the economy of the Basque region with small farms and sheepherding. Like all stereotypes, this one is only partly true. Besides being a land of shepherds, the region is, in the words of *The Economist*, the "anvil" of the Spanish economy.[11] Two-thirds of Spain's integrated steel plants are located on the Basque coast, as are one-third of Spain's shipyards, constructing trawlers as well as supertankers. Well over half of all steel produced in Spain is made in the Basque region, as are two-thirds of all machine tools. And more than 50 percent of all employed adults in the region labor in a workshop, factory, mine, shipyard, or construction site, about a quarter of them in factories and worksites with five hundred or more employees.[12]

In terms of size of plants, levels of investment, proportion of the gainfully employed in secondary- and tertiary-sector jobs, and the extent to which commercial firms have merged and been consolidated, the Basque coast is an economically advanced area of Spain. This is hardly a new situation. During the last half of the nineteenth century, with the help of British markets and investments, mining, steel manufacturing, and shipbuilding developed quickly along the coast. Hounded by depressions and prompted by an innovative spirit, Basque industrialists experimented with mergers, joint stockholding, and oligopolistic collusion long before capitalists in other parts of Spain did so. According to economic historian Robert Graham, during the early twentieth century the leading industrialists of the Basque coast were unquestionably the most cohesive and powerful economic group in Iberia.[13]

The focal point of this remarkable economic development is Bilbao. It has grown in a single century from a sleepy seaport into a metropolis with three-quarters of a million residents; a major stock market; one of the largest financial districts in southern Europe; a modern, busy port; and the first organized chamber of commerce in Iberia. The commercial and engineering achievements are impressive, but not all is rosy. Indeed, the signs of prosperity can hide a paradox: many residents live not in splendor and ease, but in crowded quarters among industrial structures. And they literally live in a stench. Snaking through Bilbao is the Nervión River, whose mouth serves as a deep-water harbor for international tankers. The sludge, odor, and yellowish color of the Nervión help make evident the breakneck pace of economic growth. Bilbao is "a warren of smelly, smoky plants cheek-by-jowl with housing," once remarked a writer for *Business Week*.[14] "Grey, coal-stained Bilbao, with its dismal workers' suburbs jammed against smoke stacks [sic] and blast furnaces, still looks like northern Europe's industrial cities at their dreariest, half a century ago," stated a writer for *The Economist*.[15] "Ancient smokestacks belch waste into the already grimy, almost unbreathable air," recently reported a correspondent for *The New York Times*, who added that the city "would be the ideal setting for a film on the death of the industrial revolution."[16] Local reports are hardly more glamorous. According to the newspaper *Correro Español*, a speaker at a medical colloquim held in Bilbao in 1975 said, "Bilbao is a paradise for contamination. From Archanda one sees smoke that is yellow, red, green . . . all colors. It is a rainbow of fume, and one must not forget that contamination is the most important cause of chronic bronchitis."[17]

Most of Bilbao's furnaces, shipyards, railroad terminals, and machine shops lie on the western bank of the Nervión River. Mixed in with them are teeming tenement houses, garbage-strewn streets without sidewalks, police stations, and myriad bars. During the 1960s, the normal overcrowding of the western bank worsened considerably when a short-term boom in mining and metallurgy (steel production increased 249 percent between 1964 and 1973)[18] drew tens of thousands of new workers from other parts of Spain. Settlements of tin shacks, called *chaboles,* soon encircled the downtown section. The new immigrants soon were acculturated into the militantly proletarian society of the west bank, with its clandestine unions, workers' social clubs, underground newspapers, and memories of past strikes.[19]

Immediately to the east of the river is a bluff, beneath which are shopping districts of small shops and boutiques. Among them is a highly prestigious Jesuit institution, the University of Deusto, whose schools of law, business, and engineering have educated many of the business and government leaders of the region. On the bluff itself and overlooking the plants and shipyards of the west bank is Neguri, a plush residential area. Two bridges connect the eastern bank—with Neguri and its surrounding neighborhoods—to the blast furnaces and the tenement houses on the western or "Left Bank" of the river. Until the 1930s, the population of Neguri was largely limited to the extended families of the thirty wealthiest industrialists of the area. During the first half of the century, these families either held controlling interests in or sat on the governing boards of almost all big businesses in Spain. Today, many nouveau riche families also reside in Neguri and its environs.

Little is known about the social norms and interfamilial organization of Neguri. There are rumors that monthly meetings are held among the leading financiers in Neguri, and it is said that at these meetings, current economic and political issues are analyzed and programs of action are forged. But there is also evidence that the residents of Neguri seldom formally coordinate their public actions or systematically discuss politics, and that they in fact differ considerably in their political prejudices and economic priorities. At least until more systematic information is available, it remains an open question whether the leading families of Neguri provide a rare example of an organizationally cohesive "power elite," or whether political organization and political and economic consensus among the residents are much less developed.[20]

Despite its relatively high degree of mechanization and organization, the industrial economy of the Basque coast has never enjoyed sustained prosperity. Since the 1860s the coal, iron, steel, and naval industries have suffered severe depressions every twenty to thirty years. The declines in sales have led to very high rates of bankruptcies, cutbacks in production, and widespread unemployment. After World War I, for example, there was a drop-off in the overseas sales of ore and metal products; and 40 percent of the miners in Bilbao were dismissed.[21] Similarly, a depression in steelmaking and naval construction occurred in the wake of the international oil crisis of the middle 1970s; and by the early 1980s, almost a quarter of all coastal workers were officially unemployed.[22]

There is no simple explanation for the periodic depressions. Undoubtedly, many short-term factors are involved, such as spiraling labor costs, company mismanagement, rash overexpansion, and a general lack of quality controls. But there are also long-term causes. For instance, the coal and iron deposits, which once were conveniently located along the coast, have been depleted during this century, and newer technology and metal products require ores not commonly found in the region. In addition, because of the lack of transportation networks with the interior of Spain, and because of the metallurgical sector's traditional dependency upon overseas sales, the coastal economy must bear the vagaries of international prices for iron and steel, which throughout the century have undergone severe and unexpected swings. Whatever the mix of short-term and long-term causes, heavy industry historically has been a highly unstable sector of the economy; and by the mid-1970s another deep downswing had begun.[23]

Heavy industry, of course, hardly accounts for all urban economic activity on the Basque coast. Along with the giant and technologically up-to-date firms there are thousands of family firms, particularly in the service sector.[24] They make up approximately 60 percent of all coastal businesses. Each of these small establishments, such as jewelry shops, corner groceries, and local bars, normally employs fewer than six workers. The division of labor is primitive: often the owner runs all operations, from ordering supplies to stocking goods to greeting customers. Work in the shops also tends to be labor intensive and involves few power tools.

However, the Basque coast (with the possible exception of the famed tourist port, San Sebastián) is hardly a haven for small businesses. Most urban workers are employed by large firms with more than seventy-five employees.[25] Recent expansion of department stores and shopping centers has threatened to drive many small firms out of business, for they cannot compete with the low overhead, wholesale purchasing, and mass marketing techniques of the larger companies.[26] Small shopkeepers, of course, are far from extinct on the Basque coast; but they are an endangered species and vastly outnumbered by the urban proletariat.

CLASSES AND CLASS RELATIONSHIPS
IN THE CANTABRIAN MOUNTAINS

For most of the twentieth century such phenomena as large industries, crowded cities, and cycles of booms and busts never extended very far inland. Because the mountains obstructed free movement of goods and services, mass production of goods was prohibitively costly. Instead, small firms manufacturing inexpensive consumer durables—such as stoves, bicycles, furniture, kitchenware, and the like—have evolved.[27] The firms usually have experienced difficulty both in expanding production and in surviving inevitable slumps, for most coastal banks prefer lending to large industrial firms, usually the more dependable debtors.

One consequence of the chronic shortage of investment capital has been experimental producer cooperatives, in which workers regularly invest a share of their earnings. Such cooperatives have existed in the Basque mountains since early in the century. For various reasons they declined in numbers during the early Franco years, almost disappeared, and then suddenly flourished again during the 1960s and 1970s.[28]

The most famous of the newest generation of the cooperatives originated during the late 1950s in the town of Mondragón. Five ambitious mechanics pooled their savings and established a moderately sized manufacturing firm. Local workers who wished to join the firm first had to buy a share of stock, agree not to sell the stock while employed in the cooperative, agree to contribute shares of their salaries to the firm for future capital investment, and agree not to join or organize a union. In exchange, their jobs were protected; they were provided with extensive health, recreational, and educational benefits; they were allowed to elect representatives to a management board; and they were permitted to attend grievance hearings.

The Mondragón firm was highly profitable and inspired scores of imitators. By 1980 there were more than seventy producer cooperatives throughout the Cantabrian Mountains, involving more than sixteen thousand workers.[29] About one in ten nonagricultural workers in the mountains was a member of a cooperative, and about 15 percent of the total industrial output of the mountains came from cooperatively organized businesses.[30]

During the late 1950s and 1960s overall productivity levels in the mountains rose rapidly. Both capitalist firms and the cooperatives began to specialize in new types of manufactured goods, such as butane stoves, oil heaters, vitamins, perfume, and accessories for cars and motorcycles, which were suddenly in demand because of Spain's rapidly expanding economy and the concomitant rise in consumer spending. It was not unusual for mountain entrepreneurs to buy foreign patents and then monopolize the production of particular goods within Spain. In addition, many firms (especially the cooperatives) concentrated on turning out unusual metal products, such as atypical machine tools and seed drills, then in demand overseas. The per capita income level in Guipúzcoa skyrocketed, and it became one of the two wealthiest provinces in Spain. Hundreds of new companies were founded; hundreds of existing companies expanded production; and thousands of jobs were created.[31]

In contrast to the industrial evolution of Bilbao, the manufacturing boom in the Cantabrian Mountains tended not to lead to huge concentrations of capital, specialization in a few goods, or immense and anonymous labor forces. Moreover, there were no enormous urban centers surrounded by working-class suburbs that were populated overwhelmingly by non-Basques. In 1975 the biggest manufacturing towns in the mountains were Eibar and Mondragón, with 38,000 and 26,000 inhabitants respectively; most manufacturing communities had between 10,000 and 15,000 residents. In the evenings workers, employers, and friends would stroll and mingle in the streets. In the words of Linz, "The relations between medium and small industrialists, often of working-class origin, in many of the well-to-do small industrial towns of the Basque country with their Basque skilled workers—who often were part-time peasants—were probably better than in any other part of Spain."[32] Economic growth had occurred, but within small towns and with a good deal of comity and daily interaction between classes.

Still, not all was well in class relationships. As early as the First World War, organizations of workers and working-class families in the mountain communities had challenged sellers of food, who were denounced for unfair price increases. Women were particularly active protesters. Many union locals became militant after World War I, when job security and wages were threatened.[33] During the 1960s and 1970s strikes occurred repeatedly—even occasionally in the cooperatives.[34]

The Catholic church has greatly affected the formation, goals, and strategy of labor organizations in the mountains and on the plains. Although during most of the Franco years the Spanish church hierarchy was less than friendly toward groups contesting the authority of social and political elites, priests in the Basque region were much more sympathetic and supportive, and occasionally were themselves participants.[35] Priests openly discussed social issues during masses and sacred rites—for example, at funerals of political and social activists. Churches in several small and midsize towns also furnished organizational resources, such as meeting places, to groups challenging the regime. For many youths, the only affordable postelementary education was offered by seminaries. During the 1950s and 1960s Basque seminaries were frequently places for subversive learning, where the works of Karl Marx, for one, could be read and discussed. According to one anxious government official during the twilight of the Franco regime, "Illegal meetings were occurring without interruption" in Basque parishes, and priests were collaborating with "Marxist groups, well prepared and genuinely revolutionary."[36] The official may not have been entirely a victim of a fevered imagination, for in the words of one former resident of the mountains, "The only possible counterbalance to overt authoritarian assaults upon one's self-identity and cultural pride was the church."[37]

Informally organized youth gangs, or *cuadrillas*, also mediated class relations.[38] These long-lasting groups of five to ten companions regularly walked the streets of their towns, shared leisure activities, ate and drank together, gave solace to each other during times of crisis, and attended one another's family events, such as birthday celebrations and marriages. Partly because of ongoing face-to-face interaction within the cuadrillas, members often came to share social and political outlooks and support similar political parties and social organizations. Because of the strength of intragroup relations, cuadrillas often functioned as communication networks by which formal political and social organizations, such as parties and unions, would contact, recruit, and train new members. Depending in part on the class homogeneity of a given neighborhood, a cuadrilla could contribute to either interclass harmony (as members of different classes became lifelong companions) or interclass hostility (as members of a single-class cuadrilla came to see cuadrillas from neighborhoods with different class compositions as strangers or even rivals). Constantly active in the streets of the midsize mountain towns, cuadrillas not infrequently viewed those streets as their turf and during the Franco years would sometimes try to defend it when police tried to control local residents' behavior.

At the close of the 1970s, expansion in manufacturing came to a halt. Domestic demand for Basque metal and electrical goods plummeted as the national economy foundered. At the same time because of a world recession, the bottom fell out of the export market. Many previously thriving companies cut back.[39]

Even the producer cooperatives, which had adopted a very cautious approach to expansion, were forced to trim wages and hours, close plants, and occasionally transfer and release workers (although not at the same rate as other private firms). For the first time in two decades there was a negative growth rate for industrial production as a whole in the mountains. By 1981 even the annual profit rate of the once highly successful producer cooperatives fell to negative 7 percent.[40]

As on the coast, more than one type of productive activity existed in the mountains. Surrounding the small manufacturing towns, with their fluctuating prosperity, were partly self-sufficient and dispersed farmsteads. On these compact plots homes and barns were combined; people normally lived on the upper floor and livestock on the lower. Families raised a variety of crops, used either hand tools or simple power tools, seldom hired outside laborers, consumed much of what they raised, and sold some cash crops and dairy products to local markets and distributors.[41]

As we shall see in the next chapter, many of these socially and economically independent farmsteads were abandoned during the 1960s and 1970s, due in part to the new job opportunities in nearby towns, in part to the more exciting life-styles of the cities, in part to government-imposed fiscal burdens and product regulation, and in part to intensified competition from the larger and more mechanized farms on the plains. Fewer and fewer young people wanted to follow the plow. Indeed, some farming parents encouraged their children to leave home for the opportunities to be found in urban society. Some of the second generation labored in manufacturing during the day and returned to the farmsteads at night or during weekends. Still, the agricultural population of the mountains dwindled. According to sympathetic observers of Basque mountain communities—such as William Douglass—during the second half of the twentieth century, "Basque household agriculture has become an anachronistic way of life."[42]

COMMERCIALIZATION OF
SOUTHERN AGRICULTURE

Before the 1960s the southern plains of the Basque region were bereft of factories, militant unions, and sizable cities. Agriculture was the primary economic activity. Three-fourths of all food companies in the region were located on the plains, and over half of the paid work force on the plains had labored in farms or food-processing plants.[43]

Agricultural production on the plains traditionally has involved far greater status hierarchy and income inequalities than has family farming in the mountains. At the beginning of the twentieth century, local nobles and their descendants leased large portions of their estates to tenant farmers and sharecroppers, who generally used hand tools. Then in the late 1950s and early 1960s, several technological changes made specialized, mechanized, and capital-intensive farming more attractive to owners of estates. In particular, a new railway line connected the plains with potential markets in the interior of Spain. The number of tractors in the south grew from under 2,500 in 1959 to almost 10,000 in 1970. Agricultural output correspondingly increased: the aggregate tonnage of many commercial crops doubled within a decade.[44] Yet, the highly unequal distribution of land persisted and perhaps even was exacerbated. By the middle 1970s, almost 45 percent of all land under cultivation was owned by about 10 percent of the commercial farms.[45]

The sudden profit-maximizing behavior of the southern landowners had several social and political consequences. First, a new type of intraregional conflict evolved. As the technological gap between the mechanized production of the south and the nonmechanized production of the mountains increased, so too did tensions between the commercially oriented southern farmers and the relatively more subsistence-oriented farmers of the mountains. Producing more goods, investing in expensive machinery, borrowing from banks for newer equipment and chemicals, and constantly searching for ways to pay off accumulated debts, the commercial farmers began to look to the nearby mountains for potential customers, and began to ship large quantities of produce and milk into the previously isolated communities. Because their products could not compete with the cheaper and better-quality goods from the south, mountain farmers lost some of the few local customers they traditionally had serviced. They coped with the worsening situation in a variety of ways: some abandoned farming; some relocated into more economically isolated valleys; and still others, as we shall see in more detail later, publicly demonstrated against the economic and political advantages of the larger, southern farmers.[46]

Meanwhile, a second novel conflict of interest emerged on the plains, where small farmers were being squeezed out of business by the larger estates, and where sharecroppers, tenant farmers, and seasonal wage laborers found their services no longer needed as landlords increasingly turned to machinery. Total plains land under cultivation had increased dramatically during the 1960s and early 1970s, but the total number of jobs, ironically, had decreased. The overwhelming majority of southern towns and villages experienced a net population loss as farmhands, small farmers, renters, and their families desperately moved to nearby cities in hopes of securing their livelihoods.[47]

The depopulation of the plains and the deterioration of mountain farming were two unanticipated consequences of the rise of commercial farming in the south. A third was the sudden industrialization of local towns that once had been small trading centers, where farmers bought equipment and manufactured goods and delivered their harvests for processing and transportation. During the 1960s the provincial and municipal governments of the south—with the strong support of the now commercially oriented southern farmers—aggressively wooed outside industrialists through a campaign of transportation and energy programs, attractive zoning laws, and tax incentives. The strategy of government-prompted industrialization seems to have worked. Over sixty multinational corporations opened new branch plants in the south by the early 1970s, and the number of bank branch offices in the south doubled between 1950 and 1975.[48] The profile of the local work force also changed dramatically. In 1960, 41 percent of the paid work force was in agriculture, and 30 percent in industry and construction; fifteen years later, 17 percent was in agriculture, and 45 percent in industry and construction.[49]

Rapid industrialization was especially noticeable in and around the two provincial capitals, Pamplona and Vitoria. By 1975 each city had over 150,000 residents and had doubled its population in less than ten years. The expansion placed great strains on the towns' infrastructures and public services, such as schools, water, sewerage services, housing stock, and hospitals. Complicating the potentially explosive political situation was the fact that many of the newcomers were former farmhands, who recently had lost their livelihoods because of the mechanization of agriculture. Anthony Giddens has speculated that when farmers from rural settings in which inter-class resentments are intense migrate to urban settings where public amenities are scarce, they are prone to become radical in their politics.[50] This hypothesis fits well the experience of Pamplona and Vitoria. Even before Franco's death in 1975, the newly built, over-crowded suburbs of these towns had become the bases for many clandestine unions and strike committees. The working-class suburbs later became electoral "Left" strongholds, not so much for the Spanish Socialist party, but for Maoists, Trotskyists, the Herri Batasuna, and other openly revolutionary parties.[51]

CONCLUSION

The Basque economy, when perceived in terms of specific classes and productive activities, has had a paradoxical history. Relatively high levels of overall productivity have coexisted with economic displacement and dislocation. During the past three decades, large estates were mechanized; metallurgy enjoyed a boom, at least during the 1960s; and hundreds of new firms and manufacturing plants opened on the plains and in the mountain valleys. Meanwhile, many traditional jobs were lost; family farming was being relegated to the periphery; international demand for regional exports fluctuated dramatically; and rural-urban migration meant housing deficits and needed goods in short supply.

Of course, these diverse economic problems ultimately may not have had any bearing on political unrest. For a variety of reasons—ranging from state repression to socialized feelings of futility—people who suffer economic discomfort and relative deprivation may choose not to resort to political activity in hopes of improving their social or economic circumstances.[52] Nonetheless, the abundant examples of hard times give us reason to look more closely at how local residents responded politically to their situations and whether (and how) local popular responses affected the development of ETA and armed struggle.

CHAPTER TWO

TRADITIONS OF PROTEST IN
NONURBAN AREAS

*D*uring the past two decades, several eminent social scientists have urged students of extrainstitutional politics, such as protest and rebellion, to adopt a "meso," or middle-level, mode of analysis.[1] This entails seeing people as embedded in local institutions—churches, schools, friendship networks, civic organizations, and the like—that determine their political behavior. The local ecology is interpreted as having causal significance independent of the influence of large-scale phenomena like nationwide patterns of urbanization, secularization, or industrialization. Granted, the larger changes may generate feelings of discomfort and dissatisfaction within individuals, but their political responses are mediated by local institutions.

Take, for example, the U.S. civil rights movement. "Contrary to popular belief among outsiders, a black community is usually well stocked with organized groups," observes one specialist on black politics.[2] According to mesosociological studies, it was these local institutions—for example, churches, colleges, and beauty parlors—that conditioned individuals' responses to feelings of relative deprivation and experiences of discrimination. The institutions provided meeting places, leadership structures, office equipment, labor, money, and/or tactical training. Without such institutions, the bus boycotts, jail-ins, and sit-downs at lunch counters arguably would not have occurred.

Scholars who emphasize the causal significance of local institutions have identified at least three ways in which they can facilitate the emergence of a social movement. First, they provide the organizational resources that are needed if planned and coordinated action is to take place. Second, certain of their activities, such as a sit-down strike by a local union, may provide tactical models and/or embody values that members of a nearby movement will adopt. Third, their ongoing activities can impart to observers in other movements a sense of confidence in their own effectiveness and in the possibility of mobilizing others.[3]

This chapter and the two that follow describe three sets of Basque institutions that engaged in local political struggle and that indirectly affected the emergence and evolution of ETA between 1960 and 1980. They are (1) social protest movements in nonurban areas that appeared in the 1970s, (2) the long-standing Basque labor movement, and (3) the urban-neighborhood association movement. Each set of institutions contributed to ETA by supplying key organizational resources for the fledgling ETA organizations (such as a pool of recruits and communications networks), by embodying an inspiring vision of a future "socialist" order, and/or by suggesting through repeated collective actions that the times were ripe for a widespread revolution from below. Like the civil rights movement in the United States, which grew out of indigenous black institutions of the time and was not simply the outcome of spontaneous expressions of anger, the self-consciously radical ETA movement was indirectly a product of the region's ongoing traditions of protest.

Because many etarras came from rural and semirural backgrounds,[4] it is worth looking first at the mobilizations that occurred in the Basque countryside between 1960 and 1980. According to Basque newspapers, protests—from peaceful demonstrations to truck burnings—were widespread, especially during the 1970s. One can categorize these protests according to geographic zone, social groups, and economic grievances, and distinguish (1) protest by fishing communities, (2) protests by family farmers in the mountains, and (3) protests by small agriculturalists and former agriculturalists on the southern plains.

PISCATORIAL PROTEST

Spain has the largest fishing fleet in Europe and third largest in the world. Many deep-sea trawlers have their home ports in Basque harbors. During the 1960s and 1970s, deep-sea fishing provided livelihoods for approximately 9,000 men in the Basque region, or about 2 percent of the coastal work force. The industry also generated thousands of jobs in packing, transporting, and marketing the catches, and for persons who produced supplies and equipment for the industry.[5]

The Basque fishing industry is decentralized. Roughly 80 percent of the seven hundred trawlers are owned not by corporations but by single individuals, and each boat has a temporary crew of between twenty and fifty, the vast majority of whom are not unionized.

Commercial fishing also is an expensive business. A fully equipped deep-sea trawler—with shortwave radio, echo sounders, winches, and cold-storage rooms—cost about $3 million during the 1970s. And it cost per ship about $1.5 million each year to stock supplies and pay wages. In short, private ownership of a commercial deep-sea trawler requires money, and lots of it.

Most anglers and sailors, however, live poorly, and have no expectations of ever owning their own trawlers. It is not unusual for an owner of a single trawler to have an annual income topping $50,000, but most fishermen earn only between $200 and $500 a month. They do not receive wages, unemployment compensation, or health benefits between jobs. They are aware, moreover, of their correspondingly low social status. In the words of one deep-sea fisherman, "To be a fisherman is the lowest thing. When you're no good for anything else, you become a fisherman." The foregoing statement, according to Basque anthropologist Joseba Zulaika, is typical of the view of social hierarchy held by coastal villages.[6]

Despite their low status and economic insecurity, organized class conflict in Basque fishing villages was virtually unknown until the late 1970s, when strikes broke out in several villages.[7] One possible explanation for the relative quietude is cultural: arguably there was a strong sense of interclass cooperation and personal loyalty on the boats that offset feelings of frustration, deprivation, and anger. Perhaps during the long trips, often lasting over three months, boat owners and employees gradually come to know each other, and the feelings of familiarity, personal respect, and mutual enjoyment smother interclass jealousies and resentments.

The problem with the foregoing hypothesis is that most boat owners during the 1960s and 1970s had little direct contact with their employees. Inshore anglers, who take day trips and work on small boats, often work side by side with a skipper owner. But the owners of the larger trawlers and freezer boats usually hired captains and master anglers to select crew members and manage the fishing expeditions, and seldom went themselves. In addition, the owners normally released all employees after each expedition, even though most fishermen wanted a permanent arrangement. Finally, face-to-face contact between owners and employees normally was restricted to a private signing of an employment contract, a ritual filled with suspicions and acrimony. According to Zulaika, owners regularly tried to entice anglers and sailors with oral promises of lavish commissions on large catches not included in the written contract. Then, after the boats returned, the owners paid a much lower commission rate per ton of fish caught. The employees were conscious of the owners' duplicity but held their tongues for fear of losing jobs in a highly competitive labor market.[8]

A more persuasive explanation for the absence of overt class conflict involves the obvious inequality in political power during the Franco regime. At least since the origins of the regime, maritime laws have defined all strikes and slowdowns on ships as "acts of sedition." They have also prohibited such "very grave faults" as "drunkenness in an act of service, habitual blasphemy, voluntary and continued diminution of the normal output of work, and simulation of illness and accident." If charged with sedition or other "grave faults," fishermen are subjected to trial by military courts, in which the rights of defendants are severely restricted. Zulaika noted in his field research that Basque fishermen were quite aware of the strict laws against misbehavior, and that they therefore vented their frustration through under-the-breath cursing instead of open mutiny. Thus, perhaps the threat of state repression—rather than warm friendships with boat owners—best explains why the low incomes and prestige of many Basque employees in the fishing industry did not give rise to overtly rebellious behavior prior to the late 1970s.[9]

Fishermen's strikes, however, were hardly the sole or even the most prominent form of piscatorial protest during the 1970s, when the Franquist regime imploded. In addition there were large antigovernment demonstrations and truck burnings unrelated to the villages' internal class struggles. The immediate origins of these protests were twofold. First, there was the worldwide rise in oil prices, which made fishing decreasingly profitable as rising energy costs cut into profit margins. In many cases, the general problem of fuel costs was exacerbated by recent purchases of government-subsidized fishing boats that were up to date in fishing and navigational technology, but were also heavy and not designed with fuel costs in mind.[10]

The impact of the international oil crisis was made worse by the second and arguably more serious condition, which involved international politics. During the 1970s Western nations began to adopt protectionist policies with respect to their fishing industries. Both the European Economic Community and Canada extended their territorial waters from fifty to two hundred miles offshore. Citing both economic necessity and the goal of environmental protection, North Atlantic countries refused to permit Basque fishing boats to enter these waters, even though the boats traditionally had done so. In desperation, several boats raided the newly nationalized waters. The nations whose waters were repeatedly trespassed upon, France and Ireland, responded by having their navies shoot at the trespassers, and at least a half dozen were injured in the confrontations.

Excluded from customary fishing waters and unable to purchase fuel for long trips, Basque boat owners, fishermen, and outfitters turned to the Spanish state for help. Members of diverse classes petitioned the government for dramatic and decisive actions, such as new price regulations on fuel, a naval blockade around Gilbraltar, and a prohibition against the importation of fish from all nations in the European Economic Community. Government officials publicly expressed sympathy with the unemployed fishermen and indebted boat owners, but insisted that deregulation was necessary for the future development of Spain's energy resources. They further held that economic relations between Spain and the European Economic Community needed to be strengthened, not strained, so that Spain could enter the EEC at the earliest moment. Rejection of the dramatic measures that the coastal groups proposed was firm.[11]

Many in the Basque fishing communities not surprisingly concluded from the inaction of the government that they were not genuinely represented within the Spanish political system. Frustrated by traditional methods of politicking, they adopted nontraditional methods. By 1978 they were organizing petitions and marches to denounce both the new international laws regulating the use of coastal waters, and the Spanish state's neglect of local interests. They began to attack and burn trucks carrying produce into Spain from France and other EEC countries. These forms of organized dissent continued well into the 1980s. The marches, petitions, traffic blockades, and truck burnings did not succeed in changing government policy, however, and more and more idle trawlers were tied to the docks. In the opinion of one visiting journalist, by the middle 1980s, residents in the villages began to suffer "authentic psychoses."[12]

FARMER PROTEST IN
THE CANTABRIAN MOUNTAINS

The swift decline of the Basque fishing industry was surprising. In contrast, the disappearance of family farms on the mountains and coastal hills had been widely anticipated.[13] There are no reliable overall statistics on the disappearance of family farms since the end of the nineteenth century, but the available statistics for particular farming villages and for short periods of time corroborate the general hypothesis of a steady drop in the number of inhabited farmsteads. In the mountain village of Murelaga, for example, there were 131 inhabited farmsteads in 1950 and 121 in 1966. Around the coastal town of Fuenterrabia, there were 256 inhabited farmsteads in 1920, 168 in 1969. The mountain village of Echalar contained 114 inhabited farmsteads in 1955, 95 in 1966. And in the mountain region of Itziar-Deba, there were 307 inhabited farmsteads in 1962, 220 in 1972.[14]

The farmstead situation partially overlapped another social trend: the commercialization of mountain farming. Before the mid-1920s, almost all highland agricultural production was geared toward immediate family consumption. Each farmstead (*baserria*) was home to a single stem family, and each made most of the goods it used or consumed. The upstairs of the dwelling building usually provided the room for four to six family members; the downstairs usually served as a barn. There was a dearth of nearby markets in which to sell or buy, and in any case the products and machinery that would have raised the livelihood above subsistence level were unaffordable. The agriculturally inhospitable land and climate meant that to survive the stem family had to painstakingly raise a score or so of diverse crops.

The nature of Cantabrian farming conditioned local life in numerous ways. Before 1925 almost all farm work was done with hand tools and rudimentary equipment. Members of each baserria were also jacks of all trades. Baserriak lacked the amenities, such as electricity, plumbing, and motorized equipment, that would have eased the onerous labor exacted by husbandry. Seasonal wage laborers were almost unknown. To maximize its contact with the soil and changing weather, each family lived on its own plot of land. Each farmer could literally step directly from farmhouse to farmland. Surrounded by land, the dwellings were distant from one another, each dwelling a self-contained society, whose members lived, worked, and socialized almost entirely with each other.

Since 1925 many Cantabrian baserriak have become more commercial and mechanized. Partly because of the growth of nearby urban markets, the necessity of paying taxes, and the attractiveness of cheap manufactured goods, family farmers increasingly cultivated cash crops. Almost half of each day was spent preparing, transporting, and selling produce. Money that came to the family coffers was reinvested to generate future profits. The average size of family plots increased from thirteen hectares in 1962 to nineteen hectares in 1972.[15] By the early 1970s about one-third of the farm families in the Cantabrian Mountains owned power tillers, and about one-fifth owned small tractors.[16]

The commercialization and mechanization of the Cantabrian farms led to more comfortable living. The ground floors of the dwelling building began to be constructed of concrete instead of packed dirt, which greatly eased the cleaning of animal stalls. A majority of farmhouses were electrified, usually using power from a privately owned generator. Forms of recreation expanded. According to anthropologist William Douglass,

> Today [1976] a person whose childhood was spent in a subsistence-oriented peasant household and who regarded leaving his natal community as a major undertaking now thinks little of driving his own car fifty kilometers to Bilbao on a casual shopping trip before rushing home in the late afternoon so as not to miss a favorite television program. . . . In oversimplified terms, the Basque peasantry became increasingly attracted to twentieth century consumerism in which, to take one example, within the period of three or four decades, the bicycle replaced walking, the motor scooter replaced the bicycle, and the automobile replaced the motor scooter as the commonplace form of transportation in rural Basque society.[17]

The observable improvements in farm life notwithstanding, farmsteads kept being abandoned. Indeed, some anthropologists believe the pace accelerated during the 1960s.[18] Thus far, social scientists have focused on three main causes: (1) the pleasantness of urban life, (2) inhibitory government regulation, and (3) growing competition from the larger estates on the southern plains. Each factor seems a convincing partial explanation, and the third seems especially valuable for understanding why political protests occurred during the 1960s and 1970s. Let us briefly review each factor.

Attractions of Urban Life

Not all farming families left their holdings reluctantly. Even with labor-saving machinery and mechanical conveniences, such as gas stoves and washing machines, farming in the mountains meant lonely, long, and physically taxing days. A family farmer worked on average ten hours a day, six or seven days a week, and without regular contact with other human beings, except immediate family members. Anthropologist Davydd Greenwood has argued that the intensity and ubiquity of family life was unusually stressful.[19] Understandably, city life lured many in the younger generation. And as commercial contacts with the burgeoning cities became more frequent, aging farmers found that their children were less and less interested in following their footsteps. As Douglass observed during the 1970s,

> The trend is clearly one of a progressive inability of the elder generation to recruit one of their offspring to the farming way of life, and even if one is willing to inherit and remain, there is little chance of securing a suitable spouse.[20]

Government Policies

Government intrusions encouraged abandonment of even the more prosperous farmsteads. If the leisure and diverse social life of the city pulled some young farmers from the land, government requirements and mandates psychologically pushed many other farmers off the land. New building codes, higher health and sanitation standards, and zoning of pasturelands for industrial development made farming an increasingly unreliable vocation. Many farmers simply left for poorer paying jobs in the cities rather than trying to deal with officialdom and regulation. An illustration of the legal origins of farm abandonment was the 1973 rezoning decision in Fuenterrabia. According to Greenwood,

> This legislative act converted most of the farming areas into urban property which is subject to restrictions that virtually rule out agriculture. As a result, nearly 50 farms had already been sold and others were up for sale. The young Basques, who had rejected farming and its profits, were being joined in the cities by their parents who never intended to be anything but farmers. What could have taken a generation occurred in four years.[21]

Another set of problems grew out of government pricing policies for agriculture. From 1920 until the late 1930s, prices for crops and dairy products in the Basque region were relatively constant in comparison to the fluctuating prices for manufactured goods. During the Great Depression, when prices for manufactured goods plummeted while prices for agricultural produce remained stable, many family farmers acquired machinery, plumbing, radios, and other conveniences.

Since the Civil War, however agricultural prices have not risen as quickly as have prices in the industrial sector. Stated differently, over the years farm families have been receiving less purchasing power (in terms of manufactured goods) for the same amount of produce sold. At first, the Franco government forced farmers to sell at low, fixed prices, which benefited consumers. Later, the government allowed farm prices to fluctuate seasonally and yearly, according to market pressures. Again, agricultural prices tended to decline in relation to manufactured goods. The government in Madrid has generally not provided any price supports for smaller farmers, intervening in the market only when prices for agricultural goods seem too high for consumers by lowering tariffs and importing large quantities of produce. This reduces the cost of food for the urban consumer but does not help family farmers who are seeking parity. Frustrated by the inadequate monetary return on labor invested and by coming up short in a comparison with city workers, some members of baserriak have questioned the wisdom of remaining under the government's thumb.[22]

New Market Competition

For purposes of understanding nonurban protest, perhaps the most important cause of rural depopulation was the entrance into local markets of larger and more efficient producers from the southern plains. Completion of an all-weather road across the Cantabrian Mountains gave plains farmers access to the northern slope. Using large machines on flat terrain and abundant cheap labor, the southern farmers successfully competed against family farmers. Many of the latter (particularly in the dairy and poultry sectors) went bankrupt. Others, seeking refuge from the larger agricultural entrepreneurs, moved to smaller towns. But inevitably trucks from the southern farms would follow and again undersell.

Not surprisingly, mountain farmers failed to see the new situation as just, good, or economically inevitable. They charged that the large agricultural enterprises in the south could undersell only because they enjoyed unfair banking advantages, ruthlessly exploited workers, and were helped by state transportation policies, labor laws, and regulations concerning product quality.

Farmers on the northern slope soon channeled their resentment into sporadic acts of protest. As early as the 1950s, they periodically organized illegal marches to government capitals. Government officials usually dismissed the farmers' demands for help, declaring that it was failure to modernize that had caused their problems, not southern estate owners. In consequence, the marches often ended in rock and food throwing, and fisticuffs between marchers and jeering onlookers. By the early 1970s the protests were attracting a thousand or so marchers, and on grounds of preserving social peace, government authorities routinely arrested the most outspoken.[23]

The church tried to help family farmers by forming youth groups (the Besarri Gaztedi, for one) that would launch literacy campaigns, teach young people new farming techniques, and encourage the formation of cooperatives. In some church-sponsored organizations, such as the Herri Gaztedi, rural youths read criticisms of capitalism and sympathetic descriptions of socialism. It was not unusual that when the youth groups dissolved, former activists would join clandestine groups with revolutionary ideologies, including the Maoist ORT, the Trotskyist LKI, and ETA.[24]

Of course, the illegal marches and episodic violence by the family farmers might be interpreted in a different way—as an emotional reaction by residents of highly integrated and unchanging rural communities against the threateningly anonymous, atomistic, and innovative culture of modern cities. It would be natural for the family farmers in the mountains and coastal hills to feel insecure and to vent emotions through actions that circumvented normal political processes. Little evidence directly supports this hypothesis, however, and there are at least three reasons to question it. First, it is dubious that the family farmers were wholly unfamiliar with and frightened of solitude, market competition, and social anonymity. They worked their fields by themselves and engaged in transactions on their own. It is quite conceivable that they perceived their own atomized and self-reliant rural habits as fully compatible with and even complementary to the individualist ethos and market competition of local urban society.

Second, if community is viewed as a natural human need, one might argue that the family farmers saw in the nearby cities and towns opportunities for—not limits to—expanded social contacts. Of course, at least since Louis Wirth's seminal essay "Urbanism as a Way of Life," numerous social scientists have contrasted the supposed cold loneliness of industrial cities with the supposed warm communal relations of rural life. In recent years, however, other social scientists have rediscovered the presence of intimate social relations in industrialized cities in the form of neighborhood churches, ethnic societies, union halls, sports leagues, and the like. At the same time, recent anthropological research into Basque cities has revealed an enormous number of communal networks and institutions.[25] It could very well be that the farmers of the mountains were aware of the rich social life of the nearby cities, and perhaps were attracted to it rather than repelled by it.

A final reason for questioning the hypothesis of an acute anti-urban sentiment in the mountains has to do with opinion polls. To the author's knowledge, none of the polls taken during the 1960s and 1970s has provided hard evidence that the family farmers there dreaded the rise of urban culture. To the contrary, most surveys indicate that they tended to admire and enjoy urban life-styles and modern conveniences. In one survey carried out in a Cantabrian valley during the early 1970s, (1) 83 percent of the sample said that watching television and movies was a "positive way" to spend leisure time, (2) less than 20 percent wanted their children to pursue farming as a lifelong vocation, and (3) 21 percent of the families said that they were saving money to buy a home in a city. Social psychologist Miguel Olza Zubiri concluded from the survey that family farmers in the mountains were generally in favor of industrialization and industrial life, and that they manifested "a realistic attitude of adaptation to new times."[26] Using the methods of anthropological fieldwork, Douglass similarly argues that "the Basque baserritarra is committed to the new way of life":

> I was struck by the fact that in both villages there were markedly similar reactions to improvements in the lot of one's neighbors. The initial reaction is to scorn him and belittle his acquisition. The neighbor is accused of being a foolhardy spendthrift (serious charges in Basque society). The item purchased is denounced on a wide variety of seemingly practical grounds. "What does a farmer want with a television set when he must be in bed by dusk if he is to be up at dawn?" "Television sets burn too much electricity." "Television programs are immoral." However, the man who criticizes his neighbor today buys a television set tomorrow. It is then his turn to remain sheepish and defensive in the face of criticisms.[27]

In summary, the atomistic and competitive modes of farming in the Cantabrian Mountains and the results of opinion surveys suggest that the instances of political violence and unruliness there probably were not simply an expression of farmers' traditionalist fears of urban, commercial life. They were, in addition, responses both to new and unwanted market competitors from the southern plains, and to the government's initial unresponsiveness to the smallholders' economic complaints.

AGRARIAN CAPITALISM AND
POPULAR PROTEST ON THE SOUTHERN PLAINS

Popular protest also occurred on the Basque plains. There it was more formally organized than in the mountains, and was more class-based and socially radical in its demands than protest on the coast. A partial explanation for the differences involves the distinctive economic structures and history of the plains and the distinctive pattern of class struggle that evolved there.[28]

On the southern plains, a local, household economy had begun to yield to an impersonal, market economy long before the close of the nineteenth century. Wanting to sell to markets in the interior of Spain, larger landowners were early supporters of the Bourbon dynasty's establishment in the 1870s of a single market, and of its dismantling of tariff barriers between different regions of Iberia. The landowners, many of whom were also moderately wealthy aristocrats, also supported the dynasty's disentailment of church lands, which they hoped to purchase.

By the 1930s two types of commercial economy had developed. On the one hand, there were many small farmers, tenant farmers, and sharecroppers who cultivated plots of approximately twenty to sixty hectares (about two to three times the size of the plots found in the Cantabrian Mountains). They produced a few crops in mass quantities that they sold to distributors and absentee landlords. On the other hand, there were a few dozen extremely large private estates of over three hundred hectares. The owners usually also owned, through government charters, food-processing plants. They used large numbers of seasonal wage laborers, yet also constantly mechanized operations to lower labor costs and intensify cultivation.

During the 1960s and 1970s agricultural output on the plains rose to unprecedented levels. The annual harvest of tomatoes increased from 315,000 tons to 674,000 tons between 1960 and 1967. Similarly, asparagus production approximately doubled, from 59,000 tons to 102,000 tons.[29] The rise in productivity was due partly to the greater use of chemicals, such as fertilizers and insecticides, and partly to further mechanization of equipment. Moreover, a new rail line to the interior of Spain gave the commercial farmers improved access to some growing urban markets, an incentive to increase and intensify production.

As mentioned in chapter 1, despite the impressive rise in aggregate productivity, many persons on the plains were threatened by the technological changes in commercial agriculture. Because of the new labor-saving machinery and the owners' concern with maximizing profits and minimizing costs, many unskilled and semiskilled farm laborers found themselves without jobs. Smaller producers, who could not afford the machinery or chemicals and whose prices were not competitive, often faced bankruptcy. The laborers and farmers who were able to hang on discovered that their incomes steadily fell behind the rising costs of staples. One consequence was that many rural residents left for nearby cities in search of better economic opportunities: approximately four-fifths of the plains towns underwent losses in permanent population between 1960 and 1970.[30] Persons who remained on the plains typically resided in small, compact villages from which larger landowners were conspicuously absent. It was a socially dense and socially homogeneous living situation, with limited differences in income. It was the type of situation that, according to the theoretical speculations of Tony Judt and Seymour Martin Lipset, would favor the formation of well-organized and reform-oriented movements.[31]

By the 1960s rural wage laborers and low-skill construction workers (many of whom were former farmhands or children of farmhands) began to protest their economic plight through illegal blockages of traffic and other disruptions of social routines. The smaller commercial farmers on the plains also acted. They were angered by having to pay new taxes for the financing of industrial growth on the plains; by the irrigation regulations that seemed always to favor larger landowners; by the low prices for foodstuffs offered by local distributors, who had been given licensed monopolies by the state; by the high interest rates that private banks charged; and by the exclusion of small farmers, sharecroppers, and tenant farmers from the social security and retirement programs that the Spanish government had established for industrial workers. Throughout the 1970s small farmers and tenant farmers expressed their discontent by holding back foodstuffs from distributors, illegally blocking traffic on highways, putting obstructions on railroad tracks, and throwing rocks and produce at police.[32]

The popular protest against unemployment, declining wages, high interest rates, and other economic conditions often was neither short-lived nor programmatically shortsighted. In fact, there was a great deal of permanent organizational structure and historic and architectonic vision behind many of the events. For example, in 1976 small plains farmers established a union. More than 3,000 persons attended its first congress in 1978. At the meeting, there were cries of "long live the freedom of the men of the countryside!" and "long live the struggle of the agrarian sector!" Participants booed, hissed, and shouted catcalls whenever the name of the civil governor was mentioned. The speakers identified the "great enemies" of the farmers in terms of social institutions and roles and not only personalities: "large capital, the middlemen, and the monopolies." The speakers advocated "democratizing" credit rates, reestablishing "just prices" for farm goods, and reforming social security laws so as to make life in the countryside "more dignified and stable." They also stated that "industrial workers share the same problems and enemies as small and medium agriculturalists. Therefore, it is necessary that we work together." It was argued that in the past the private lobbying of government officials had been unproductive, so future lobbying should be complemented with dramatic and even technically illegal acts—picketing, mass marches, and boycotts—that would attract the attention and earn the respect of government officials. To persuade the audience, union officers cited the unorthodox tactics of farmers in France as examples of the types of direct action needed.[33]

The 1978 congress was more than an isolated meeting to discuss political tactics and goals in the abstract. The plains farmers were militant in practice, not just in the officers' words. In 1977 the farmers' union sponsored a massive information picket demonstration in conjunction with other rural groups in Spain. Approximately 5,000 pieces of farm machinery were parked along highways and thoroughfares of the Basque plains, and thousands of farmers held banners and posters demanding "protection of the countryside."[34]

The union's actions and social programs did not occur spontaneously, but had precedents. For almost a century, popular protesters in the farming villages of the plains had identified the owners of the nearby estates as politically dangerous rivals who had monopolized access to government. Large landowners, according to popular myth, were a politically cohesive oligarchy that controlled vital river waters and received excessive and often illegal government favors, such as tax exemptions, access roads, and government contracts and licenses. Moreover, members of the largest landowning families allegedly held most of the important offices in local government and made biased and unjust decisions about tax increases, irrigation projects, and other policy questions deeply affecting local farmers.

Even though it was probably exaggerated, the myth of an oligarchic conspiracy was not wholly unfounded. Recent historical research on Navarrese politics has shown that most legislative authority in this southern Basque province was invested in an indirectly elected senate composed of seven persons; that the members of the provincial senate almost always belonged to the largest landowning families in the province; and that the nominal powers of a larger, more directly elected, and more socially heterogeneous provincial parliament were primarily ceremonial. Of course, the myth of an oligarchic conspiracy probably exaggerated the uniformity of interests within the senate and neglected obvious conflicts of interest among landlords. But it was not a totally inaccurate first approximation of how the formal organization of the provincial government impeded the representation of a broader variety of social forces within the region.[35]

Since the 1930s much of the hostility on the plains toward the large landowners had been channeled into support for parties that advocated the dismantling of the provincial senates, direct election of all legislators, and redistribution of farmland. For example, during the short-lived Spanish Second Republic (1931–36), many agrarian villages elected Socialist majorities to their town councils. The reason was partly programmatic: the Socialist candidates had promised land redistribution, improved education and social services for the nonwealthy classes, emergency loans to small farmers, higher taxes on the profits of the rich, and direct election of all local legislators. Of course, when Franco came to power, the Socialist party was outlawed and driven underground. But other political organizations carried the reformist torch. For example, during the early 1950s the radical Catholic labor organization HOAC actively organized small farmers and rural wage laborers against the large estates. During the 1960s HOAC activists also organized clandestine unions in local industrialized cities and tried to forge a rural-urban coalition against the "rural oligarchy" that allegedly controlled the cities' administrations as well as the provincial governments on the plains.[36]

Another organization, the Carlist party, also attempted to form an alliance between small farmers, rural wage laborers, and urban workers against large landowners during the 1950s and 1960s. It is difficult to generalize about the goals and ideologies of the Carlists, for the party underwent several schisms and purges during the Franco years. After one particularly bitter congress, the party officially declared itself Maoist in ideology and strategy, and committed to the principle of worker self-management in all urban and rural workplaces. The Carlist movement was and remains small, very obscure,

Table 2.1. Percentage of Seats on Labor Arbitration Boards Won by Rival Unions in 1978 Elections

Union and Dominant Political Leanings	Province and Geographic Characteristics				
	Alava (inland, mountainous)	Guipúzcoa (coastal, mountainous)	Navarra (inland, plains)	Vizcaya (inland, mountainous)	Spain
CCOO (Communist)	26	27	21	24	35
UGT (Socialist)	26	17	15	21	22
ELA-STV, ELA-STV(a), and LAB (Basque Nationalist)	19	36	7	35	1
SU and CSUT (Maoist)	8	6	36	2	5
USO (Christian Democratic)	4	1	5	5	4
CNT (Anarchist)	—	—	—	—	0
Others	17	13	16	13	33
TOTAL	100	100	100	100	100

Sources: Adapted from *Punto y Hora*, February 16–22, 1978, p. 46; Robert Fishman, "The Labor Movement in Spain: From Authoritarianism to Democracy," *Comparative Politics* 14 (April 1982): 291.

and secretive, but it may have had a profound impact on the nature of popular politics on the plains. In terms of election results during the late 1970s, the Carlist candidates received between 3 and 6 percent of the plains vote on the whole, but between 10 and 20 percent of the vote in smaller farming communities. These figures probably understate the ideological impact of the Carlists on members of the rural classes who moved to nearby industrialized cities for gainful employment. In the rapidly growing cities of Pamplona and Vitoria, avowedly Maoist trade unionists won pluralities in the union elections administered by the Spanish government during the late 1970s, a phenomenon that did not occur elsewhere (see table 2.1).[37]

Because of the frequent public unruliness of poorer classes after the mid-1950s, the southern plains had become notorious among Spanish capitalists by the early 1970s. Angered by the prices offered by government-licensed retailers, farmers threw produce at police and government officials. Former agricultural workers then employed in cities constantly initiated wildcat strikes—so many that in 1973 almost 12 percent of the recorded strikes in Spain took place in the newly industrialized cities of the plains, which contained less than 2 percent of the country's industrial labor force.[38] Troubled by the multiple manifestations of class conflict, a former president of Navarra's senate wrote a personal letter to Carrero Blanco (at the time, Franco's handpicked successor) requesting his aid in ending "the very grave disorders" in Navarra. He then wrote an official letter to the landlord-dominated Navarrese senate denouncing the present "dangers of social radicalism."[39]

CONCLUSION

This chapter has described some of the turbulence that co-incided with the early years of ETA—clearly, armed actions by ETA did not occur in a social and political vacuum. Fishermen, family farmers, sharecroppers, and farmhands were being economically threatened. In addition, they perceived that the government was not immediately responsive to their needs or calls for help. To energize officials, extrainstitutional forms of political action were undertaken.

As several scholars have emphasized, many of the supporters of armed struggle in ETA came from the countryside. They were often farm born and bred but worked in small manufacturing towns that were ringed by baserriak. In debates within ETA, they justified violence by saying it would detonate the revolutionary dynamite of the countryside.

It seems that many of these semirural etarras were sympathetic to the plight of the dispossessed in the countryside and viewed capitalism as the root cause of the economic decline of particular rural classes. Their militancy expressed not simply cultural discomfort with modern ways but personal familiarity with ongoing economic crises. Zulaika, who has closely studied an ETA cell in a single mountain community, comments:

> It cannot be accidental that, of the four members who formed an ETA cell during the middle 1970s, the baserri house of one of them was demolished for the construction of the Bilbao-Behobia freeway and rebuilt nearby; the baserri family of

another of them sold its land to industry and moved into a newly built apartment in Itziar's center. The brother of one of them, heir of the baserria, who for years experienced the typical situation of being unable to find a wife, committed suicide. . . . Membership in ETA and anticapitalism, although ideologically distinguishable, were in fact inextricable in the experience of the activists. Perceiving the baserri property of their parents at the complete mercy of capitalism, the revolutionary goal became evident: the motherland—"our" land— had to be rescued from the greed of outsiders and given the *askatasuna* (freedom) of a native and collective ownership.[40]

Using police reports, Clark has similarly documented that violent attacks by ETA usually occurred in the small towns and semiagricultural communities of the Basque mountains, and often were committed by individuals who earlier had participated in nonviolent forms of economic protest.[41] These findings are consistent with Zulaika's view of ETA's violence being at least in part an attempt to deal with capitalist dislocation in the Basque countryside.

Perhaps their awareness of both the economic worries and the grass-roots political activism and acts of protest in rural and semirural areas explains why the proponents of armed struggle argued so steadfastly that the everyday people of Euskadi were on the verge of rebelling spontaneously against existing government institutions and economic arrangements. Such a judgment may have rung true for these etarras, given their personal experiences in the nonviolent rural movements of the region. Perhaps in a more passive political environment such an argument about the region's potential for popular insurgency would not have found as many serious advocates, and their proposals would have fallen on deaf ears. It is tempting to speculate that the mobilizations of the countryside inspired hopes in these etarras that popular radicalism was possible.

Still, economically motivated unrest in the region cannot fully explain the rise of Basque political violence. After all, most members of ETA who advocated armed struggle probably would not have planned for action had there not first been a highly visible, regionwide, avowedly anticapitalist movement that could attract and recruit them. Indeed, many advocates of armed struggle during the 1970s had not known about ETA or thought about joining until they first had learned from state-controlled media of widespread urban mobilizations to protest the trial of sixteen political prisoners who belonged to the militantly nationalist and anticapitalist movement called ETA.[42]

Where did ETA come from? What sort of anticapitalist ideology did it have? And why were so many labor groups demonstrating for the release of the ETA prisoners? For answers, it will be useful to look further at local political struggles but to shift the focus to the cities, their factories and their work forces.

CHAPTER THREE

WORKING-CLASS MOVEMENTS IN
THE BASQUE REGION, 1890–1980

*T*he activist-historian Francisco Letamendia (political pseudonym "Ortzi") once wrote that the history of ETA is inextricably
connected with the history of the region's labor politics, especially the militancy of the 1960s. In the words of Letamendia:

> The Basque workers' movement was always present in the
> minds of ETA militants during those early years, as a radical-
> izing factor, as a source of sympathy and loyalty, as a magnet
> drawing them toward socialist postulates, and also—why not
> say it—as a root of discord among the different sectors of
> opinion which began incubating within ETA from that time.[1]

According to Letamendia, not only did the workers' militancy encourage hopes among etarras of a regional revolution by the economically disadvantaged, but the labor movement's temporary demonstrations of support for ETA, especially during the 1970 Burgos
trial (to be described in more detail in chapter 8), gave ETA additional
visibility (needed to attract new recruits) and reinforced the hopes of
etarras that an alliance with local labor organizations was possible.
Finally, several ETA activists, many of whom either began to participate in labor politics or came from labor-organizing backgrounds,
became key protagonists within the movement during debates over
the effectiveness and purpose of armed struggle. Their efforts to limit
the ambitions of advocates of armed struggle and their decisions to
separate and form organizations apart from the latter had important
implications for the evolution of the movement's politics.

Letamendia insists that ETA did not exist in social isolation. It was nourished by local proletarian militancy that provided it with some recruits, sustained hopes of popular insurgency, fostered visions about a future socialist order, and ultimately pulled the movement into radically different political directions. Let us accept for the moment Letamendia's argument and assume that to understand the evolution of ETA one must know something about the local proletarian environment. What was the evolving labor movement that the etarras beheld? In particular, what were its goals, activities, and strategies?

EARLY LABOR MOVEMENTS

The region's physical geography, in particular the central location of the Cantabrian Mountains, has long affected its labor politics. For a century, the mountains have impeded communication and coordinated actions throughout the region. And within the mountains organized movements for the improvement of conditions almost always have been splintered, with workers in each manufacturing town pursuing their own priorities and plans of action.

Working-Class Protests and Organizations in Bilbao

The most famous Basque city in terms of labor militancy is probably Bilbao. Its social geography was discussed in chapter 1. Hence it suffices to say here that its two "societies" on opposite sides of the Nervión—the poorer, proletarian community of the western bank and the wealthier, bourgeois community of the eastern bank[2]— live in isolation from each other. According to Basque social satirist and political cartoonist Juan Carlos Eguillor, it is not unusual to meet people in Bilbao who have lived there their entire lives but who never have crossed the river to see how the other side lives.[3]

Socially and physically isolated, the working-class neighborhoods have developed their own self-consciously proletarian culture, with its own newspapers, music, celebrations, and meeting places. Today, buildings and parks are covered with posters and graffiti denouncing the monied interests and wealthier classes of the town and their purported allies in government. Bars catering to specific working-class parties ranging from Socialist to Maoist easily can be found in the older downtown section of the city.

This proletarian culture is not simply a post-Franquist phenomenon. Explicitly working-class ideologies and exclusively proletarian organizations have existed in Bilbao since the middle of the nineteenth century. In September 1868 local industrial workers formed one of the earliest chapters in Western Europe of the First International. After Marx and Bakunin's feud, a group of local workers organized one of the first chapters of the Socialist party in Spain. By 1910 there were more than seventy local Socialist chapters on the Left Bank, and dozens of Socialist meetinghouses. Meanwhile, the mining and factory settlements had become the first in Spain to elect Socialist candidates to municipal office, and Bilbao was the first district to send a Socialist representative to the Spanish parliament.[4]

In 1890 a group of miners on the Left Bank called for a general strike to protest low wage levels, the management of company stores, and the conditions of company bunkhouses. More than 20,000 workers from different industries in and around the city participated, and the strike was bloody. Dozens of miners were shot, and many strikers gleefully destroyed expensive machinery. Partly because they were pressured by the Spanish state, the mine owners gave in temporarily to the workers' demands; and several improvements were made in terms of workers' rights and treatment. The strike was a landmark event: the first general strike to be called in an Iberian city. Perhaps more important, the strike worked, at least in the short run. It was a collective action that attracted workers' attention and prompted emulation: between 1890 and 1910, industrial workers in the greater Bilbao area launched seventeen major industrywide strikes and four citywide general strikes.

Extant labor songs from Bilbao convey the class consciousness, organizational infrastructure, and political militancy that were evolving along the western bank:

A Song for the First of May

Arise, fellow workers
For the day has dawned
It is the First of May

When the general strike is called,
You will see how quickly
We workers will come forth,
Telling the big shots,
"You'll exploit us no longer."
Let's sing together
Of the glory of labor
For having thrown off
The yoke of slavery.
Down with capitalism
That lives on injustice.
Long live the workers
United in brotherhood!

A Song for the Picket Line

The scab is a social derelict
Who helps the boss steal from the workers
The right to a better life.
Traitor!
The worker who betrays a strike
Will get what he deserves
Before very long.
He will see his children scorned,
Despised and shut out
Because of him.
Some day he'll realize
The dirty work he's done
Against his own interests.

*A Song Commemorating the Anniversary of
the 1905 Russian Revolution*

Don't lose heart, Russian people,
Go on fighting, do not weaken,
For the International supports
Your revolution.
We, too, demand revenge upon
The autocratic rabble.
Let the blood of the oppressor
Run through the streets like a river.[5]

The memoirs of labor organizer Oscar Pérez Solís also express the energy, optimism, and activism of the labor movement on the Left Bank during the early decades of the twentieth century. Solís, originally a republican activist in a rural, non-Basque province, had been exiled from that province for libeling a landlord. Arriving in Bilbao for the first time, Solís reported feeling immediately "more virile, more intrepid, and more vigorous in spirit."

> The ambience of Vizcaya (which for the first time caused me to be an actor in the real class war—not the simulacrum of social war that I had experienced in Castile), opened a profound breach in my anti-Bolshevik opinions . . . The masses were beginning to make me theirs, drawing my thinking and my will toward theirs . . . I began to slide toward Communism in the heated ambience of Vizcaya labor of 1920.[6]

In the wake of the Russian Revolution of 1917, the rapidly evolving proletarian culture in Bilbao underwent a profound ideological and organizational split (as did working-class movements throughout Western Europe).[7] Inspired by romantic reports about the quasi-anarchistic soviets, a small group of Socialists in Bilbao helped establish the Communist party of Spain. They believed that the Russian Revolution had demonstrated the efficacy of relentless workplace militancy in developing revolutionary class consciousness as well as laying the institutional foundation for a successful postcapitalist society. Basque Communists, such as Oscar Pérez Solís, Dolores Ibárruri, and Facundo Perezagua, argued that local strikes, slowdowns, and public articulation of grievances provided the psychological and organizational experiences necessary for a future proletarian revolution. They also called for the immediate secession of the Basque region from the Spanish state as well as an immediate social revolution in the region that would mimic the legendary soviets of the early Russian Revolution. In its 1933 booklet of resolutions, the Basque chapter of the Spanish Communist party declared its formal objective to be the creation of a "Free Soviet Republic of the Workers and Peasants of Euskadi." They therefore advocated protest and rebellion against evils in the factories. "We were criticized for 'anarchist tendencies,' " recalls Ibárruri in her memoirs. "Our party might well have served as the model for the kind of errors Lenin described in *'Left Wing' Communism: An Infantile Disorder.*"[8]

During the 1930s the Basque chapter of the Communist party

of Spain officially renamed itself the Communist party of Euskadi (or the Communist party of the Basque Homeland). The Communist party also denounced the organizing attempts of the Spanish Socialist party's union, the Unión General de Trabajadores (UGT), as "social fascism" because the union seemed to be seeking a strong Spanish state that would intervene in the economy at the bureaucrats' and parliamentarians' will and in which workplace democracy would not be a preeminent priority.

Despite the Communists' constant efforts to organize future soviets in the villages and factories of the Basque region, most politically active workers in Bilbao chose to belong not to the Communist party of Euskadi, but to the Spanish Socialist party and its union, the UGT. For a number of reasons—not the least being the legal protection that during its dictatorship the Primo de Rivera government gave the Socialist party—the party had enjoyed a large number of dues-paying members during the 1920s and 1930s. It reportedly had more than 30,000 members in Bilbao during the early 1930s, in contrast to the less than 9,000 members of the Basque Communist party.[9]

Several American and British labor historians have emphasized the centrality of the Basque region for the dissemination of socialist ideas throughout Spain. Gerald Meaker, for example, has described the Bilbao area as "the heartland of Spanish socialism," and Gerald Brenan has described the Basque region as "chief center for the diffusion of Socialism to the rest of Spain."[10] Socialism, however, is an ambiguous term with many meanings, depending on the historical period being considered and a user's orientation or intent. Accordingly, regarding the traditions of labor activism in the Basque region, it is useful to ask: What was the substance of the Basque Socialists' goals and strategies? And how did they differ from the current goals and strategies of the Basque Communists?

In contrast to the Communist party of Euskadi, most Socialists in and around Bilbao advocated a popularly elected parliament for Spain. In principle, it would be sovereign over all other social and political institutions. It would (1) protect the rights of industrial unions to organize, negotiate, and strike, and (2) represent workers' interests in domestic policy making. They also wanted the Spanish state to provide welfare services for the downtrodden and to redistribute land among individual renters so as to increase farm production. Further, most Socialists in the region wanted industrial unions to be statewide in scope and to fight for uniform wages and work conditions. In short, through a program of parliamentary sovereignty and industrywide collective bargaining, the Socialists hoped to improve the standard of living and workplace conditions of all employed workers in Spain.[11]

To attract future parliamentary allies, especially among middle-class republican parties, the leaders of the Basque Socialists, such as Indalecio Prieto, tried to minimize the use of strikes in labor conflicts and to soften militant and radical rhetoric about the need for an imminent overthrow of the capitalist system. They argued that openly radical behavior was politically irresponsible. Allegedly, it was necessary first to secure a parliamentary form of government and legal rights for unions, if the conditions of workers were ever to improve. The Basque Communists, however, viewed the strategy of interclass compromise as unlikely to succeed in the long run because of the disinterest of the middle class in workers' issues and its distrust of workers' political power. They believed also that in the short run the strategy entailed the willful sacrifice of the needs of industrial workers and the possible weakening of workers' loyalties to proletarian organizations.[12]

During the 1920s, the ideological and strategic differences between the Basque Socialists and Basque Communists deepened. Correspondingly, organizational rivalries between them became extremely heated. Both fought for control of local union halls and other scarce organizational resources. Periodically, the rivalry evolved into gunplay, with both sides suffering casualties. Among major Spanish cities during the 1920s, Bilbao ranked only after Barcelona in terms of labor-related shootings; it ranked first in terms of labor-related gun users as percentage of total population.[13] The chasm between the Communists and the Socialists deepened, if anything, by the early 1930s as both parties competed for similar constituencies. A temporary truce was reached in 1935, when both groups became alarmed by the unexpected electoral and paramilitary strength of the Spanish Right. A popular front was established. Their alliance of convenience was strengthened in the short run by the triumph of Franco and the subsequent repression of both groups by Spain's new authoritarian regime.

Working-Class Protests and Organizations in the Mountains

Until around 1910 urban workers in factory towns of the Cantabrian Mountains lacked the proletarian consciousness, trade-union organizations, and explicitly working-class parties typical of the miners, metalworkers, and transportation workers in and around Bilbao. The absence of a vibrant, self-conscious proletarian culture —with its own organizations, songs, symbols, meeting places, and memories of collective actions and rebellious undertakings—can be attributed to two factors: residential patterns within the factory towns and the small-scale workplaces.

Located in narrow river valleys, the manufacturing towns of 10,000 to 20,000 people are physically compact. Members of different classes do not live miles apart in distinct neighborhoods, but together in close communication. Institutions and activities they have in common, such as churches, stores, schools, and recreational activities, traditionally have softened conflicts of interest generated in the workplace. Familiarity and informal social pressures, and the absence of a large labor pool, have prevented workshop owners from being too ruthless toward employees, and thus have allowed wage earners to influence the running of workshops, generally without recourse to strikes of any consequence.

Moreover, before the 1950s manufacturing in the mountains tended to be labor intensive and highly skilled. Whereas production in the steel mills, iron mines, and naval yards of Bilbao often involved heavy machinery and multitudes of unskilled or semiskilled laborers, production in the mountains characteristically involved small workshops with handsful of highly trained and difficult-to-replace craftsmen, making furniture, handguns, hand tools, and other finished products. Workers with scarce skills had leverage over owners who needed them; they could negotiate by temporarily suspending their labor or by threats of walkouts, without having to resort to more extreme measures.

The first large-scale association of urban workers in the Cantabrian Mountains occurred in 1911: 179 skilled craftsmen formed the Solidarity of Basque Workers, or SOV (later the ELA-STV).[14] The SOV was radically decentralized in its formal organization. In each shop artisans with similar skills were expected to establish their own self-financing and self-directing chapter. Even though it was hoped that chapters within a town would cooperate with one another, each chapter was formally autonomous with regard to determining its issues, priorities, and methods of influencing owners.

During the confederation's first two decades, each chapter acted on its own when addressing specific problems such as job classification, promotion schedules, hours and wages, duties, pace of production, and introduction of new machinery. Leaders of the SOV did not dispute the right of a private individual to own a workshop and to keep a fair share of its profits. Indeed, they saw such persons as part of the "producing classes" that physically made things, in contrast to nonlaboring financiers, rentiers, and state bureaucrats who did not earn their livelihoods through the sweat of their brows and the creation of physical goods. The leaders often denounced "capitalism" as a system of production in their public speeches and writings. However, their "capitalism" involved not private property per se but large-scale, impersonal firms in which workers have no voice.

SOV leaders usually argued that there was a natural harmony of interests between skilled artisans and owners of small workshops: both classes wanted financially successful enterprises in which high-quality goods were made by well-treated workers. It would follow, then, that either side's grievances could be handled harmoniously. According to some publicists in the movement, what sometimes prevented constructive give-and-take was not objective and unavoidable conflict of interest but personal attributes, such as inordinate greed or pride, especially on the part of the owners. Some SOV leaders explained these personal vices in terms of Christian metaphysics (such as humankind's innate moral depravity since leaving the Garden of Eden). But a number of leaders offered a more secular and sociological explanation, laying personal shortcomings at the door of large-scale capitalism: owners' excessive wealth fostered the avaricious and arrogant personality.

One theoretical current within the SOV argued strongly for workers' cooperatives as the best way to combat the imminent rise of large-scale capitalism in the mountains. In the cooperatives, a company's permanent workers would own shares of its stock, would not be fired unless the company went bankrupt, and would be able to vote for a governing board empowered to appoint and dismiss managers and to review all important management decisions. Favoring unmediated dialogue between workers and owners, most SOV leaders opposed the intervention of government in labor issues. Indeed, they commonly portrayed the Spanish state as the promoter and protector of large industry and financiers on the coast, and as the opponent of small businesses and skilled, self-directing crafts.

By the 1930s labor-saving machinery and the world depression had weakened the bargaining power of skilled workers in the mountains. Many leaders in the SOV began to accept strikes and walkouts as legitimate methods by which craftsmen should protect their interests. In 1932 the SOV for the first time endorsed and aided strikers in the lumber industry. The confederation also struck with the Communists and Socialists during the short-lived Asturias Revolution of 1934. Despite the increasing militancy and coordination of strike activity by the SOV, it remained largely an apolitical organization. Members were more interested in protecting the rights of existing crafts within isolated workshops than in capturing the state electorally and then using it to discipline and reform capital at large. The SOV may have become more militant and confrontationalist by the 1930s, but it still was not radical in the specific senses of endorsing new state regulations of the economy, proposing nationalizations of industry, or advocating the extension of welfare services.

Between 1937 and the middle 1950s the SOV, like the Basque Communists and Socialists, was driven underground. But many of its programs and strategies reappeared during the late 1960s and 1970s. The Basque Nationalist party tried to direct the union's activities during the Francoist years, as there was some overlap of the party's and the union's leadership, but many SOV activists rejected the party's authority by the early 1960s, especially in Guipúzcoa, the union's provincial stronghold.

QUIESCENCE AND MILITANCY DURING
THE FRANCO REGIME

The military forces supporting Franco captured the remaining parts of the Basque region in 1937. Franco immediately banned all proletarian organizations designed for political and social conflict, such as political parties and trade unions. Laws were passed making strikes of any kind illegal. The new government tried in 1938 to redesign labor relations according to an organic theory of society. Spanish society theoretically resembled a huge body, and the overriding duty of its members (or organs) was to promote the body's preservation. The specific duty of the producing organs—such as companies, entrepreneurs, and employees—was to generate sufficient material goods to save the society from domestic and foreign dangers.

To insure a high output of appropriate goods, the government required that all employers and employees (with very few exceptions, such as domestic servants) join a gigantic, nationwide syndical organization that would coordinate production. Many local officials within the syndicate, such as the shop stewards, were elected directly by the producers affected, but only after the government first investigated and approved of the candidates' political commitments. Middle-level and regional officials were elected indirectly. The syndicate's top officers, such as those who sat in the Spanish *Cortes* (parliament) were appointed directly by the government, and often by Franco himself. Until 1967, the syndicate's hierarchy was to be staffed solely by Falange militants (a requirement thereafter dropped).

The national syndicate's powers vis-à-vis workers were many. Its officers recommended labor policy, such as wage levels and safety standards for workplaces, to officials in the labor ministry. In addition, syndicate officers administered many of the regime's social insurance programs and helped construct public housing. They also ran vacation centers for workers, medical centers, an apprentice system, a placement service, five labor universities, and over 120 craft schools.[15]

Many industrial workers were not convinced that their interests were being adequately represented through the syndical organization. Of course, several benefits resulted from the new social system: employers no longer could easily dismiss redundant workers, and fringe benefits (especially in comparison to earlier decades in Spanish history) were generous. According to Charles Anderson, "In terms of protections against layoffs and firing, holidays, and insurance and social benefits, the total package of welfare programs was comparable to most European practice."[16] Nonetheless, workers' real wages declined during the 1940s, as the wage increases decreed by the government always fell behind price increases. Sima Lieberman is typical of economic historians who study Francoist Spain when she reports:

> The real value of wages and salaries in 1956 was probably 15% to 37% below the pre–Civil War level; although nomi-

nal wages and salaries had increased by about six times since 1936, prices of meat had increased by ten times, those of bread by twelve times and those of potatoes by eighteen times.[17]

Feeling overlooked in the Francoist policy-making process, many urban workers, particularly in the Basque region, resorted to large general strikes from time to time. Obviously such actions were highly hazardous because of police repression, but another problem was high unemployment (hovering around 10 percent during the 1940s and 1950s), which meant that employers often did not feel economically compelled to rehire those workers accused by the government of illegal strike activity. Because of the clear risk to one's employment, strike activity was sporadic, and it was not unusual for a dramatic general strike, such as the political-economic strike of 1947 in which 6,000 Vizcayan workers were arrested and 15,000 Basque workers subsequently sacked, to be followed by years of passivity.[18]

But the economic and political circumstances dampening labor activism were not fixed. The Basque economy grew rapidly after 1960. There was a sudden rise in demand for Basque industrial and manufactured goods in Spain and the West in general. Between 1960 and 1963, 893 new industrial and manufacturing firms arose in the coastal province of Guipúzcoa alone; and another 694 such firms expanded.[19] The number of employees in regional chemical companies rose from 26,000 in 1965 to 33,000 in 1970.[20]

Increased production meant, among other things, that Basque businesses needed more employees, creating a temporary shortage of workers. Business leaders began petitioning the Spanish government to encourage surplus populations from the interior of Spain to move to the Basque region, where new and expanded factories were badly shorthanded.[21] Each year tens of thousands of rural people, often from the partially educated lower-middle classes of rural Spain, came in search of employment. By the late 1970s more than 40 percent of all permanent residents were either recent immigrants or children of recent immigrants.[22] Still, the labor market remained tight, as the new enterprises required more machine hands and skilled laborers than existed in the region.

To keep their workers and attract new ones, employers made numerous concessions, such as wage increases. And aware of their

Table 3.1. Strike Activity in the Basque Region and Spain during the Closing Years of the Franco Regime

Year	Number of Government-Reported Labor Conflicts in the Basque Region	Number of Government-Reported Labor Conflicts in Spain	Reported Basque Labor Conflicts as Percentage of All Labor Conflicts in Spain
1963	100	640	15.6
1964	146	384	38.0
1965	60	164	36.6
1966	54	179	30.1
1967	184	567	32.5
1968	76	351	21.6
1969	257	491	52.3
1970	668	1,595	41.8
1971	174	616	28.2
1972	280	853	32.8
1973	326	931	35.0
1974	1,028	2,290	44.8

Source: Adapted from Luis C-Núñez Astrain, *Clases sociales en Euskadi* (San Sebastián: Editorial Txertoa, 1977), p. 198.

temporary bargaining leverage, workers used threats of walkouts and strikes to extract even greater concessions. Nor did they limit themselves to threats. Every year Basque workers engaged in scores of collective actions—including wildcat strikes, spontaneous walkouts, solidarity strikes, and some citywide general strikes—despite stringent prohibitory laws (see table 3.1).[23]

Meanwhile, a new political and economic institution, the Jurado de Empresa, or factory jury, became more widely used.[24] Factory juries originally were established by the Spanish government in 1953, apparently as part of a broader set of policies aimed at increasing trade between Spain and other countries in the West. Between 1939 and the middle 1960s most Western governments had refused to permit trade with Spain, partly on grounds that because independent trade unions were outlawed in Francoist Spain, wages were artificially low, and Spanish businesses therefore could undersell foreign competition. The Spanish government attempted to counter this argument by requiring that every plant with fifty or more have a factory jury—composed of representatives of workers and management—before which employees' grievances could be presented, reviewed, and resolved without the intervention of the state. The jury was also to collect money from the employers and employees for educational and welfare services, such as summer camps and schools for workers' children. The Franco regime often cited the more successful projects as examples of the superiority of its institutional alternative to independent trade unions.

The factory jury was required to have an equal number of representatives from three groups: management, technical workers, and nontechnical workers. Each group was free to nominate and elect its own representatives without interference from the other two groups. The ministry of labor had the right to suspend any or all rights of a factory jury if its behavior threatened overall "harmony" within an industry.

Even though by law the factory jury was formally representative, until the 1960s most industrial workers viewed it as a publicity stunt and a cruel joke. After all, the original jurisdiction of the factory jury was quite narrow. For example, it was not permitted to address layoffs and demotions. Further, many employers and state officials disregarded the laws requiring factory juries, arguing that they were another unnecessary fetter on entrepreneurial energy. Workers also feared that their more outspoken representatives would be sacked on trumped-up charges (laws protecting labor leaders from unjustified dismissal, in fact, were not rigorously enforced until the late 1960s). And some workers who believed in the principle of proletarian unity feared that the decentralized organization of factory juries would undermine class solidarity, for through participation in them, workers might become preoccupied with their own immediate interests to the detriment of the interests of industrial workers elsewhere.[25]

The outlawed Communists of the Basque region were among the first group of workers to experiment seriously with the possibilities of the factory jury as an instrument to protect and promote working-class interests. After being driven underground in Francoist Spain and expelled from Socialist trade unions, the Communists decided to gain working-class visibility, gratitude, and support through participation in all available public institutions, such as factory juries and the neighbors' associations. In addition, many Catholic labor activists vigorously participated in the juries, especially in Navarra, where the Communist party was weak and Catholic labor groups combined recent Catholic social doctrines with Maoist and Leninist ideas. Only leaders of the Socialist party and a handful of local anarchists officially refused to participate. They argued that the juries legitimized the Franco regime in the eyes of foreign powers and domestic classes, thus artificially extending the regime's longevity.[26]

By the middle 1960s the factory jury had become an important institution to thousands of Basque workers because in many plants it had become an effective method for redressing certain grievances. The factory jury's sudden effectiveness was due in part to the rising militancy of the workers. Factory owners desperately wanted a disciplined work force and hoped that through the use of the factory jury closings due to strikes could be avoided. Meanwhile workers continued to use strikes and the threat of strikes to extract the best deal possible. Partly because of the unending need to remind owners of the consequences of not taking workers' grievances and demands seriously, the annual number of strikes trebled during the 1960s, and the region soon gained notoriety among capitalists for its walkouts, picketing, slowdowns, and solidarity strikes. Even though less than 11 percent of all industrial workers in Spain lived in the region, 37 percent of all officially recorded strikes between 1967 and 1974 occurred there; 30 percent of all workers who went on strike during those years worked there; 36 percent of all working hours lost because of strikes between 1968 and 1974 were lost there; and in 1969 alone more than half of all officially recorded strikes occurred there.[27] Hoping to minimize future disruptions, factory owners increasingly turned to the factory jury as an alternative forum for resolving disputes.

In addition, workers in the Basque region began to organize general strikes and solidarity strikes during the 1960s (1) to put pressure on companies with multiple plants in the region and (2) to demand new political rights from the regime, such as the right to create independent trade unions, to have labor parties, and to have factory juries in all plants regardless of size. After 1967 more than half the recorded strikes in the region included demands for broader political reforms. In terms of popular support, the general strikes and semipolitical strikes were extremely successful, sometimes receiving the support of more than 75 percent of all industrial workers in the region. "No other part of the working class in Spain showed such a level of solidarity," declares José Maravall.[28]

During these waves of wildcat, solidarity, and general strikes emerged two novel working-class institutions known as the factory assembly (*asamblea de fabrica*) and the workers' commission (*comisión obrera*). At a factory assembly all interested workers in a plant could discuss their grievances and plans, irrespective of their political or union affiliations and sympathies.[29] The principle of direct democracy (or, as Basque workers sometimes phrased it, "democracy without adjectives") was taken seriously in most assemblies. Indeed, sometimes democratic norms were followed so scrupulously that promanagement workers freely attended assemblies and afterward reported what went on to managers. At a typical meeting organizational leaders, such as representatives from the factory juries, presented issues and policy alternatives. Then any worker could pose questions to the leaders and speak before the assembly. After discussion was exhausted, votes were taken, and the majority prevailed. Until the middle 1970s no single party or union openly monopolized discussions or rammed decisions through, even though members of underground labor organizations were present in almost all assemblies.[30]

The second institutional innovation, the workers' commission, was a temporary, ad hoc strike committee.[31] It had developed originally to collect and distribute strike funds, formulate strike demands, and negotiate with owners. Once a strike was over, it dissolved itself, and its decision-making authority returned to the plant's assembly. For a variety of reasons—including increasing state repression—the strike commissions became permanent, ongoing organizations by the late 1960s.

Employers in the Basque region differed in their judgments about the legal factory juries, the quasilegal factory assemblies, and generally extralegal workers' commissions. Some companies, such as Laminación de Bandas en Fria, adamantly refused to meet with factory juries, fired workers' representatives on the juries, and hired strikebreakers. In contrast, managers in plants owned by Firestone encouraged the formation of factory juries and factory assemblies, apparently in the hope of improving relations with workers and avoiding future disruptions in production.[32]

The Spanish government responded to the militancy of Basque labor in two ways. First, hoping both to cool workers' tempers and to limit their demands, the government legalized narrowly defined "economic" strikes in 1966; that is, strikes whose aims were limited to immediate plant-level demands and that were not acts of sympathy for workers in other plants or strikes against the existing regime. Earlier (1958) the government legalized local-level collective bargaining, with contracts subject to approval by the Spanish Syndical Organization. Many manufacturers and industrialists supported the government's new toleration of economic strikes and plant-level negotiations. The owners hoped that by making strikes and plant-level collective bargaining legal, it would be easier to identify bona fide representatives of local workers and negotiate quickly. However, the new legal right to strike also made factory juries legally more powerful vis-à-vis management. Henceforth if management tried to ignore the grievances presented to the jury, representatives of employees could legally threaten an economic strike and be less fearful of state repression. (Workers still had to fear, of course, decisions by the Spanish government about the levels of strike violence; for destruction of company property and bodily harm to nonstriking workers remained punishable offenses.)[33]

The state's second and very different response to the seemingly endless economic and political strikes in the Basque region was to increase repression. In 1967 the government declared a "state of exception" in the Basque region and temporarily suspended civil liberties. It was the first of more than a dozen states of exception declared in the region between 1967 and 1981. The supreme court ruled that workers' commissions were subversive and illegal. The rights of assembly, press, and habeas corpus were formally ended throughout the region. The Spanish police arrested all workers who had held elective posts in the factory juries. Many labor leaders were beaten badly while incarcerated.[34]

Because of the simultaneous successes and repression of factory juries, factory assemblies, and workers' commissions, industrial workers in the Basque region were deeply divided over how best to advance their interests. Trotskyists, Maoists, and Marxist Catholics such as the Catholic Worker Vanguard and the Catholic Worker Youth, generally argued that illegal solidarity strikes were necessary tactics for compelling employers to take workers' demands seriously. Further, democratic assemblies and factory juries were important institutions for educating workers about workplace problems and the intransigence of employers. Members of the Communist party of Euskadi, however, increasingly favored restrictions on discussions and public votes in factory assemblies because of the need for internal security. They also advocated greater prudence in the use of solidarity strikes and the creation of industrywide negotiating teams that would bargain peaceably with organized groups of employers. The Communists believed that factory assemblies and solidarity strikes had provided the Spanish government and police with pretexts for repression and the suspension of civil liberties, thus making future labor organizing difficult if not impossible. What was needed was a constitutionally liberal state with an elected parliament and legally protected rights for unions. This required that workers' groups moderate their behavior and demands so as not to frighten middle-class groups working for the democratization of the Francoist regime. Thus, the Communists increasingly adopted a position with respect to strikes and plant assemblies that, ironically, resembled the position typical of the Socialists before the rise of Franco.

Angered by the Communist party's proposals, several revolutionary proletarian organizations, including the Movimiento Comunista (or Communist movement), the Trotskyist ETA-VI, and the Maoist "ORT," formed a separate coalition within the Comisiones Obreras and tried to push them in a more radically syndicalist direction. The new coalition praised factory assemblies, solidarity strikes, and wildcat strikes; expressed opposition to continued use of factory juries and other legal channels; and considered the assemblies to be prototypes of a future postcapitalist order in Spain. They also accused the Communist party of aspiring to a bureaucratic dictatorship over the working class of the region. Purportedly, members of the Communist party wanted professional bureaucrats to decide questions about workplace grievances and workers' priorities and needs, and wanted ordinary workers to be mute.[35]

ECONOMIC RECESSION AND THE POLITICS OF UNION CENTRALIZATION

After the death of Franco in 1975 the political and economic circumstances of urban workers in Spain again dramatically changed. As the new constitutional order was being determined, the future of factory juries, union rights, and job tenure became increasingly unclear. Scholars often characterize these years simply as a time of liberation for Spanish workers, when they won rights to form independent unions and working-class political parties. But such generalizations tend to be too cheery, and they minimize ambiguities in the changing political and economic status of Spanish workers. For example, even though independent unions had the legal right to exist as early as 1977, their right to organize at the workplace and their future roles as interlocutors in collective bargaining were not clearly established until 1980. During the interregnum government, harassment of union organizers and strike leaders continued, and according to some international observers such as Amnesty International and correspondents of the *New York Times*, there was a significant amount of torture of labor leaders by the police, as well as occasional shootings of unarmed demonstrators. During the late 1970s and early 1980s, employers also gained new rights to dismiss redundant workers; factory juries were either ignored or disbanded by employers and the state; and solidarity strikes and political strikes remained illegal. Workers, in other words, lost, as well as won, legal rights immediately after Franco's death; and the trade-offs were sources of controversy and concern among labor leaders and within the laboring community in general.[36]

At the same time, the recent pattern of rapid economic growth in Spain (and in the Basque region in particular) suddenly reversed. According to government estimates, unemployment within the region soared from under 1 percent in 1973 to over 11 percent in 1978, and to over 15 percent in 1982. Jobs quickly disappeared as many industrial firms went bankrupt. The number of employed workers shrank by more than 16 percent (160,000 workers) between 1975 and 1982. Total sales of machine tools in the Basque region (an indicator of levels of overall industrial production) declined 16 percent between 1975 and 1976. By the end of the 1970s, for the first time in three decades, more people were emigrating from the region than immigrating into it.[37]

Under these new conditions of political uncertainty and growing unemployment and plant shutdowns, strikes and militancy no longer seemed viable ways of improving the conditions of wage laborers. Strikebreakers could easily be found, and walking off a job could lead to permanent idleness. Consequently, there were 100 fewer officially reported strikes in 1980 than there were in 1979; and only 2 million hours of work were lost because of strikes in 1980, whereas 5 million had been lost in 1979. Even attendance at May Day marches

Table 3.2. Numbers of Basque Workers Officially
Unemployed, Selected Years, 1960–80

Year	Alava	Guipúzcoa	Navarra	Vizcaya	Region
		Province			
1960	622	1,804	254	944	3,624
1962	108	545	263	604	1,520
1964	210	482	646	588	1,926
1967	255	922	657	1,623	3,457
1969	397	1,617	595	2,313	4,922
1971	520	1,828	3,663	3,006	9,017
1973	643	2,784	1,335	4,291	9,053
1975	480	3,287	1,342	3,645	8,754
1976	1,217	8,465	5,326	8,751	23,759
1977	3,037	19,090	6,836	18,763	47,726
1978	4,140	21,939	9,088	25,376	60,543
1979	5,939	27,249	11,249	38,150	82,587
1980	8,772	28,365	14,901	52,001	104,039

Sources: Adapted from 1960–1973: Milagro García Crespo, Roberto
Velasco Barroetabeña, y Arantza Mendizabal Gorostiaga, La Economía
vasca durante el franquismo (Crecimiento y crisis de la Economía vasca: 1936–
1980). (Bilbao: Editorial la Gran Enciclopedia Vasca, 1981), p. 151;
1975–1980: Anuario estadístico de España (Madrid: Ministerio de Economía, 1980, 1981).

dropped. In the words of ERE, a Basque newsweekly with a prolabor
editorial line, the poorly attended 1980 May Day march in Bilbao
was "neither spectacular nor glorious."[38]

Almost every labor organization in the Basque region was con-
fronted with a crisis of identity, for it was far from clear how best to
respond to the altered circumstances. For example, there was a split
in the craft union of the mountains, the ELA-STV: a procapitalist faction (which advocated more cooperative relations with employers,
and favored the new technologies and job opportunities generated
by business prosperity and capitalist investment) versus a more militant and procooperative faction (which strongly opposed the labor-
saving technologies introduced by big businesses, was increasingly
hostile to private employers as a social class, and advocated the creation of producer cooperatives in lieu of private ownership of the
means of production). The ideological differences soon crystallized
into an organizational schism and two rival labor confederations:
ELA-STV(a), which favored greater cooperation with businesses, and
ELA-STV, which did not.

Despite political aid from the Basque Nationalist party and financial aid from various business groups, ELA-STV(a) remained small. For example, during the 1978 elections for representatives in plant-level collective bargaining, it won less than 3 percent of the negotiating posts that were contested. Nonetheless, other unions in the region were troubled by its existence, for it seemed that business leaders always could use the cooperative union to delegitimize the assertions by more militant unions that they were the genuine representatives of employees. Following such reasoning, the rival unions initiated a smear campaign. For example, Manuel Robles Arangiz, the president of ELA-STV, insinuated to the Basque press that ELA-STV(a) was directed by a wealthy Basque industrialist, by former Francoists, and by an underground and conservative Catholic organization, Opus Dei. Not surprisingly, the leaders of ELA-STV(a) vehemently denied these charges.[39]

Meanwhile, the original ELA-STV continued to be an extremely decentralized union, with each craft in each plant acting as its own bargaining unit and, if necessary, strike committee. Such decentralization was justified in public on grounds of democratic participation. It was alleged that centralization of authority within a union, which was typical of Socialist unions on the coast, provided few opportunities for the rank and file to participate in day-to-day decision making and hence a bureaucratic and impersonal tyranny replaced the face-to-face tyranny of a boss in a workshop. ELA-STV, in contrast, stood for the moral principle of "free unionism" that gave skilled workers in each workplace frequent opportunities to discuss and decide policies.[40]

In addition, leaders of ELA-STV increasingly criticized and opposed the use of wildcat strikes in other than dire circumstances. Their grounds were prudence: in the prevailing economic circumstances, dismissal for labor militancy could lead to permanent unemployment. The leaders argued that it is much better to negotiate in good faith and temporarily limit demands than to risk livelihoods through rash militancy.

> In these years we have lost strikes, lost hours of work, lost millions. This does not benefit us. Nor does it benefit workers. . . . This can be avoided, and must be avoided, precisely through clarification of representation. . . . The owners want to deal directly with workers, and workers likewise want to

deal directly with owners, without interference by vertical syndicates.[41]

Like the crafts-union tradition of the mountains, the Socialist industrial union, the UGT, also underwent internal organizational and ideological struggles immediately after the death of Franco. Although both the UGT and the Socialist party had officially refused to participate in the factory juries, members of the union and the party had been active in various clandestine projects throughout the Franco years. Exiled Socialists, for example, had started a school in France for labor organizers. Graduates of the school then secretly returned to Spain to rebuild Socialist organizations, particularly in Catalonia and southern Spain. In addition, many individual members of the UGT, particularly in the Basque region, had participated unofficially in the workers' commissions and factory assemblies, and also in the general strikes called by these two bodies.[42]

The first congress of the UGT to be held in Spain in almost four decades took place in Barcelona in 1978. It was the first of four annual congresses in which bitter fights occurred over the future direction of the Socialist party and the UGT. The issues that gave rise to the disagreements involved, on one level, four largely technical and procedural questions: (1) levels and distribution of membership dues, (2) authority of local chapters of the UGT to call strikes at their plants without prior approval of the national board of the UGT, (3) the UGT's future approval of the austerity plan designed by the non-Socialist Spanish government, and (4) rules concerning the direct representation of local chapters in future UGT congresses. Underlying these seemingly narrow procedural questions was, however, a growing ideological tension between the cautious and socially conservative national executive council of the UGT and the more innovative and militant leaders of local chapters, many of whom had participated in factory juries and workers commissions during the late 1960s and early 1970s. The executive council wanted to continue the nationwide and parliamentary strategies of the pre-Franco years. But many local leaders were intrigued by the experiments in factory juries and factory assemblies and advocated a more plant-level labor movement with regular assemblies open to all interested workers.[43]

The executive council won a majority of the struggles at the 1978 congress and also at the next three. The national congress voted to prohibit factions, which had the effect of atomizing opposition to the executive council. Henceforth, the writing of minority reports and rival platforms was to be considered grounds for punishment, including expulsion from the union. The executive council also successfully initiated changes in procedural rules concerning membership dues and budgeting. Dues, which always had been collected by each chapter at each plant, now were to be sent to a nationwide steering committee for each industry—a process that greatly reduced the local plants' financial resources to pursue their own activities. Formal rules concerning representation at the national congresses also were changed, so that the directly elected leaders of local chapters collectively constituted a smaller proportion of all representatives present. Prompted by the executive council, the union officially endorsed the principle of supporting only "winnable" strikes and dropped "socialism" as one of its explicit aims.[44]

The executive council also proposed annual negotiations between the official leaders of the union's industrial branches and the representatives of major business associations. Such negotiations allegedly would allow representatives of almost all major economic interests in Spain to meet face-to-face and solve the "global" economic problems of the time, such as the current depression, double-digit inflation, and technological renovation. The council argued that the negotiations should involve only labor leaders representing entire industrial branches because leaders of plant-level chapters were simply not well enough informed about the issues. Moreover, the latter lacked official authority to make binding promises for workers in other than their own plants; this would lead to uncertainty and frustration rather than constructive discussion and agreements. In any case, the individual plants were too weak to deal with the most important economic issues of the day—for example, unemployment and inflation—and therefore should not have a large voice in deciding upon policies. An instance of high-level negotiations that the executive council wished to institutionalize was the Moncloa Pact, a recent voluntary economic agreement between representatives of a national business organization, of national trade unions, and of the Spanish government. The pact was comprehensive—dealing with such things as tax reforms, voluntary controls on price increases, and voluntary controls on wage demands—and according to the executive council, was the outcome of patient discussion between informed and accountable leaders of all major economic interests.[45]

As in the past, several UGT chapters in the Basque region disagreed strongly with the moderate tone of the UGT. Their leaders openly criticized the decision to support the Moncloa Pact and warned of the hidden costs of national-level pacts in general. A few Basque trade unionists also proposed that the UGT publicly distance itself from the Spanish Socialist party by having all national-level officers in the union resign from any posts that they might hold within the Socialist party. Further, several Basque leaders urged increased cooperation between the UGT, the workers' commissions, and the ELA-STV in matters involving plant-level strikes and plant-level negotiations. This was essentially a policy proposal for increased decentralism that implicitly contradicted the centralist and "global" strategy advocated by the executive council. The dissenters consistently lost in key votes at the national congresses of the trade union and were under increasing pressure to muffle their criticism of the union's national leaders. Supporters of the executive council were a numerically larger faction (even within the Basque region). In 1980, after heated debate, the Basque regional congress of the UGT passed bylaws stating that it would support and obey all decisions made by the national congresses and decision-making bodies of the UGT.[46]

Heated debates over the future of plant-level militancy and assemblies also took place within the Communist party of Euskadi. As noted, the party began to participate in the workers' commissions around 1964. By 1970 it was by far the largest organized faction within the workers' commission movement. Indeed, it had become extremely difficult to untangle the history and activities of the party from the history and activities of the workers' commissions.

Between 1964 and 1970, many Communists in Spain saw the factory juries, plant-level assemblies, and ad hoc strike committees as the basis for a new type of socialist society. They enthusiastically watched the Italian experiments with factory councils during the late 1960s. In 1966 an anonymous group of Communists published an illegal pamphlet, *Toward a Syndicalist Future*, which proposed the creation of a confederation of autonomous factory councils throughout Spain. The first national congresses of workers' commissions, which met in 1968 and 1969, publicly criticized "vertical unions" (or hierarchically structured industrial unions) and advocated solidarity strikes and general strikes as proper tactics for winning benefits. Workplace democracy and workplace militancy were, for the moment, the guiding stars of both the workers' commissions movement and most members of the Communist party.[47]

After 1966 police repression increased considerably, especially in the Basque region. States of exception lasted three to six months and brought suspension of civil liberties. Many leaders of the workers' commissions were rounded up, and many labor organizers who were suspected of being members of the Communist party were tortured. In 1972 the entire national coordinating committee of the workers' commissions was incarcerated.

For the first time, significant numbers of Basque Communists who had been active in the workers' commissions saw workplace democracy and diffuse workplace militancy as unsatisfactory in terms of winning benefits. A split soon developed between the increasingly cautious members of the Communist party and the more enthusiastic supporters of workplace democracy and workers' councils, such as the members of the Communist movement and the Trotskyist International Communist League.

In 1976 representatives of the workers' commissions throughout Spain held their first legal nationwide meeting. A new permanent coordinating committee of forty-two persons was elected, thirty-seven of whom belonged to the Communist party. In addition, a professional staff was hired to aid the coordinating committee—a first. Several leading Communists openly ridiculed the extensive use of factory assemblies during strikes and contract negotiations as being amateurish and naive. Their derision presaged more serious actions against the traditional practice of workplace assemblies and factory juries. In 1978 the coordinating committee ordered workers' commissions to hire technical teams of professional negotiators or else be dismissed from the national confederation. According to Juan Pablo Landa Zapirain, the maintenance of technical staffs seriously depleted the meager financial resources of local workers' commissions. Soon, they were too poor to finance local-level strikes. In 1980 the coordinating committee also urged local workers' commissions to limit their demands for wage increases and immediate improvement of workplace conditions because the deteriorating condition of the Spanish economy required increased cooperation if companies were to survive.

Like the Executive Council of the Socialist party, the coordinating committee of the comisiones obreras recommended state-level negotiations between national representatives of business and of labor. In theory, it was better for businesses and workers to learn about their common interests and needs through peaceful dialogue than through strikes. In such fashion, they could in principle discover ways to improve profitability, job security, and wages, and then commit their sides to any jointly reached program. Clearly, the dominant vision of the comisiones obreras of the mid-1960s—of a radically decentralized confederacy of factory assemblies constantly engaged in wildcat strikes and solidarity marches—had been laid aside, or perhaps forgotten.[48]

The steady centralization and increasing quiescence of the workers' commission movement was not passively accepted by all members of the commissions, especially in the Basque region. Many still wanted to realize the ideas outlined in *Toward a Syndicalist Future*. Members of the Communist movement and the International Communist League began to disrupt congresses of workers' commissions with shouts of "general strike!" whenever announcements were made from the podium.[49] On the Basque plains, large numbers of so-called *asamblistas* deserted the comisiones obreras and joined the newly organized Maoist unions. Elsewhere in the region, the asamblistas (often belonging to the Communist movement, the International Communist League, or the Communist party of Euskadi) became a loud dissenting faction within the broader Spanish workers' commission movement.

In 1979 the coordinating committee of the workers' commissions began to purge asamblistas from the commissions in Bilbao after they had participated in some unauthorized labor demonstrations. Basque Trotskyists and members of the Communist movement in turn accused the national leadership of the comisiones obreras of "Stalinist tactics" and refused to march with members of the Communist party during the 1980 May Day celebrations. Severely hobbled by internal disagreements over the degree to which the workers' commissions should continue to be radically decentralized, overtly militant, and participatory bodies, the Communist party of Euskadi finally dissolved itself in 1981. Although some former Communists stayed within the workers' commissions and acted as militant gadflies, a large number left the commissions altogether and joined the much less hierarchical and much more decentralized Basque craft union, ELA-STV.[50]

CONCLUSION

Born at the end of the 1950s, ETA arrived on the scene at a time in Basque labor history when urban workers were increasingly rebellious, when plant-level activism and organizations characterized the labor movement, when participatory assemblies were coming into vogue, and when traditionally powerful organizations—such as the Socialist UGT—were momentarily weakened and new organizations—such as the CCOO—needed militants.

Some etarras, as we shall see, viewed the regional labor movement during the 1960s and 1970s with indifference and even hostility, as a further expression of Spanish influence within the region.[51] Other etarras were fascinated with the labor movement, speculated about possible alliances, and, especially during the late 1960s and early 1970s, worked in the comisiones obreras both on the Left Bank of Bilbao (with immigrant workers) and in the manufacturing towns of Guipúzcoa.[52] In turn, labor activists—many of whom were immigrants or children of immigrants—became sympathizers of the early ETA and the general goal of regional autonomy (although notions of territorial independence were never embraced).[53] By the close of the 1960s, the Communist party of Euskadi proclaimed regional autonomy one of its goals, and police arrest records suggest that growing numbers of etarras came from immigrant backgrounds (some arrestees had non-Basque surnames).[54]

The local labor movement inspired and activated ETA, brought some recruits, and provided tasks. It gave the fledgling movement political definition and organizational resources.

The Basque labor movement, however, also caused deep schisms within ETA. Etarras increasingly disputed (1) who were "the Basque people" deserving liberation from bondage (the working class, the immigrants, only native Basques, only Basque speakers); (2) how the Basque people should be liberated (armed struggle, labor organizing, cultural revitalization, or some other hybrid of methods); and (3) what liberation should institutionally look like (a future social order with factory assemblies, with government-owned industries, with powerful unions, or with none of these arrangements). These were provocative matters that stirred up fundamental disagreements within ETA. What some etarras viewed as the liberating sword of labor militancy would prove double-edged for the ETA movement.

CHAPTER FOUR

NEIGHBORS AND
NONVIOLENT PROTEST

*W*hat we find in political and social history is determined in part by what we are looking for. This seems to be the case with the neighborhood political organizations that first appeared in the Basque region during the twilight of the Franco regime. Many scholars and journalists have been preoccupied with the bombs and gunplay and with the social nostalgia that seemed to be the activists' underlying motivation; few outside the region have explored the history of largely nonviolent, urban neighborhood politics.

A cursory reading of local newspapers suggests that legalized neighborhood associations were one of the key elements in the region's urban politics during the middle and late 1970s. Several articles in every issue were devoted to the associations' activities and pronouncements. No wonder: the associations were pressing the state on issues ranging from nuclear safety to garbage collection. Their tactics included mass demonstrations, alternative publications, petition drives, and face-to-face lobbying. And they successfully experimented with quasi-anarchist projects, among them the opening of public libraries, youth centers, and small-scale transportation systems in lower-income neighborhoods.

The neighborhood associations—in other words—were novel and newsworthy (at least by local standards) attempts by subordinate classes in the cities to defend their interests and influence the state. Moreover, they represented a type of politics that fascinated generations of etarras. As early as 1966, members of ETA's workers' front were publishing extended discussions about the potential uses of neighborhood associations for developing an alternative to the political status quo.[1] Exhortations to join neighborhood organizations appeared in ETA handbills and documents throughout the 1970s.[2] After the legalization of parties in 1977, some members of nonmilitary offshoots of ETA—such as the Herri Batasuna and Euskadiko Ezkerra—participated in the neighborhood associations with hopes of using them as springboards for electoral power.[3]

The neighborhood associations' collective actions may seldom have been centralized, large scale, or violent—the sorts of actions that would attract international press coverage—but the associations appear to have inspired, and enlisted the energies of, many activists within the ETA movement. They therefore deserve a short recounting.

THE ORIGINS AND EARLY ACTIVITIES OF THE NEIGHBORHOOD ASSOCIATIONS

Legal Status

The neighborhood associations in the Basque region began in 1964 as quasi-legal bodies, licensed by the Spanish state. Until then most private associational activity in Spain had been prohibited unless formally sanctioned by the Catholic church or the Falange party. That year, however, the Franco regime permitted voluntary social, cultural, and professional associations to form.

To become a legal asociación, a group of individuals would submit a statement of purpose, a constitution, and a list of members and members' addresses to the government for approval. Approval depended in part on whether the membership list included the names of known members of illegal trade unions or clandestine political parties, which could be sufficient grounds for rejection of an application for an asociacional license. Approval also depended on whether the constitution met certain requirements, such as that officers be elected periodically by the membership at large.

Once legalized, an association was free to undertake almost any project its members decided upon so long as it fell within the law and furthered the spirit of the regime's social-political philosophy, articulated in the Principios del Movimiento. It was required to notify local government officials of upcoming meetings, and to allow interested

Table 4.1. Population Growth in Selected Cities and Towns in the Bilbao Metropolitan Area, 1950–70

City	1950 Population	1970 Population	Percentage Population Increase (1950 Population = 100%)
Bilbao	229,334	405,908	177
Baracaldo	42,240	109,185	258
Basauri	11,637	42,037	361
Portugalete	12,211	45,803	375
Santurce Antiguo	10,224	46,417	454
Sestao	19,969	37,345	187

Source: Adapted from Alfonso Pérez-Agote, "Racionalidad urbana y relaciones sociales. El Gran Bilbao, 1945–1975," in *Saioak* 3 (1979): 16.

officials to attend the meetings. The officials could prohibit a meeting if they believed laws would be violated.

Among those who applied for association status were groups of neighbors, who formed *asociaciones de vecinos* (associations of neighbors); groups of parents, who formed *asociaciones de familias;* and groups of housewives, who formed *asociaciones de amas de casa* (associations of housewives). The groups utilized a geographic criterion for membership, restricting it to people living or working within an administrative or electoral subunit of a city. In everyday discussion, the term *neighbors' association* informally referred to all local groups, regardless of composition.

Social Origins

More than a hundred neighbors' associations were formed in the Basque region between 1964 and 1979.[4] Most were established in and around Bilbao, but every industrial and manufacturing city with 30,000 or more residents had several.

The associations appeared first not in the wealthiest but in the poorest sections of a city, typically where immigrants had flooded into a half-developed district and had begun to construct shantytowns.[5] The post–World War II decades saw the populations of Basque industrial and manufacturing cities grow very quickly, sometimes tripling in size in only two decades (see table 4.1). The population of the steel and shipyard town of Baracaldo, to take one instance, increased from 42,240 in 1950 to 109,185 in 1970.[6]

Not surprisingly, the sudden urbanization resulted in severe shortages of public services and urban amenities, such as low-cost housing, elementary schools, hospitals, and water and sewage systems. For example, in 1977 there was classroom space for only 148,000 of the 211,000 school-age children in Vizcaya province. And as late as 1975 (the closing year of the boom period in the region), 40 percent of the homes in the province lacked heating. One Bilbao shantytowner sardonically commented, "Our streets are marvelous. There is trash, bottles, rats, water. . . . There are two exposed high voltage cables above our grade school—security for students!"[7]

According to available studies and seven early participants in Bilbao's associations whom I have been able to locate and interview, the first associations were spontaneous responses to specific, local problems, such as refuse in the streets or the need for schools. At first, the participants combined with no long-term goals, ambitions, and/or plans. Thereafter the groups' undertakings multiplied.[8]

The well-known Asociación de Familias in the Recaldeberri district of Bilbao comes to mind. One of the first associations, it was established in the middle 1960s primarily to pressure the local government for more schools and teachers. In 1971 it opened a community library and began a bimonthly newsmagazine that featured muckraking articles about municipal politics and a regular column by local labor lawyers on underground trade unions and strikes. In 1975 it organized a lecture series that the Spanish government periodically prohibited (the first lecture, "Workers and Culture"). In 1976 the library staff opened an adult school, the Popular University of Recaldeberri, whose motto was "Neighbor, if culture can be an instrument for your liberty, seize a book." The next year, 6,000 adults were studying, among other things, anthropology (an anthropological dig was begun in the middle of the district), family psychology, family sociology, fine arts, labor history, labor law, photography, and industrial sociology. By the end of the 1970s the association had launched more than seventy community projects and organizations, including committees investigating services for the elderly, housing codes, street sanitation, and fire prevention. It also helped to finance and administer a consumer cooperative and annual musical festivals. More than 3,000 residents belonged to the library, the only "public" library in the district. One correspondent for the Madrid newsweekly, La Calle, predicted that the association "will be remembered in golden letters in the history of citizens' movements in the Spanish state."[9]

The neighbors' association of Recaldeberri may have been unusually successful in terms of sheer number of undertakings, but its steadily expanding agenda was not unique within the region. To take another example, the neighbors' association in the immigrant district of Ariznabarra in Vitoria formed initially to press the local government to remove uncollected garbage in the streets. Members never neglected this goal, and spent three years lobbying for public trash cans. But in the meantime, the association created a volunteer sanitation corps, a park and playground, a senior citizens' center, a cooperative taxi company, and several other novel neighborhood projects. Similarly, the neighbors' association in the Adurza district in Vitoria was founded in 1972 to accomplish a relatively limited and straightforward goal: to organize athletic activities for adults. By 1976 it had also established a women's center, a recreational club for teenagers, a music program for small children, and a permanent lobbying committee, which was primarily concerned with acquiring public schools and a medical center for the neighborhood. That year the immediate plans of the association included a twenty-four-hour emergency medical center, a movie house for small children, and a complaint bureau, where residents could file grievances and petitions with a special administrator appointed by the municipal government.[10]

Organizational Decentralization

The neighbors' associations seldom cooperated with each other. There were, of course, occasions when asociaciones joined forces. For example, in 1975 in Bilbao twenty-seven associations organized a quasi-illegal petition drive to unseat an unpopular, nonelected mayor.[11] Such coordinated efforts occurred sporadically, however; they were exceptions rather than the rule.

One obvious explanation for the absence of routinized cooperation was governmental repression. Spanish law prohibited municipal, provincial, and regional federations of asociaciones; and on occasion the law was vigorously enforced.[12]

Still, fear of government repression was only part of the explanation. In addition, an undeterminable but large number of participants in the associations feared that acting in concert might lead to loss of local control. An official in the association of Basauri warned that a municipal or metropolitan federation could lead to an alienation of power from the grass roots, and could create "a new summit above smaller summits."[13]

Further, the "go-it-alone" mind-set reflected differences in priorities and aims. Even though the asociaciones typically began in immigrant and relatively low-income settlements, and thus can be considered sociologically homogeneous, each responded to problems and goals pertinent to that neighborhood, such as a lack of parks, the absence of refuse collection, or a shortage of classrooms in a neighborhood school. This diversity of interests made regular cooperation with other asociaciones seem unnecessary or even costly in terms of time and resources.

Exceptions to the general absence of cooperation occurred in towns where a high proportion of workers were employed by a single company. There the associations often cooperated with local unions and strike committees. The association in Potasas—whose largest employer was a government-run potassium mine—typified such a townwide coalition of "proletarian" neighborhood groups. But by and large associations were not interested in wages and workplace conditions, and seldom made statements of solidarity with local strikers or actively aided local unions.[14]

INTERNAL WORKINGS OF THE ASSOCIATIONS

As we have noted, the neighbors' associations first appeared in neighborhoods with high proportions of immigrants and unskilled, semiskilled, and unemployed workers. The most active members of the associations, however, were highly skilled factory workers, self-employed artisans, shopkeepers, or such white-collar workers as teachers and bank tellers. They belonged to the lower-middle classes, and often enjoyed modest but secure incomes, a modicum of postsecondary education, and clean workplaces. Their chances for significant upward mobility in the near future usually were limited, but they hoped for better things for their children (indeed, improved public education and medical services for the young were issues on which almost all the asociaciones agreed). The few unskilled manual laborers who belonged to the associations seldom attended the general meetings, apparently because they felt uneasy among the better-educated and better-dressed members, who often used abstract and unfamiliar terms in discussions.[15]

Although neighbors' associations were most commonly found in blue-collar neighborhoods, members generally did not use the language and rhetoric of proletarian class struggle. Instead, they normally used a more populist language when discussing politics and economics. They constantly contrasted the unwarranted privileges of the rich (*la oligarquía*) with the undeserved sufferings of the local residents (*el pueblo*). The rich allegedly were nonlaboring schemers who wished to rob the people of decent livelihoods. The people, in contrast, were hardworking, honest, and generous. Moreover, because of shared interests, values, and aims, they were not divided into rival factions: "In our neighborhood there are no social classes," declared one neighborhood booklet from Recaldeberri.[16]

The myth of a homogeneous, industrious urban neighborhood collectively resisting the schemes of the rich sometimes was manifested in the graphic art of the associations. A cover of one association newsmagazine, for example, showed three bald and flabby rich men losing a tug-of-war against three virile and muscular members of the association (figure 4.1). The members wore identical clothing: white T-shirts and dark work pants. There was nothing to suggest different economic classes, occupations, social strata, or ethnic groups, or different and perhaps even antagonistic interests, values, and moral principles among the neighbors. In the symbolism of the cartoon, the only cleavage was between an extremely wealthy but morally and physically deteriorating leisure class and the physically strong and morally determined residents of the neighborhood.

The belief that the residents of an immigrant neighborhood were roughly the same in regard to goals, interests, and aspirations, and were not naturally divided into factions, classes, or social strata, also was apparent in the etiquette of meetings. When greeting one another, members typically employed the socially indiscriminate *tú* and the economically vague *vecino* (neighbor) instead of either the socially correct and implicitly hierarchical *usted* or the more proletarian *comarada* and *hermano* (forms of address common among Spanish Marxists, Communists, and trade unionists).[17]

Furthermore, editorials in association publications did not treat neighborhood problems—such as dirty streets and crowded schools—in terms of conflicts of interests within the neighborhood. Rather,

Figure 4.1. Cover of neighbors' association journal *Hauzolan: Revista del Movimiento Ciudadano*, September–October, 1978.

problems were attributed to the greed and inhumanity of financiers and big businessmen outside the neighborhood. Thus, the lobbying of local government officials for neighborhood improvements was represented in handbills and newsmagazines as "people's struggles" (*luchas populares*) against the monopolists and industrialists who controlled the city government (*la ciudad-gran capital*). One Recaldeberri pamphleteer declared that the taxes of residents of the immigrant neighborhoods were paying for lights, parks, and spacious boulevards in Ensanche (the banking district in Bilbao) and Getxo (a wealthy neighborhood on the east bank of the Nervión River), while the immigrant communities lacked sidewalks, regular garbage collection, and even paved streets. "We must not forget, for instance in Bilbao, that the mayor's office always has been given to persons connected to the elites, who have enormous wealth (members of the Hurtado de Saracho family, the Ibarra family, the Careaga family)."[18]

The notion of a hardworking, solidary "people" was also institutionalized in the very open decision-making procedures within the *asociaciones*. Whereas in the United States neighborhood groups and civil rights movements often utilize a representative system of governance—factions and organized interests are assigned a certain number of representatives—the Basque associations were radically participatory, with no methods for regulating the number and strength of intraneighborhood factions in the decision-making process. Whoever showed up at a meeting was considered to be as much a spokesperson of the "people" as anyone else. An exception to this generalization was the neighbors' association in Eibar, which was organized as a federation of small independent districts. Residents of each district elected a governing council that had the right to veto decisions made by the larger executive council for the association as a whole.[19]

By law, every registered association was required to have an elected executive council composed of a president, vice-president, secretary, treasurer, and the chairpersons of the standing committees. In addition, every association was required to hold periodic assemblies open to all members in good standing, in which officeholders would review past decisions and discuss upcoming issues with those present. Further, every *asociación* had to comply with its constitution, which had been filed in the office of the local civil governor. The constitution specified (1) the frequency of meetings of the executive council and the standing committees, (2) the procedures for selecting officers, and (3) the duties and rights of members and officeholders.[20]

Despite the legal mandates, there remained considerable leeway for an association to develop its own distinctive decision-making arrangements. For example, every asociación was allowed to create its own rules and procedures for ad hoc committees and for its *asambleas de barrio* (assemblies open to all residents in the district). And it was up to the association to determine the policy-making powers of the executive council, standing committees, and general assemblies. In some associations, almost all important policies were decided in the general assemblies. In a few associations, the executive councils made almost all policy decisions during weekly meetings that were closed to outsiders. In the remaining associations, decision-making authority was divided among the standing committees, each of which was responsible for a specific policy area.

In associations where policy questions were decided primarily in assemblies open to all members (such as those of the Casco Viejo districts in Bilbao and Pamplona), the executive council typically would arrange the time and place for an assembly. During some weeks, no assembly might be held; during other weeks, two, three, or even four. The formal agenda normally contained three to five items worded by a member of either the executive council or a standing committee. The president usually chaired the meeting, introducing each agenda item with a brief presentation of background information and of the views of the executive committee and relevant standing committees. Discussion then opened up. According to the participants interviewed, discussions were lengthy, not infrequently lasting more than two hours. In the manner of participants everywhere at such meetings, some became tired and distracted, others highly animated. In Pamplona, and perhaps in other cities, there were no formal time constraints, but the president as moderator could declare "*último turno*" (last turn). Thereafter, each interested person was permitted one final speech before the vote was taken.[21]

How many people attended a typical general meeting? Most participants whom I have interviewed estimated somewhere between one hundred and two hundred. In every association, however, the numbers appear to have dwindled as the years passed and as the association ceased to be a novelty.[22] The numbers correspond to the periodic estimates in Basque newspapers and newsmagazines—roughly one hundred to five hundred participants.[23]

As we have noted, there were no formal procedures within most associations for representing organized interests within a given neighborhood. There were, however, many members of clandestine political parties and, after the post-Franco reforms of 1977, legal political parties. The partisan backgrounds of members varied from place to place. For example, members of Maoist parties regularly attended meetings of neighborhood associations in Pamplona (as mentioned, the center of the Maoist trade-union movement in Spain), but they seldom participated in San Sebastián or Bilbao.[24]

Although sometimes most officers in a given association belonged to some political party (ranging from the socially conservative Basque Nationalist party to the avowedly revolutionary International Communist League), they seldom all belonged to the same party. Diversity prevented most associations from being manipulated by particular local parties, but there were other reasons as well. During the Franco years, most clandestine parties wanted to protect the associations' always tenuous right to assemble, partly because they afforded a rare opportunity for party members to work with and recruit local residents. Therefore, many party members avoided any sectarian behavior that might either scare away nonpartisan members or raise suspicions and concerns among police. In addition, most parties did not have official positions on the local issues discussed in neighborhood associations. Therefore, party members were seldom bound by specific instructions; they were free to act within associations according to personal judgments, loyalties, and sympathies.[25]

PATTERNS OF COLLECTIVE ACTION

The neighbors' associations gained most of their local fame and notoriety from unorthodox protest activities, especially open demonstrations of strength. One association rally against the construction of a nuclear plant outside metropolitan Bilbao, for example, attracted almost 90,000 persons (at the time the largest antinuclear demonstration in European history). In 1975 a rally against the licensing of an ammonia plant in a crowded, west-bank community drew approximately 50,000 protestors. And antitax marches in the industrial towns of the west bank typically involved between 5,000 and 15,000.[26]

Neighbors' associations also attempted to influence public opinion and government officials through exhibitions of photographs and paintings. One association in Tudela, for example, organized an exhibition of photographs highlighting traffic problems and accidents in the city; it reportedly attracted 2,000 visitors in its first month. A similar exhibition in Pamplona attracted 2,500 visitors during its two-week showing.[27]

Associations sometimes collected and published statistics about local food prices, garbage problems, and school matters in hopes of generating public concern and greater government sensitivity. At least ten associations published periodicals that reviewed and openly criticized municipal policies and government activities. One association tried to draw the government's attention to shortages of public services in its neighborhood by seizing an abandoned building and transforming it into a community center; the police expelled the trespassers after two weeks.[28]

During the Franco years, most of the above-mentioned and similar other actions technically violated the law. Even shortly after the death of Franco, leaders of neighborhood groups periodically were arrested for acts of public disorder, such as chaining themselves to government buildings to protest local educational policy. The groups' frequent criticism of government policies and their occasional resistance often annoyed government officials, a few of whom even accused the associations of inciting mob violence. None of the major demonstrations organized by the groups during the late 1960s and 1970s, however, directly led to widespread physical violence. A possible exception to this generalization was a riot in Pamplona in the summer of 1978, when youths burned dozens of cars, looted stores, and broke hundreds of windows. Most analysts, however, have attributed the riot primarily to the misjudgment of local police, who fired into a crowd within a bullring and thus apparently provoked the aftermath.[29]

Besides demonstrations of strength and attempts to inform local residents about current policy issues, almost all the associations patiently lobbied government officials. The Association of Recaldeberri, for example, repeatedly sent delegates to Bilbao's city hall to present petitions, read speeches, submit data, and talk informally with officials about traffic regulations, recreational programs, enforcement of fire and building codes, and the construction, maintenance, and policing of local roads. Similarly, delegations from the association in Bilbao's Casco Viejo district repeatedly met with municipal officials to discuss traffic regulations, parking ordinances, bus transportation, and rubbish collection. Delegations from a group of associations in several mining towns of Vizcaya traveled to Madrid to lobby the Spanish Ministry of Health for medical centers that would provide vaccinations and inexpensive checkups. And representatives of the association in the Berango district of Bilbao lobbied the governor of Vizcaya province for a larger allocation of drinking water in Bilbao.[30]

The attitude of the association leaders and lobbyists toward local officials varied from town to town, depending in large part on the accessibility of officials. Where town governments were open to the neighborhood groups, a cooperative spirit tended to prevail; where they were not, relations grew strained. The city council of Vitoria, for example, actively sought constructive dialogue with the associations, and even appointed part-time "neighborhood mayors" to routinize communication between the associations and the council. The government of Llodio (a rapidly growing manufacturing town in Alava) likewise viewed lobbying as legitimate, and organized a "chamber of neighborhood organizations," where representatives of the associations could meet regularly with city officials and discuss city policies. In contrast, officials in San Sebastián repeatedly refused to meet with or discuss written statements of grievance from the associations. Consequently, the city government came to be viewed as an adversary by many members of the associations; in the words of one local newspaper, "The municipal government is considered 'enemy number one' by the neighborhoods."[31]

An episode in Bilbao about a year before Franco's death and three years before the legalization of political parties, illustrates the import that some associations placed on good-faith lobbying, and also suggests the complementary relationship of lobbying and public protest. For several months the recently appointed mayor of Bilbao refused to discuss local issues with representatives of the city's associations, charging that members of the associations behaved rudely and disrespectfully during discussions, and justifying the suspension of consultative meetings on the grounds that the associations had improperly held "tumultuous gatherings" in the lobbies of public buildings. Whereupon twenty-seven associations launched an audacious petition campaign, demanding that the Francoist governor dismiss the appointed mayor. They collected more than 46,000 signatures (a remarkable achievement at that time) and held enormous rallies and traffic blockages. Shortly after receiving the petition, the provincial governor dismissed the mayor, and the number of street-level demonstrations declined.[32]

HOW POWERFUL?

The power of the associations vis-à-vis the Spanish government (especially during the Franco years) is difficult to assess. As U.S. scholars who study urban politics frequently emphasize, "power" is a contextual and historically rooted phenomenon. Consequently, any generalization about a group's political power is problematic because it is in constant flux, varying according to the group's current goals, adversaries, allies, legal opportunities and constraints, and mobilizable resources.[33]

Still, there are some journalistic anecdotes (such as the successful petition drive) that suggest that the associations at times were formidable forces in local politics, even during the Franco regime. For example, according to a news story in *Business Week*, during 1975 the associations in Lejona prevented the Spanish government from issuing a license to Dow Chemical Company, a major multinational corporation, for a new insecticide plant. According to the correspondent:

> Dow obtained a investment permit from the Madrid government, expecting that the construction permit and operations license issued by local officials would follow in due course. . . . The Lejona Assns., a powerful group of citizens' organizations in the predominantly Basque area, complained that the plant would aggravate pollution in an area whose air is perhaps the foulest in Europe. Dow called public meetings to refute the charges, explaining that it planned to spend $1.8 million on antipollution equipment. But local officials, unable to cope with the pressure, agreed to ask federal experts stationed in Vizcaya Province, which includes Lejona, for an environmental impact report.

In January, the experts reported that Dow's plant would not be a polluter. But Lejona officials, still under heavy pressure, informed the company that it could only open the new plant if it closed two others that make sulfuric acid and titanium oxide in its existing Lejona complex.

Dow countered by offering to cut back twice as much sulfuric acid emission from its other chemical plants as the new plant would add to the air. Lejona officials first agreed, and then, in a tense meeting attended by excited townspeople, did an about-face. At the same time, the federal experts who had declared the plant clean reversed themselves.[34]

The defeat of the new Dow plant and the dismissal of the mayor of Bilbao, both during Franco's lifetime, offer some empirical grounds for entertaining the possibility that the associations were at times formidable forces in Basque politics, even when opposing Francoist officials and multinational corporations. "How powerful?" and "Powerful with respect to what issues?" are complex questions, nonetheless, that perhaps can never be completely answered, especially given the fragmentary data at our disposal and given our dependence on state records (which tend to minimize the impact of social pressures on state officials) and on newspaper accounts (which tend to report only the most dramatic political activities by social groups).[35]

ETA AND THE ORIGINS OF
THE NEIGHBORHOOD ASSOCIATIONS

Given the current dearth of information about the day-to-day activities of ETA before the death of Franco, it is difficult to describe in detail and then generalize about possible clandestine ties between ETA and the neighborhood associations. Víctor Urrutia Abaigar, a student of Bilbao's neighborhood associations, has suggested that individual *etarras* indirectly nurtured some associations by encouraging urban priests, who at the time viewed nationalist groups with sympathy, to provide the fledgling associations with meeting places, office accoutrements, and a modicum of legitimacy in the suspicious eyes of government officials.[36] Unfortunately, Urrutia does not marshal any evidence that directly supports his hypothesis; for example, he does not name particular associations in which etarras were unusually active.

Some ETA pamphlets from the late 1960s portrayed the associations in a positive light and encouraged etarras to participate in them.[37] And as late as 1977 ETA publications urged members to become active in them.[38] The associations were deemed valuable because of their contributions to political decentralization, participatory democracy, and proletarian unity, and thus had the potential to become "instruments of Basque popular revolutionary counter-power" against the Spanish state.[39] So perhaps ETA was among the factors contributing to the associations' growth.

The involvement of ETA would help explain some peculiar features of Bilbao's associations, most of which exist in predominantly immigrant neighborhoods. For example, according to surveys of a small sample of association leaders, which Urrutia administered in the early 1980s, most were partially or completely fluent in the Basque language. In contrast, less than 15 percent of the associations' members at large whom Urrutia surveyed (n = 404) could speak Basque.[40] In addition, Basque words were often used in association slogans and names (for example, the metropolitan periodical for the associations was titled *Hauzolan*), even though the vast majority of members neither could speak Basque nor wanted to learn how.[41] As well, 62 percent of the leaders surveyed reported casting ballots in political elections for candidates sponsored by electoral organizations commonly associated with branches of ETA: the Euskadiko Ezkerra (commonly associated with ETA-pm), the Herri Batasuna (ETA-m), and the Movimiento Comunista de España (ETA-berri). In contrast, only 24 percent of the association members who did not hold leadership positions and only 16 percent of all voters in metropolitan Bilbao voted for such candidates.[42]

In sum, the leaders of Bilbao's associations in the early 1980s seemed to have linguistic and electoral characteristics compatible with the hypothesis of long-standing ties between ETA and the neighborhood associations. Surely it would be rash to view the associations simply as by-products of ETA activism. Other influences, such as church leadership and economic grievances, undoubtedly contributed to the emergence of the associations, and urban associations exist outside the Basque region, where ETA is not active. But perhaps

ETA had a more significant role in the founding of the associations than is commonly recognized.

CONCLUSION

The standard picture of Basque politics during the 1960s and 1970s is one of violence and destruction: a world of gangs, assassinations, and intimidation, where more civilized modes of politics—periodic consultation, dialogue, mutual aid—are absent. The picture contains many elements of truth. After all, there was physical and verbal violence in great abundance. Still, the picture in many ways oversimplifies and caricatures. Alongside the violence were novel forms of cooperation, peaceful discussion, and mutual aid. Some occurred in working-class neighborhoods that provided members of ETA with institutional spaces in which to work. And neighborhood associations also influenced the thinking of etarras—in particular, their goals and strategy.

Inspiration for radical politics can come from many sources, and novel social institutions are one. In thinking about how to transform Basque society, some etarras perceived in the neighborhood associations a model for a new society in which hierarchy and inequality would be eliminated. The associations were often radically participatory in policy-making procedures, often egalitarian in symbols and norms, and often provided badly needed services to the less advantaged. In the context of late-Franco Spain, the associations seemed to many etarras refreshingly free and democratic.[43]

> From our point of view, socialist and democratic, life in a neighborhood must become progressively more autonomous. That is to say, members of each urban community must become responsible for it. . . . In a neocapitalist regime, the struggle for the autonomy of neighborhoods (as of that of municipalities, of the region, of Euzkadi, etc.) has a highly revolutionary significance.[44]

For some ETA activists, the associations also furnished evidence —alongside the growing militancy of the labor movement—that the region's disadvantaged populations could launch a social and politi-

Table 4.2. A List of Known Asociaciones de Vecinos in the Basque Region of Spain, 1975–1980

Alava	13. San Jorge
1. Adurza	14. Villava
2. Amas de Casa de Vitoria	*Vizcaya*
3. Aranako	1. Andra-Mair
4. Aranbizcarra	2. Arangoiti
5. Ariznabarra	3. Artaza
6. Burlada	4. Atzuri
7. Casco Viejo (Vitoria)	5. Basurto
8. Errekaleor	6. Begoña
9. Llodio	7. Berango
10. Lourdes	8. Bolueta
11. Pilar	9. Casco Viejo (Bilbao)
12. Txagorribidea	10. Elexalde
13. Zaramaga	11. Erandio
Guipúzcoa	12. Gure-Etxea
1. Antiguo	13. Iralabarri-Torreurizar
2. Eibar	14. Iturrigorri-Peñascal
3. Eguía-Atocha	15. Lamiaco
4. Goiherri	16. Larrabezua
5. Inchaurrondo	17. Mazustegui
6. Tomas Gros	18. Plencia
7. Ulía	19. Portugalete
Navarra	20. Otxarkoaga
1. Ansoain	21. Ortuella
2. Barañain	22. Recaldeberri
3. Berriozar	23. Romo
4. Burlada	24. San Adrián
5. Casco Viejo (Pamplona)	25. San Ignacio-Ibarrekolanda
6. Casco Viejo (Tudela)	26. Santutxu
7. Chantrea	27. San Vicente de Barracaldo
8. Echavacoiz	28. Sestao
9. Estella	29. Sopelana
10. Milagrosa	30. Txurdinaga
11. Rochapea	31. Zubarán
12. San Juan	

This list was compiled from articles from the following Basque newspapers and newsmagazines: *Deia, Egin, Punto y Hora,* and *Berriak.*

cal revolution "from below." Residents in poorer neighborhoods appeared neither too despairing nor too apathetic to be trusted with political power. They were not politically passive, nor were they helpless. After all, these social institutions of and by the nonwealthy, from which militant actions often flowed, existed independently of the Franquist state, despite constant police surveillance.

The associations thus contributed to the revolutionary dreams motivating etarras and reinforced their optimistic assessment of the prospects for imminent popular insurgency. They were another part of the local environment that affected etarras' thoughts about social and political change. In turn, they were a part of the Basque society that individuals and groups within ETA may have assisted.

CHAPTER FIVE

ATTITUDES TOWARD REGIONAL SELF-RULE AMONG BASQUE BUSINESS LEADERS, 1976–1980

*T*hus far we have looked at local economic struggles and collective actions that coincided with the appearance and evolution of ETA and that may have influenced the thinking of individual etarras. But members of ETA were not shaped only by emerging forces within civil society. Many etarras also studied contemporary political tracts, and some were impressed by social and political ideas propagated by the Basque Nationalist party.

What were the party's ideological orientations? Scholars disagree, and the disagreements in part reflect different assessments about the social bases of support for the party. Some contend that the rapid social transformations of the region during the twentieth century have generated profound feelings of insecurity among the region's small-town and rural residents. These feelings have been channeled into political movements for the revitalization of premodern culture. The party, it is said, is an excellent example of such a movement. Its leaders frequently criticize commercial values and urban life, and celebrate religion, family, and the small community. Its social basis of support is largely limited to small property owners and the traditional middle classes. The modern business leaders of the region, who have a much more positive attitude toward recent cultural change, are said to be offended by the antimodern rhetoric of the party and tend not to join its ranks. Instead, if they are politically active, they oppose its goal of regional self-rule. Their behavior thus indirectly corroborates the dominance of an antimodern ideology within the party.[1]

Some historians and social scientists, however, have reached very different conclusions about the relationship between commercial interests and the Basque Nationalist party. These scholars believe that substantial numbers of modern business leaders have supported the general goal of political decentralization of the Spanish state, and many have participated in the party. Jean-Claude Larronde, for example, maintains that as early as 1898 some prominent industrialists and manufacturers were highly active in the party and even held important posts in it. These personages gradually increased their influence over party policies, and by the 1930s the anticommercial rhetoric of the early years had almost completely disappeared.[2]

Joseph Harrison similarly has argued that modern business leaders have had cordial relations with the Basque Nationalist party, at least since the late 1910s. He also holds that they became so active that the party developed a dual ideological character early in the twentieth century and was able to enjoy the best of two worlds: "It was to pick up the electoral support of the reactionary countryside, while its wealthy industrial supporters hobnobbed with the plutarchy in Bilbao."[3]

Like Harrison, Antonio Elorza has depicted the Basque Nationalist party as containing easily discernible probusiness and antibusiness factions, at least since the 1910s. But whereas Harrison suggests that the factions often cooperated, Elorza says that they battled endlessly over control of the party's organizational apparatus. The winners thus far have been the leaders from the business world, who repeatedly have purged virulent antimodern groups from the party and then readmitted them only after their popularity and militant spirit had waned. In the meantime the party increasingly has advocated rapid capitalist development under direction of an autonomous regional government. To support his belief that the party has a generally favorable orientation toward business concerns, Elorza cites the works of several probusiness party theoreticians, for example, Jesús de Sarriá, who declared:

> For us Basque Nationalists, national wealth is connected to the substance of nationality itself. . . . The wealth that we have is a fundamental element, like a shield and fortress, for nationality and citizenship. We are a people with a practical sense, with concrete notions, with a spirit of solidarity within the national economy.[4]

Two very different views exist, then, on the relationship between modern business and the ideas of the Basque Nationalist party. On the one hand, some eminent scholars, among them Fusi, Linz, and Payne, assert that the attitudes of businessmen toward the nationalist movement tended to be hostile, a consequence of the party's anti-modern and anticommercial ideological orientation. Contrariwise, other scholars emphasize the ongoing presence of business leaders within the party and view the party, at least in part, as a vehicle for the interests and beliefs of modern big business.

This chapter looks at the opinions concerning regional self-rule voiced by several Basque business leaders and business associations during the late 1970s.[5] Their statements suggest that at least during the late 1970s many manufacturers and industrialists did not see regional self-rule (and therefore possible rule by the Basque Nationalist party) as antithetical to their interests. If this is true—if more classes were open to the goal of regional self-rule and, by implication, open to Nationalist rule than the modernization interpretation would lead us to believe—then perhaps a more diversified view of the ideologies within the Basque Nationalist party is in order.

ECONOMIC CIRCUMSTANCES DURING THE 1970S AND POLITICAL DECLARATIONS OF BUSINESS LEADERS

The 1970s was a time of uncertainty for most Basque business leaders. The Spanish government recently had legalized unions, parties, and freedom of the press. Dozens of new political parties were being organized in the region, including explicitly working-class parties. After the 1977 and 1979 general elections, the Basque Nationalist party and the Spanish Workers' Socialist party suddenly emerged as the two strongest parties in the region. It was becoming increasingly obvious (1) that some sort of regional government soon would be established, and (2) that the new government could have considerable power over local economic affairs.

In this political situation, business leaders in the region did not sit still and passively observe history unfold. At least six major associations of industrialists and manufacturers began to issue statements of support for the creation of a new regional government. Some business spokesmen even offered openly to help leaders in the Basque Nationalist party negotiate the transfer of political authority from Madrid to a new regional government and to consult with party leaders about its future economic programs.[6]

The six associations that endorsed regional self-rule were the Democratic Association of Businessmen of Guipúzcoa (ADEGUI), the Basque Council of Entrepreneurs (EKOR), the Union of Alavese Businessmen (SEA), the Confederation of Basque Businessmen (CEV), the General Confederation of Businessmen in Vizcaya (CGEV), and the Chamber of Commerce, Industry, and Navigation of Bilbao. Together, they represented more than 10,000 business leaders and entrepreneurs, many of whom were large industrialists, large manufacturers, and financiers.

Of course, not all businessmen viewed current events the same way. For example, the Bank of Bilbao warned against extensive decentralization through large newspaper advertisements.[7] Antinationalist books sold at the Corte Inglés (a chain of Spanish department stores) suggest that some Basque merchants feared the unexpected and growing electoral strength of the Basque Nationalist party (at the same time, it is worth noting that Corte Inglés also sold, since 1978, a wide range of nationalist articles, such as flags). Nonetheless, as we shall see, officials for the largest and most prestigious business associations in the Basque region did openly express strong support for regional self-rule; and their endorsements suggest that a sizeable number of politically interested business leaders looked favorably (at least for the moment) upon the founding of a regional government.

Why did so many business leaders favor a novel and untested form of government? Part of the answer seems to lie with the region's sudden and largely unanticipated economic depression. During the 1960s and early 1970s, the Basque economy grew at an average annual rate of 7.75 percent, faster than the GNP growth rates of almost all industrialized nation-states of the time.[8] The region also received 19 percent of all new investments in Spain between 1971 and 1975, despite the fact that it constitutes only 3.2 percent of Spain's total territory and has only 6.5 percent of its total population.[9] Then around 1975 economic activity suddenly declined. Statistical measurements of the new depression are abundant: yearly housing construction in Guipúzcoa province declined 70 percent between 1975 and 1979; yearly cement consumption in the region dropped from 1,284,000 tons in 1975 to 554,000 tons in 1979; and the number of

Table 5.1. Basque Bankruptcies during Regional Recession, 1974–80

Year	Registered Bankruptcies	Workers Affected
1974	229	7,369
1975	448	26,229
1976	702	21,862
1977	1,086	25,000
1978	2,169	50,826
1979	3,553	106,960
1980	3,922	127,792

Source: Adapted from *Euskadi 1982* (Donostia: Egin, 1983), p. 168.

Table 5.2. Annual Growth Rate of the Basque Gross Regional Product and of Spain's Gross National Product, 1975–80

Year	Annual Growth Rate, Basque Gross Regional Product (%)	Annual Growth Rate, Spain's Gross National Product (%)
1975	1.4	1.0
1976	0.8	3.0
1977	0.7	2.6
1978	−4.3	2.9
1979	−6.3	1.1
1980	−2.7	0.8

Source: Adapted from Jesús Lobo Aleu, "Política industrial en la Comunidad Autónoma del País Vasco," in *Información Comercial Española*, no. 598 (June 1983): 67.

firms that filed for bankruptcy each year increased from 229 in 1975 to 3,922 in 1979 (see table 5.1).[10] The region had annual growth rates (with respect to total goods and services sold) of −4.3 percent in 1978, −6.3 percent in 1979, and −2.7 percent in 1980 (see table 5.2). The official unemployment rate in the region rose from 1 percent in 1973 to 11.2 percent in 1980, and some observers believe that the actual unemployment rate may have exceeded 17 percent.[11] According to one local newsmagazine, unemployed fathers who needed to feed and house families were seen crying in the streets of Bilbao and sometimes took to robbing food markets.[12]

Throughout the late 1970s and early 1980s, industrialists and other business leaders in the region expressed not only support for regional self-rule, but also concern over the unexpected depression. Officers of the Chamber of Commerce, Industry, and Navigation in

Bilbao, for example, said that the condition of the economy was "frankly alarming" and declared 1980 to be the worst year in the recent history of the Vizcayan economy.[13] Officers of the Chamber of Commerce and Industry of Alva said at a press conference that they were "deeply pessimistic" about the immediate future of their province's economy.[14] Officers of the CGEV asked the Spanish government to declare the Basque region a "zone of catastrophe" and to provide funds for economic recovery.[15]

Interestingly, when endorsing the creation of a regional government, representatives of business associations usually argued that regional self-rule was a necessary precondition for ending the local depression. For example, Luís Olarra, a steel magnate and the president of the CGEV, said that he favored a regional government partly for reasons of political liberty but primarily "for reasons of pure efficiency."[16] The research department of the Chamber of Commerce, Industry, and Navigation in Bilbao stated that "the fullest autonomy possible" for a Basque region government was an "absolutely primordial economic necessity" for ending "the deterioration . . . of economic activity."[17] Spokespersons for the EKOR argued that economic recovery, at minimum, required creation of an independent regional government with authority (1) to promulgate rules for collective bargaining, (2) to create a bank for industrial development, and (3) to raise and lower taxes.[18] An officer of the CGEV stated at a news conference that he considered "full, total autonomy" a necessary condition for ending high unemployment in the region.[19]

Hard times help explain the business leaders' support, but the slump alone does not fully account for their proautonomy statements. The business leaders in addition wanted autonomy because they distrusted the meddling of Madrid's bureaucrats. One high-ranking executive of a major Basque bank exclaimed, "God liberate us from the Spanish administration! We presently are traveling on a road of concubinage and nepotism. . . . This country needs to be decentralized."[20] Market analysts for Bilbao's Chamber of Commerce, Industry, and Navigation warned:

> We must not forget that behind each so-called economic problem—the inadequate size of the public sector, the crisis in traditional agriculture, the failure of exports, the absence of an indigenous technology, the problems with labor, etc.—

we find a previous, fundamental political problem linked to some administrative structures whose inertia is remarkable.[21]

According to one spokesperson for the ADEGUI, Spanish government bureaucrats had constantly "obstructed the genuine dynamic of businesses and the mental agility necessary to contemplate the long-term fortunes of a business."[22]

Basque business leaders also complained about apparent fiscal inequities and geographic maldistribution of government expenditures. Spanish tax policies seemed unusually onerous and unjust because the Spanish government seemed to receive far more tax money from the Basque region than it returned in the form of public expenditures. According to Clark,

> While Madrid took out of the Basque provinces in 1970 more than 30,000 million pesetas, it returned to those provinces slightly more than 8,500 million pesetas. . . . Vizcaya received only 24 percent of what it paid out in taxes; Guipúzcoa received only 19.9 percent. Further, what funds Madrid did expend in these provinces went primarily for the maintenance of order, and the support of the Spanish central administrative bureaucracy, and relatively little went to finance needed social-infrastructure improvements.[23]

It also seemed that the Spanish government constantly shortchanged the Basque region when distributing public services. For example, of the new industrial research centers financed by the government, 70 percent were located in Madrid; almost 10 percent were located in Catalonia; and none was located in the Basque provinces.[24] Similarly, educational funding seemed geographically skewed. In 1974 the Spanish state spent on average 2,501 pesetas per child on classroom education, and in most industrialized provinces the state spent far more. Yet in the Basque provinces of Guipúzcoa and Vizcaya (which together contained almost three-fourths of the region's total population), the state only spent 1,371 and 1,755 pesetas per student.[25]

Perhaps equally troubling was the economic program advanced by the newly elected ruling party in the Spanish parliament, the Unión del Centro Democrático (UCD). The economic ministers were staunchly free-market liberals who opposed restrictions on international trade, on the free movement of labor, and on interest rates.

They wanted to reduce the large subsidies to Spain's heavy industry and to dismantle the high tariff walls established by the Franco governments.[26] In the words of analysts for *The Economist*,

> In its programme of social and economic reforms announced after the elections, the Spanish government has committed itself to some radical structural changes. The phasing out of the "privileged circuits" and the introduction of much stiffer personal and corporate taxation, the liberalisation of interest rates and the commitment of the state to increase its share of social welfare contributions are all innovations which, if implemented, will have a profound impact on industrial and banking practices.[27]

Throughout Spain, business leaders maintained that they needed government subsidies, tax exemptions, and protective tariffs if they were to expand production, update plants, and hire unemployed workers.[28] As a form of protest against the UCD's radical free-market reforms, the CEOE, the largest and most prestigious business association in Spain, soon removed its officers from all research commissions sponsored by the Spanish government.[29] During the early 1980s, the president of the Spanish bankers' association advocated street marches by business leaders and entrepreneurs as a method of resisting the government's economic program.[30]

Similar objections were heard in the Basque region. Officers of the ADEGUI declared that UCD policies on taxation and credit were directly responsible for the bankruptcies of several large companies that otherwise would have been profitable.[31] Spokespersons for the CGEV advised local businesses to stop paying social security taxes, at least for a month, until the government changed its economic program.[32] One president of the CGEV initiated bankruptcy proceedings in connection with his steel plant and threatened to leave thousands of unpaid workers permanently jobless unless the government provided financial aid to the steel industry. (In addition, he may have encouraged some of his unpaid workers to march on a local bank and demand changes in the government's interest-rate and credit policies.)[33] A speaker at a prestigious business club in Bilbao told a sympathetic audience that UCD economic policies threatened to bring only further bankruptcy and unemployment to the region. The policies, he warned, could become "the tomb of Spanish democracy";

moreover, "if the Government does not change its economic policy, it will risk a coup d'etat."[34]

CONCLUSION

There were, in short, numerous instances of business leaders deploring the region's economic crisis, criticizing the economic policies of the Spanish state, and advocating regional autonomy. The statements of Basque business leaders suggest that, at least during the late 1970s, the interests motivating residents to support regional self-rule were more diverse than the modernization interpretation presumes. This in turn adumbrates that perhaps not all people active in the Basque Nationalist party have been antimodern and anticommercial in their beliefs and ideologies.

Of course, demonstration that the Basque Nationalist party was in fact ideologically plural requires direct examination of political declarations of several of its chief theoreticians and leaders. But the discovery of the willingness among members of the Basque business community to embrace regional self-rule (a relatively radical position during the late 1970s, especially given the local electoral strength of the Basque Nationalist party and the Socialists) gives us reason to launch such an investigation and to be open to the possible discovery of more than one ideology predominating within the party.

If research discloses that there has been more than one major ideology within the Basque Nationalist party, then a further conjecture merits our attention: that the causal relationship between the multiple ideologies propagated by the party and the beliefs held by members of ETA is knottier and less direct than is commonly assumed. Indeed, perhaps the political beliefs of etarras have multiple sources and are not simply an echo of the beliefs of an earlier established antimodern nationalist party.

The next two chapters will consider these themes, describing first the multiple aims and strategies articulated by leaders within the Basque Nationalist party, then examining the diverse revolutionary theories advanced by members of ETA.

CHAPTER SIX

RIVAL SOCIAL VISIONS WITHIN
THE PARTIDO NACIONALISTA VASCO

The advocacy of regional autonomy by Basque industrialists and manufacturers and their explicitly economic justifications suggest that the modernization interpreters' view of the social and psychological characteristics of the Basque Nationalist party tends to oversimplify. During at least the late 1970s, many persons from modern, bourgeois-class backgrounds supported regional self-rule, and did so for reasons other than a desire to resurrect preindustrial culture and society. Briefly, at least, local business leaders' interests seemed to coincide with the activities of the Basque Nationalist party, which was working for an autonomy statute.

What about the party's leading activists? For them was the party a rural populist organization whose members were hostile to industrialization, urbanization, and scientific culture, and who wished a return to a significantly less industrial, urban, and secular world? Or was it a vehicle for values and goals that were considerably more complex? This chapter argues that at the elite level, the party was never merely populist and anti-industrial. It was, rather, an ideologically variegated organization with two seemingly contradictory ideological traditions: (1) a theocratic and anticapitalist tradition that tended to be highly critical of large-scale production and of capitalists' exploitation of employees, and (2) a more typically "Western" or "modernist" tradition that favored rapid industrialization and private entrepreneurship as a way to organize society.

This chapter will illustrate the two ideological traditions through a survey of statements and actions by spokespersons of the party since its inception nearly a century ago. Then, the chapter will interpret some recent intraparty struggles in light of the enduring ideological traditions.

HEAVY INDUSTRY AND THE ORIGINS OF TWO NATIONALIST IDEOLOGIES

Political ideologies become popular in part because they address the salient social concerns of people living at a particular time. Therefore, to understand the logic and emotional meaning of an ideology, it is necessary to know something about the social context in which it first attracted a following.

Both major ideological traditions within the Basque Nationalist party first gained adherents in the aftermath of the Second Carlist War, which officially ended in 1879. Speaking broadly, the Carlists were a coalition of social conservatives who favored the ancient prerogatives and rights of the Catholic church, of the small nobility, and of the peasant villages of northern Spain. In contrast, many opponents of the Carlists tended to be social liberals. They wished to transform the culture and social evolution of Iberia by moving Spain's customhouses from the southern edge of the Basque region to the Basque seacoast, by repealing most of the regional laws that limited extraction and exportation of natural resources, and by permitting foreigners to invest in Spain. They also wanted to weaken the power of the Catholic church through disentailment of church lands and experiments in secularized education.

The struggle over the economic and cultural future of Spain coincided with the second industrial revolution in England, when machines for what we now call heavy industry were first being invented. One particularly important invention, in terms of the social and political history of the Basque region, was the Bessemer furnace, which allowed the inexpensive production of railway tracks, steel plates, and metal tubing. The process required a type of iron ore that was scarce in the British Isles but plentiful around Bilbao. Once the social liberals won the Second Carlist War and inaugurated their economic reforms (especially those facilitating the exportation of natural resources), British orders for iron ore transformed Bilbao almost overnight from a small trading port into a major international center of iron mining and refining. More than 250 iron mines were being operated in the region by 1900. At that time Spain produced 21 percent of the world's iron ore, and the Vizcayan mines alone produced more than 13 percent.[1]

The extraction of iron ore for international markets created thousands of jobs in mining and ancillary industries. The population of the municipality of Bilbao grew from 17,923 in 1857 to 81,956 in 1900. By 1900, 26.4 percent of the population of Vizcaya had been born outside the province.[2] The new industrial proletariat of the region generally lived within walking distance of mines, furnaces, and other work sites, and in neighborhoods socially isolated from the bourgeoisie. Soon the workers began to resort to industrywide work stoppages and the election of Socialist candidates to government posts in attempts to protect and assert their class interests.

During the three decades of unprecedented industrialization, urbanization, and overt class conflict (roughly 1880 to 1910), two new types of social and political thinking appeared on the Basque coast. They provided the intellectual assumptions and inspiration for new political practices that gradually would become the Basque Nationalist party. Both styles of theorizing included the proposal that the Basque region rule itself, but differed fundamentally in their assumptions, analyses, and judgments regarding recent capitalist industrialization and its possibilities, benefits, and costs.

EARLY EUSKALERRÍACOS (1890–1920) AND THE IDEOLOGY OF RAPID CAPITALIST DEVELOPMENT

One prototypically "nationalist" ideology endorsed recent social and economic changes in the region and sought ways to continue them. The organizational crucible for this ideology was Bilbao's Euskalerria Society, a private club made up of successful businessmen. The so-called Euskalerrians greatly admired the British industrial revolution and hoped to duplicate British social history on the Basque coast. To do so, they believed, required political decentralization, especially self-government for the Basque region. They reasoned that if there were political decentralization, they would have a greater influence over local economic policies and could then legislatively recreate northern England in northern Spain.[3]

The Euskalerrians' early demands were modest: restoration of an earlier decentralized system of taxation, in which each province would decide its own contribution to the Spanish treasury as well as how taxes should be levied. Many favored a regressive, consumption-based tax that would provide funds for public works without bleeding profits from business. In addition, they advocated a decentralized system of tariffs, in which each province or region would decide upon which goods would carry tariffs and at what levels.

Contemporaneous political events in Madrid cast light on why some Basque industrialists wanted a decentralized tariff system. A socially liberal governing coalition under the leadership of Prime Minister Práxedes Mateo Sagasta was advocating lower tariff walls, international free trade, and legalized trade unions. It argued that lower tariffs and therefore greater competition between Spanish producers and foreign firms would accelerate technological innovations, modernize the economy, and allow Spain to become a world power. Landowners would benefit from additional markets for their goods and from less expensive manufactured imports, and legalization of trade unions would promote social peace between classes.

Basque industrialists saw things differently. Unlike Sagasta, they were profoundly suspicious of trade unions and of working-class associations. Moreover, many in the Basque region and Catalonia thought that the proposals for free trade, if implemented, would only permit foreign companies to undersell and destroy Spain's infant industries. Accordingly, industrialists and urban businessmen on the coast of the Basque region formed anti-Madrid tariff leagues for the purposes of protecting and, if possible, raising tariffs.[4]

Though obviously advocating fundamental changes for Basque society and the evolving Spanish political system, the members of the Euskalerria Society never saw themselves as engaging in seditious politics. They carefully avoided advocating secession and violent rhetoric.

The Euskalerria Society dissolved itself in 1902. Many of its former members joined a new political coalition that later would be known as the Partido Nacionalista Vasco (or Basque Nationalist party). Today, the terms "eskalerríacos" and "sotistas" are often used in the Basque region to refer to groups and individuals who advocate regional self-rule and also believe that (1) rapid industrial growth is highly desirable, (2) growth requires significant decentralization of the Spanish state, and (3) business leaders are the best persons to oversee and direct local industrialization.

Engracio de Aranzadi (whose political pen name was "Kizkitza") was one of the earliest spokespersons for the euskalerrian position within the Basque Nationalist party.[5] He edited an important party periodical, *Euskalduna*, and his *La nación vasca* (1918) was the first book-length explication of the euskalerrian position. In almost all his writings Aranzadi alluded frequently and flatteringly to England's economic history. *Euskalduna* openly sided with the Allies during World War I and accused the empires of the Central Europe of oppressing national minorities, such as the Poles and the Croatians. This editorial position generated considerable conflict within the party, for many members sympathized with Germany. Aranzadi vacillated on the subject of regional independence but sometimes stated that the goal of the Basque nationalist movement was regional autonomy in economic matters, not complete separation from Spain: "it is an error to think that the nationalist objective is independence."[6] He highlighted the economic goals of Basque nationalism (as *he* understood the movement) by giving his articles such titles as "Nationalism and Basque Riches" and publishing such essays by other nationalist authors as "Ideas and Wealth."[7]

At the same time many members of the Basque Nationalist party and its sympathizers began reading the works of another party intellectual, Jesús de Sarriá.[8] Sarriá was arguably the most controversial of the earliest advocates of the euskalerrian position because of his unqualified praise of industrialization and large-scale capitalism. His influential *La ideología del nacionalismo vasco* was published in the same year as Aranzadi's *La nación vasca*. He also edited *Hermes*, a cosmopolitan, avant-garde magazine that covered contemporary intellectual movements on the Continent. It published postmodernist poetry by Ramón de Basterra, philosophical and historical essays by Miguel de Unamuno and José de Ortega y Gasset, and extensive reviews of international art exhibitions. Led by Sarriá, *Hermes* writers and contributors insisted that the proper aim of the party was economic growth; capitalism was a unique talent of the Basque people and they could share its benefits with the rest of Spain. According to Sarriá,

> The National homeland of the Basques is an industrial and commercial democracy, working, active, rich. . . . We are an industrial and commercial people. The passive life is not part of our race. There are harmonies of interests between capital and the workers. . . . We consider it indispensable to

stimulate this public wealth of ours through a government of protection and defense.[9]

He also wrote:

For us Basque Nationalists, national wealth is connected to the substance of nationality itself. . . . The wealth that we have is a fundamental element, like a shield and fortress, for nationality and citizenship. We are a people with a practical sense, with concrete notions, with a spirit of solidarity within the national economy.[10]

According to Sarriá and the other *Hermes* writers, economic growth could best be nurtured through an administratively decentralized Spanish state. This, however, did not mean that the Basque Nationalist party should seek secession from Spain. "It must be recognized that Basque nationalism does not signify, nor does it intend to signify, a movement for separation from the Spanish state, in any manner," wrote one contributor in *Hermes*.[11] "The link with Spain is long and profound. . . . We must never act in ignorance of this link. Nor ought we violently to provoke the destruction of this link."[12]

Sarriá and Aranzadi were essentially intellectuals and propagandists in the service of the Basque Nationalist party. Ramón de la Sota, however, was different. He was an active statesman, holding many government offices, and, for this reason, was perhaps the single most influential euskalerríaco during the first quarter of the twentieth century.[13] Sota had been a member of the original Euskalerria Society, but his local influence was not due solely to that organization. Through a series of shrewd mergers, he had become president of the largest shipbuilding corporation in Spain. During World War I its annual profits soared from 2.5 million pesetas in 1914 to over 35 million pesetas in 1918. Sota also sat on the governing board of the Bank of Vizcaya, was president of Bilbao's port commission, was president of Vizcaya's shipbuilders' association (a prestigious post because in 1900, for example, 39 percent of Spain's merchant marine was Vizcayan),[14] and had been awarded a knighthood by Britain to acknowledge his cooperation during World War I.

All these achievements and activities contributed to Sota's status within the Basque Nationalist party, but his influence also reflected the growing number of local businessmen who were attracted to the party during the early twentieth century. Around 1910, the industrialized economy of the Basque coast had entered a new stage of development; local industrialists discovered innovative ways to finance expansion, such as joint-stock companies and industrial banking, and firms increasingly merged and found other ways to coordinate production. Moreover, because of Spain's neutrality during World War I, many Basque industrialists had become key suppliers of metals and metal products to the combatants. Bilbao had undergone "an extraordinary commercial fever," in the words of one contemporary businessman.[15] Total annual investment in Vizcaya rose from 164 million pesetas in 1917 to 427 million pesetas in 1918.[16] At the same time the Spanish government seemed to be stunting the "natural" economic development of the Basque region (or so Basque businessmen believed) through its taxes on war profits.[17] Basque industrialists, among them Sota, declared that the government lacked the business sense and economic skills necessary to make intelligent fiscal policy. Angered by the government's seemingly foolish policies, many Basque industrialists, such as Daniel Basaludúa (then the president of Bilbao's chamber of commerce), expressed support for an independent regional government that would decide all questions about tariffs and taxes. The slogan Por Vizcaya y Para Vizcaya (For Vizcaya and by Vizcaya) was popular among coastal industrialists by the 1920s. It was amidst this growing fiscal and budgetary regionalism that Sota enjoyed his remarkable prestige as a political leader.

THE EUSKALERRIAN TRADITION SINCE 1930

In the early years of the Spanish Second Republic (1930–36), almost all the leadership posts within the Basque Nationalist party were held by businessmen. They were neither the stereotypical ruthless types nor robber barons indifferent to the needs and wishes of other classes and callous toward their workers, but were, according to Javier Tusell Gómez, businessmen who held "advanced conceptions about politics and society," inspired in part by Roosevelt's New Deal.[18] Even though they remained hostile to most unions and to Socialist rule, this new generation of leaders in the party believed that some concessions to the working class were necessary if regional capitalism were to flourish in an orderly manner. They therefore supported proposed legislation for a forty-hour work week, a minimum wage, and the transfer of land owned by absentee landowners to sharecroppers and tenant farmers. And they continued to seek home rule, especially in areas of economic policy.

In exchange for permission to establish an autonomous regional government, the Basque Nationalist party sided with the Republican forces during the Spanish civil war. It afterwards suffered political persecution. The victorious military rebels revoked all rights of local self-rule for the coastal provinces of Vizcaya and Guipúzcoa, and refused to recognize the new regional government. In contrast, the two inland provinces of Alava and Navarra, which immediately supported the rebel forces, were granted an amount of provincial self-rule unparalleled in Francoist Spain. Partly because he was fearful that regional loyalties might undermine the "organic" society that many supporters were trying to create, Franco tried to destroy the Basque Nationalist party by ordering the imprisonment and execution of thousands of party activists and proscribing local cultural activities, such as the use of the indigenous language in public places. In exile, several party leaders wrote speculative articles about how the Basque economy might develop under their rule. Except for supporting two general strikes during 1947 and 1951, however, most Nationalists were not greatly involved in fomenting popular resistance during the first half of the Franco regime. Police repression after the two general strikes had ruined the organization's clandestine network, and no tangible benefits resulted. Therefore, most Nationalist leaders chose to play a waiting game, hoping that international pressure would soon bring about the collapse of the Franco regime and that thereafter the new democratic regime would reinstate the region's autonomous government.[19]

The Franco regime did not quickly collapse, however, and despite laws against political assembly, the Nationalists began to organize large rallies during the mid-1960s. A new generation of euskalerría-cos also appeared. One of the more outspoken was Juan Beitia. Beitia was, among other things, a co-owner of a public relations company that managed elections for socially conservative businessmen in France. He also had numerous professional contacts with members of the Spanish Unión de Centro Democrático, which was the first party after the death of Franco to rule Spain. For example, he was a friend of the UCD's minister of industry, Rodriguez de Sahagun.

Beitia first became active in the Basque Nationalist party during the late 1960s. He soon joined the party's executive council for Vizcaya province and was responsible for managing the party's budget. Beitia also was one of the founders and financiers of a conciliatory craft union, the ELA-STV(a). Despite his formal responsibilities, Beitia was never fully trusted by some Nationalists. During the 1979 negotiations in the Spanish parliament regarding an autonomous government for the Basque region, some accused Beitia of disclosing politically sensitive information about intraparty negotiations to the UCD. In 1980 he was expelled from the party, partly on grounds that he was misusing party funds and was publicly misrepresenting the party to others.[20]

Despite numerous charges and countercharges about Beitia's "true" partisan loyalties, there has never been serious disagreement about his social ideology. It was an essentially libertarian view of industrial growth, in which the entrepreneur was to be given as much freedom from government regulation as possible in his or her pursuit of profits. He believed that many of the social and economic policies of the Franco regime, such as factory juries and restrictions on the sudden firing of workers, retarded rather than encouraged local economic development, and deterred talented and intelligent entrepreneurs from making efficient use of their resources. Beitia also maintained that the existing rights of industrial workers, such as factory juries, needed to be curtailed as soon as possible in order for the Basque firms to be internationally competitive. Beitia held that the creation of a Basque regional government was a rare and historic opportunity to redefine the legal rights of the bourgeoisie, vis-à-vis organized workers and the state, and to redesign the regional economy according to free-market principles.

Three other businessmen soon surpassed Beitia in terms of prestige within the party: Javier García Egocheaga, Pedro Luis Uriarte, and Carlos Blasco de Imaz. The three were selected by the Basque Nationalist party to be the first ministers of industry, the treasury, and commerce in the Basque regional government, which was reconstituted in 1980, five years after Franco's death. Each had earned a reputation as an efficient executive and had held a post in a prominent corporation on the Basque coast—for instance, Uriarte had been the general director of the Bank of Bilbao, one of the half-dozen largest banks of Spain.

These euskalerríacos strongly favored government aid to large industries, including government inducements for mergers and the formation of cartels in the private sector. Though they were not advocates of government-owned businesses, their political thinking was far less consistently laissez-faire than that of Beitia.[21] As minister of industry, Egocheaga actively sought to subsidize what he considered to be industries with great potential for future growth, such as electronics companies. Conversely, he advised that all governments (Spanish and regional) sharply cut back their aid to industries unlikely to prosper in the long run, such as the mining and naval industries in the Basque region. Uriarte, minister of the treasury, sometimes compared the Basque economic crisis of the late 1970s to the notorious economic crisis of Weimar Germany. He argued that the depression could be ended only through labor discipline and large reductions in taxes; tax cuts would generate more private savings, more private investment, and further technical innovations and jobs. Imaz, minister of commerce, advocated stimulating economic growth in the Basque region through a new government agency called "Basque-export." Its primary mission would be to promote Basque industries abroad and to provide loans to promising export-oriented firms. Imaz also believed that it was economically imperative that the Basque regional government resist antimonopoly sentiments, and that it encourage mergers, the formation of purchasing collectives, and other types of coordination of businesses within the private sector.

Perhaps the single most influential euskalerríaco within the Partido Nacionalista Vasco during the early post-Franco period has been Carlos Garaikoetxea.[22] His political struggles within the party will be discussed later. Here, what will be emphasized is his perpetuation of euskalerrian values and concerns.

Garaikoetxea, the first president of the new Basque regional government in 1980, was a former president of the chamber of commerce of Navarra province. He had a long history of involvement in Navarra's business community, and has been described by one observer as "above all, a business executive. A man formed for, of, and by the managerial world; accustomed to discussing and haggling with diverse people, always looking to obtain a profit."[23] He portrayed himself in newspaper interviews as a "progressive" thinker who was strongly committed to economic prosperity for the Basque region. He repeatedly denied that the ultimate goal of the party was secession per se; the goal also included sustained and rapid economic growth. In his inaugural speech as president of the Basque regional government, Garaikoetxea expressed his strong commitment to regional economic development. In his opinion, he "represented the entire opinion of this Chamber in stating that the economic situation of our Homeland must be one of the preoccupations and highest priorities of the future Basque Government." Moreover, the economy of the region currently was "sick" and required "exceptional solutions" that Madrid refused to entertain. Therefore, it was necessary to win regional independence "if we really aspire to structure Basque social and economic life in accordance with our people's collective will."[24]

SABINO DE ARANA Y GOIRI AND THE SOCIALLY CONSERVATIVE, ANTICAPITALIST TRADITION OF BASQUE NATIONALIST THOUGHT

According to some observers, the euskalerríacos represent the dominant intellectual current within the Basque Nationalist party, at least since the first decades of the twentieth century. For example, Basque journalist Ramón Zallo has estimated that since the death of Franco as many as 60 percent of the members in the party have subscribed to some version of euskalerrian (i.e., rapid capitalist development) doctrine.[25]

It may be true that in recent years a majority of the active members in the party have advocated commercial prosperity and rapid capitalist growth. Many members, however, have adhered to a radically different ideology, sometimes called by local observers "Basque nationalist primitivism" or "Aranaism," after its first systematic theorist, Sabino de Arana y Goiri.

Most historians who have studied Arana have elected to separate his writings into two categories: the early writings about politics and society (1893–98), when Arana defined "Basque nationalism" in terms of religion and the complete secession of the provinces of the Basque region from Spain; and the later writings (1899–1903), when Arana increasingly defined "Basque nationalism" in terms of local economic development within a federation of Iberian regions. Most self-proclaimed Aranaists tend to dismiss the later writings as inaccurate expressions of Arana's true beliefs. We shall follow this convention, and limit our exposition of Aranaism to an elaboration of his earlier ideas and statements about politics and society.[26] The elaboration, however, is not as easily accomplished because several ideas, such as theocracy, jar with our post–World War II conceptions about politics, culture, and society. Perhaps some of his experiences before he started to write about Basque nationalism may help cast light on the logic and emotional appeal of his arguments.[27]

Arana was born in 1865 to a wealthy family on the east bank of the Nervión River in a small village that produced vegetables for Bilbao's residents. In 1890 Bilbao annexed the village (it became a crowded commercial district now known as Siete Calles), and the Bilbao General Strike occurred. According to some contemporary observers, Bilbao was buzzing with discussions and debates about the unprecedented and often violent strike. Little is known about Arana's immediate response to it, but he may have been angered by it because later in life he spoke very critically of workers' "egoism," "materialism," and propensity for dictatorship.

Arana, suffering constantly from consumption and jaundice, was sickly during most of his childhood and adolescence. (He died when he was only thirty-eight from Addison's disease.) Deeply religious, he prayed for help before a statue of the Virgin Mary during a near-fatal illness in his adolescence, and reportedly had a mystical experience, which was followed by a near-miraculous recovery.

Arana's father was a wealthy shipbuilder whose company constructed more than a hundred vessels. He was also mayor of the village and an elected member of the parliament of Vizcaya province, in addition to being an international gunrunner for the Carlist party. According to Stanley Payne, after the military defeat of the Carlists in the 1870s, Arana's father suffered deep depressions, which bordered on psychosis. He died when Arana was seventeen. Perhaps there was a complex and ambivalent relationship between the often-sick Arana and his swashbuckling father, because until his father's death Arana was an unquestioning Carlist. Immediately afterward, he underwent a legendary political transformation.

Most historians have noted that Arana's political conversion occurred on a symbolically significant day, Resurrection Sunday, 1888. According to a common but perhaps apocryphal story, he had been humbled in a political debate with his older brother, Luis, about the theoretical foundations of his father's Carlist doctrine. Sabino tried to defend Carlism, while Luis vigorously pointed out the flaws in his brother's arguments. Angered and discomfited, Sabino announced that he was going to dedicate his life to studying Basque political history and to inventing a new and compelling defense of regional autonomy from the Spanish state that would supersede his father's formal ideology.

Writers who use the modernization interpretation when accounting for the motivations that underlie Basque nationalism often speculate that the speed of cultural change generally creates acute insecurities and anxieties within persons unfamiliar with the new mores, and that they consequently often wish to return to a simpler, premodern age to escape their cultural uncertainty. Stated differently, the nationalist ideology of the region is a behavioral manifestation of deeper, intrapersonal sufferings, brought about by very rapid and widespread changes in societal norms and institutions. It may be true that Sabino de Arana's nationalism was due in part to the speed with which his sleepy village became part of modern, industrialized Bilbao (though it should be noted that the head of the Arana household obviously was not unfamiliar with modern trade, machinery, and commercial culture and that therefore Sabino de Arana probably was neither purely "traditional" in his thinking nor totally unfamiliar with the ways of Bilbao's emerging, industrial culture). If, however, one wishes to identify the psychological roots of Arana's nationalism, an alternative interpretation also seems possible. Given the familial circumstances in which he decided to seek a new defense of the region's independence, one might argue that his sudden decision was, on a personal level, a subconscious attempt by a chronically sick youth to establish his manhood and personal autonomy before his older brother and his dead-but-once-dynamic father.[28] In other words, there are probably multiple sociopsychological origins of an ideology such as nationalism; and perhaps the modernization interpretation focuses on one, but only one, of the arguably relevant historical circumstances.

In any case, shortly after his father's death, Arana went with his mother to Barcelona, where he studied for various professions, such as medicine and law, but did not successfully complete any course of study. Returning to Bilbao for a short visit, he participated with his brother Luis in demonstrations for a martyred bishop from Vizcaya. During another short visit Arana was angered by the selling of Protestant books at a local book fair. Without authorization from the organizers of the fair, he opened his own stall and sold books advocating Catholicism. The organizers ordered Arana to close down, and after being banned from the fair, he reportedly walked through the streets, giving away his books.

Arana's six-year stay in Barcelona coincided with the development of Catalan nationalism. He was aware of the trend, observed the revival of Catalan literature, and read the new theories of Catalan separatism. In 1888 he returned to Bilbao with hopes of launching a Basque cultural revival that ultimately would lead to a new type of political movement similar to that in Catalonia.

This revivalist project was an audacious and arguably unrealistic undertaking for at least two reasons. First, what outsiders call the Basque language is in fact a group of several mutually unintelligible languages, with radically different vocabularies, grammars, and pronunciations.[29] Would a serious "Basque revival" lead to cultural unity, as in the case of Catalonia, or ultimately to a Tower of Babel? Second, most indigenous Basque dialects already had disappeared from common use, except in isolated mountain villages and small fishing ports. In fact, there were not as many native Basque speakers in the region as there were Catalan speakers in Catalonia, perhaps too few on which to premise a successful political movement. Arana was not daunted by these practical problems. He wrote and published grammars, systematized existing dialects, and published regional histories (all very remarkable achievements, given that he, like other children of upper-class families in the region, had been raised speaking only Castilian). He also opened folkloric centers (*batzokis*) where Basque languages could be taught and practiced.

In 1880, at the age of twenty-five, Arana printed 2,000 copies of his first political manifesto, *Bizkaya por su independencia*. It defended the right of Vizcaya to secede from Spain (interestingly, no mention was made of the political rights of the other three Basque provinces). That year he also held a colloquium of seventeen friends, including several members of the Euskalerria Society, at which he elaborated some of his new political and social ideas. Five years later, he established the novel political and propaganda bureau, the Bizkai-Buru-Batzar (or Vizcayan provincial council), that after his death gradually evolved into the Basque Nationalist party.

In his early political writings Arana combined disparate notions about religion, the virtues of rural and precapitalist life, and the need for culturally segregating the native residents of the Basque region from the industrial workers of other parts of Spain.[30] He interpreted the centralization of political authority in Spain during the late nineteenth century as a conscious attempt by atheists to weaken the Catholic church and to advance secular and irreligious values. The Basque region, not Spain, he averred, is "the most Catholic country in the world."[31] Arana believed that the Spanish state was controlled by sinister, anticlerical forces, in particular, Republicans and Freemasons. One example of the state's villainy was its economic and social reforms after the Second Carlist War. By encouraging exports of iron and coal to England and by disestablishing the church's lands, the Spanish state had unleashed a plethora of social forces that if not vigorously resisted, would corrupt otherwise pious souls. The reformers had initiated "profound and extensive irreligiosity, and intense and expanding immorality."[32] Arana reasoned that it was imperative that the liberal impulse in Iberian politics be destroyed, and that the Catholic church be given "absolute freedom to realize its divine mission."[33]

According to Arana (at least in his earlier writings), a necessary precondition for defeating the irreligious threat posed by the Spanish government was the creation of an independent confederacy of municipalities and provinces in the Basque region of Spain (Arana sometimes extended his argument to include the Basque provinces in France, but this was not his regular practice). These jurisdictions would be politically independent of the Spanish state but under the direct authority of the Catholic church. Except for foreign affairs, each would administer its own laws according to general principles announced by the church, and would be free to secede at any time from the larger confederacy if it judged that the policies of the confederacy were endangering the religiosity of its populace. Thus, Arana's early commitment to regional self-government was inextricably connected to a broader theological commitment. He wrote:

> My patriotism is not rooted in human motives, nor is it directed toward material ends. My patriotism is rooted and every day is more rooted in my love for God, and its aim is to connect God to my blood relatives, to my great family, the Basque country.[34]

And

> Ideologically speaking, before the existence of the homeland there is God; but in practical and temporal life, here in Viz-

caya province, in order to love God it is necessary to be a patriot, and in order to be a patriot it is necessary to love God; this is the meaning of fatherland.[35]

Arana used several religious rituals, slogans, and symbols within the Bizkai-Buru-Batzar to reinforce its theocratic orientation. For example, all members of the organization had to be Catholic and had to renounce allegiance to any "atheistic" political or social doctrines, such as freemasonery, anarchism, socialism, and republicanism. Arana also coined For God and Ancient Law as the official motto of the organization, and used the acronym GETEJ in all of the organization's pamphlets; the acronym stood for "We are for the Basque homeland, and the Basque homeland is for God." He also wrote a religious poem that later became the official hymn of the Basque Nationalist party, and that included the following lines:

> Live long, live long Basque homeland,
> And glory to the good God of the heavens. . . .
> Above us we have the sacred law,
> Which will always be our emblem.
> We sing long life to our homeland,
> and glory to the good God of the heavens. . . .[36]

In addition to prescribing political confederacy and theocracy for the region, Arana argued at length about a "racial" incompatibility of native Basque residents and newcomers from other parts of Spain. But by race he had something more in mind than physical differences. He believed that physical differences corresponded to a deeper, spiritual reality—to invisible differences in mentality and styles of thinking and feeling:

> The physiognomy of a native Vizcayan is intelligent and noble; that of a Spaniard is inexpressive and gloomy. The Vizcayan walks elegantly and assertively; the Spaniard either does not know how to walk or adopts a feminine style (for example, the bullfighter).

Further, a Vizcayan dancer unites

> simple innocence and the most terrific happiness. If you watch a Spanish dance, and if you are not nauseated by its

lewd, disgusting, and cynical hugs between the two sexes, it is a credit to the robustness of your stomach.[37]

To insure racial purity, Arana required that members of his political bureau be native-born Vizcayans and also have at least one native Vizcayan grandparent. As an elected city councilman, Arana proposed separate prisons for Basque and non-Basque juvenile delinquents (the motion was not passed), arguing that close proximity between the two races would result in Basque youths learning blasphemous sayings and immoral habits from *maketo* (a derogatory term Arana invented for people from other parts of Spain) cellmates. In addition, his bureau publicly condemned intermarriage between Basques and maketos.

According to Arana, among the immoral habits that non-Basques introduced to the region were capitalistic greed and proletarian ingratitude. Prior to the "invasion of the maketos," there had been neither employer contempt of workers nor worker hatred of employers; employers and employees had spontaneously helped each other. The new industrial capitalists (many of whom, according to Arana, came from England and the interior of Spain) brought with them unbridled avarice and were unjustifiably and unnecessarily mean to their workers. "All of us know that today," he declared, "the poor are inhumanely exploited and treated like beasts by industrialists and businessmen, mine owners and the propertied."[38]

Arana often expressed sorrow over the sufferings of the industrial workers of the Basque region, but he also thought that workers' proposals for socialism were thoughtless reflections of their own immoral avarice and laziness. "Experience teaches us every day that the majority of workers and the poor are this way because they do not know how to control themselves, because they do not know how to suppress their vices."[39] Rather than seeking to control society, workers should more effectively control themselves. Furthermore, Basque Nationalists must use legal tools to help remind local businessmen of their duty to physically care for and morally educate the poor. Arana's solution to the vexing "social question" of the nineteenth century was a more loving, Christian-spirited paternalistic relationship between classes—a sort of tender subordination:

> Do Catalan nationalists, either moderates or radicals, have in their programs solutions to the social problem, which is

so important in their land? We do not believe so, because they have not fastened onto a religious theme, and there is no solution apart from Christ.

Have the Basque nationalists fastened upon a religious theme? Yes, and it is clearly demonstrated in their motto: "For God and Ancient law."

Their goal is not political but social: to Christianize the people, the poor as well as the rich—politics is to be the means.[40]

Between 1893 and 1898, Arana failed to develop an effective strategy for creating an independent Christian confederacy in the Basque region. He had declared in 1893 that "Spain must die!"[41] But his early proclamations, although colorful, were politically sterile and failed to generate a popular following. Then, around 1898, Arana's political statements and behavior suddenly changed. He invited members of the Euskalerria Society to join his organization (the Bizkai-Buru-Batzar) and even to hold key leadership posts. The two groups formally merged in 1903. More surprisingly, explicit theological defenses of regional secession disappeared from nationalist publications. Instead, under Arana's editorial direction, La Patria began to encourage readers to aspire to "a special autonomy for the Basque country . . . adjusted to the needs of modern times."[42]

Some observers and historians have attributed Arana's new behavior and sayings to his election to the city council of Bilbao and to the provincial parliament of Vizcaya. He now had tangible stakes in the political system and, it has been posited, altered his behavior so as to be more influential in government. Other people think that the changes in Arana were due to his two short incarcerations on charges of seditious activity; he may have wisely decided to tone down his militancy temporarily in order to avoid further imprisonment.[43] Whatever the motives for his metamorphosis, it led to an important organizational fusion between Arana's followers and the Euskalerria Society. Consequently, when Arana died in 1903, he left an uneasy but electorally successful coalition of theocrats, led by his older brother, Luis Arana, and capitalists, led by Ramón de la Sota.

VARIETIES OF POST-ARANA ARANAISM

The constellation of ideas articulated by Sabino de Arana inspired several later members of the Basque Nationalist party, who seized upon and developed certain themes while ignoring others. One can distinguish at least four varieties of Aranaism that evolved after his death. The four derivative traditions can be labeled for purposes of convenience: (1) the religious tradition, (2) the linguistic tradition, (3) the political tradition, and (4) the anticapitalist tradition.

The Religious Tradition

After Arana's death in 1903, a messianic spirit developed in some sectors of the Basque Nationalist party. Some Nationalists began to describe Arana as the "brother of Jesus Christ" and as "the Master." Mass marches to Arana's grave began around 1907. Party celebrations paralleled the Christian calendar, for instance, the "Day of the Basque Nation," first held in 1931, fell on Easter Sunday.[44]

Some admirers of Arana began to emphasize the theocratic arguments in his writings to the exclusion of the other elements. Regional self-rule remained an important goal in the revisionists' thinking, yet secondary to a primary goal of reviving Catholicism in an age of European atheism. In fact, they sometimes maintained that they would give up the goal of regional self-rule if, by some twist of fate, the government in Madrid fell into the hands of committed Catholics. Political independence was not a summum bonum, but merely a secular means to a religious ends. In the words of one theocratic Aranaist, "Between seeing Euzkadi in full exercise of its right, but separated from Christ, and seeing her as in 1901 [as an integral part of Spain], but faithful to Christ, the Basque Nationalists would opt for the second situation."[45]

The Linguistic Aranaists

While some admirers of Arana were refining the theocratic elements of his thought, others mined and developed his positive statements about Basque folk culture. Romantic essays about Basque peasants, fishermen, and shepherds soon became commonplace.

Some Aranaists even identified rural life as the source of Basque Christian virtues. One author, for example, maintained that "there is no important act in the daily life of a Basque peasant which is not in some way an homage to God."[46] Another author insisted that Christian morality and the life-style of a modern industrial capitalist were ultimately incompatible.[47]

One book that greatly extended Arana's ideas about culture was Luis de Eleizalde's *Raza, lengua, y nación* (1911). Eleizalde contended that Basques have a distinctive capacity to be moral because of peculiarities in their local languages. According to Eleizalde, the sounds, sentence structure, and vocabulary of an area's language determine the thoughts, perceptions, sentiments, and social relations that are possible within the area. Basque dialects, because of their unusual sounds, words, and grammatical rules, allegedly have certain advantages over Spanish and French in terms of facilitating Christian feelings, virtues, and social relations. Therefore, the preservation and promotion of the Basque languages are necessary for correct moral education, and are not "merely" the arbitrary aims of another set of parochial people who wish to preserve their distinctive heritage. Eleizalde's linguistic theory of human psychology influenced many later party members and even ethnonationalists who had only a modicum of involvement with the Basque Nationalist party—for example, Frederico Krutwig and José Luis Alvarez Enparanza (also known as "Txillardegi").[48]

The Political Tradition

Arana sometimes spoke very strongly in support of regional independence and confederacy, especially early in his political career. These sentiments have inspired a third type of Aranaist: the so-called *independistas* and confederalists (or what I will call the "political Aranaist"). One leading political Aranaist was Arana's brother, Luis. Immediately after Sabino's death, Luis Arana officially presided over the Bizkai-Buru-Batzar of Vizcaya province, the oldest, largest, wealthiest, and most prestigious Buru-Batzar in the region. During his tenure Arana strongly opposed the euskalerríacos and criticized their apparent preoccupation with money and their apparent indifference toward the principle of municipal self-government. He also wrote a book systematizing his brother's views about confederacy and regional independence, and coined the phrase "primitive Basque nationalism" to refer to his brother's early and more radical political goals, and to distinguish that program from the less politically radical ideas of the euskalerríacos.[49]

Luis Arana also helped establish a new nationalist periodical, *Aberri*. The writers for *Aberri* constantly criticized the (relatively) politically timid goals and economic motivations of the euskalerríacos. The journal chastized three prominent euskalerríacos—Ramón de la Sota (at the time the president of Bilbao's port commission), Gregorio Ibarreche (the mayor of Bilbao), and Pedro Chalbaud (the president of Bilbao's Chamber of Commerce)—for meeting with the Spanish king and joining him for a tour of Sota's shipyards. *Aberri* also raised embarrassing questions about conflict of interest involving Sota's activities within the Spanish parliament, for some of the legislation subsidized Sota's shipbuilding companies. As one might expect, most euskalerríacos viewed Luis Arana as politically inflexible and socially unrealistic. According to the euskalerrian newsletter, *Euskalduna*:

> Two forces struggle within the Partido Nationalista Vasco: the faction of artificial ideology, of "all or nothing," victims of obsessions with a lovely illusion, and because of this, intransigent to the point of enthusiasm; and the faction of the moderates, who without discarding doctrine have adapted it to present circumstances.[50]

In 1908, Ramón de la Sota succeeded Luis Arana as president of the Bizkai-Buru-Batzar. Under Sota's leadership, the Nationalist organization soon adopted a new political program. Instead of working for total and unequivocal independence from Spain or for the creation of a confederacy of Catholic settlements within the Basque region, the Bizkai-Buru-Batzar worked to establish an autonomous, administrative body in the region that would decide fiscal and other economic issues. Luis Arana protested, saying that the euskalerríacos had discarded his brother's two most important principles: national independence from Spain and municipal confederacy. Angered by the euskalerríacos' disloyalty to the principles of primitive Basque nationalism, Arana and a band of followers officially resigned from the Bizkai-Buru-Batzar, and organized a new nationalist group that gradually would come to be known as the Jagi-Jagi.[51]

The Economic Tradition

The fourth distinguishable tradition of post-Arana Aranaist thought first appeared shortly after World War I. It was first systematically developed and vigorously promoted by Elias Gallastegui, who adopted the political nickname of "Gudari" (warrior). Because Gallastegui's ideas superficially resemble certain variants of Western Marxist-humanist thinking, it is useful to review briefly Gallastegui's political career and social environment so as to appreciate better both his novel assertions and his omissions.[52]

Gallastegui was born in 1892. He belonged to what might be labeled "the second generation" of Basque Nationalists. Unlike Sabino Arana, Luis Arana, Jesús de Sarriá, and Ramón de la Sota—who were adolescents during the last quarter of the nineteenth century, when Bilbao suddenly was transformed from a quiet town into an international center of mining, steel manufacturing, and shipbuilding—Gallastegui was a young man before and during World War I, when Basque capitalism was consolidating itself. This was a time of spectacular profits and mergers among Basque businesses and banks—and a time of growing labor unrest along the west bank. Strikes, which had been infrequent and extraordinary events before the war, fast were becoming routine. Before World War I, the total number of strikes in and around Bilbao in a given year never exceeded one hundred, but more than one thousand strikes occurred in 1920 alone.[53]

Gallastegui joined the Basque Youth of Bilbao, an organization devoted to preserving local Basque languages and sponsored by the Bizkai-Buru-Batzar. He also wrote for Luis Arana's journal, *Aberri*, and in his essays frequently reproached the euskalerríacos for timid political ambitions and limitless greed. While writing for *Aberri*, Gallastegui became disenchanted with both the Aranaists' and the euskalerríacos' unsympathetic interpretations of class conflict and labor protest. During World War I there were many street fights between working-class youths and members of the Basque Youth. Nationalist journals like *Aberri* generally criticized the former for their "socialist savagery" and "vandalism," but Gallastegui had other ideas. In 1919, he began to write articles that sympathized with Bilbao's industrial workers, terming their acts of violence and lawbreaking justifiable responses to unjust, exploitative, and oppressive economic conditions. He further argued that many of the workers' demands during strikes were, upon reflection, modest, reasonable, and fair. Around 1922 Gallastegui proposed the creation of a new social and political coalition made up of industrial workers and holders of small properties. In his opinion, such a coalition would be numerically strong enough to win regional secession from Spain and to build a new social order, in which big capitalists would receive their just deserts.

In 1920 Gallastegui and several other officers of the Basque Youth organized a public meeting in San Sebastián at which they openly criticized older leaders of the Basque Nationalist party for improperly compromising the values and principles of Sabino de Arana. Shortly thereafter, the national council of the Basque Nationalist party expelled several people from the Basque Youth of Bilbao, including Gallastegui.

Gallastegui's expulsion coincided with a shocking event in 1921 that permanently alienated Gallastegui from the other major doctrinal currents within the Basque Nationalist party. Fearing a workers' revolution in northern Spain, the Spanish police attacked a meeting of a Communist cell in Bilbao and killed several unarmed workers and labor organizers. Most newspapers in the area, both Nationalist and non-Nationalist, applauded the police action. The conservative *Gaceta del Norte* insisted that Spain's police forces "siempre, siempre, siempre" (always, always, always) have good reasons for resorting to violence when dealing with workers.[54] *Euskalduna* similarly refused to condemn the massacre. Gallastegui saw the event differently. In an article for *Aberri* entitled "Fiesta de Sangre" (Festival of Blood), he berated the Spanish police, and advocated solidarity between young Nationalists and young Communists. Wrote Gallastegui:

> Profuse and warm blood ran through Bilbao yesterday, and, as always, it was the blood of humble people. There had fallen idealistic men; some men who had struggled and had suffered constantly. They are Communists, as earlier there had fallen members of Solidaridad [ELA-STV]. . . . They are very far from our goal for laborers. Yet is this important? The bullets that have entered the chests of those dead young men seemingly have been lodged in our own hearts. We feel tragedy as if they were our own because we too, like them,

are young, are idealistic, suffer, and are of modest condition. . . . [Such a person may be] good-for-nothing if one so
believes . . . but [he has] dignity within his body.[55]

Even though he had been purged from the party, Gallastegui
continued to try to influence the thinking of younger Nationalists.
And he often was successful. Inspired by the Sinn Fein's ability to
organize and mobilize in Ireland, Gallastegui organized a Nationalist mountaineering club, the Federation of Mendigoizales. He also
helped establish a Nationalist club for women, who met to discuss
the personal meaning and implications of Arana's writings. Last,
Gallastegui organized what is now commonly called "street theater":
a group of amateur but politically committed actors who perform
plays about contemporary political events and social trends in public
places.

After the military coup by Primo de Rivera in 1923, Gallastegui
fled to Ireland. When he returned during the early 1930s, he wrote
for Luis Arana's new journal, *Jagi-Jagi* (Arise). The explicit purpose
of the journal, as in the case of the earlier *Aberri*, was to propagate
Sabino de Arana's early ideas and to criticize the alleged greediness
and opportunism of the euskalerríacos. In many respects *Jagi-Jagi*
was stodgy and partisan, endlessly repeating old Aranaist arguments
and sayings about theology, secularization, confederacy, and secession. It was theoretically innovative in one important respect: many
of its younger writers, such as Gallastegui, argued that the political
struggles for local secession and the proletarian struggles for economic reform should be combined. In Gallastegui's formulation: "The
social independence of the Basques cannot be realized until political
independence has become a reality; nor will political independence
occur while there remains a single Basque suffering from the clutches
of capitalism."[56]

The anticapitalist tone of *Jagi-Jagi* is difficult to exaggerate. One
article asked readers to "join us and cry with all the force of your
lungs, 'Death to Capitalism!' "[57] The journal endorsed strikes against
big corporations, including multinationals such as Firestone.[58] In
addition, it regularly published exposés of well-known businessmen
who belonged to the Basque Nationalist party.

Though *Jagi-Jagi* constantly criticized *capitalismo*, it nevertheless was respectful toward private property and private ownership of the instruments of production. These two positions may seem logically contradictory, if one defines capitalism in terms of private property per se. But the paradox can be partly resolved if one assumes that by capitalismo, Gallastegui and the other writers for *Jagi-Jagi* usually had in mind only large enterprises, in which owners did not physically labor and in which workers received low wages and had no job security. Gallastegui and the other writers apparently wished to replace capitalismo with a vaguely described system of small-scale, privately owned enterprises, in which employers would work alongside a few skilled laborers, who would be treated in a decent, respectful, fraternal manner. The family enterprises and peasant farms in the Cantabrian Mountains occasionally were cited as examples of the type of noncapitalist production that Gallastegui and the others wished to establish, but their visions of an alternative, noncapitalist political-economic order were never very clearly and systematically stated. Nor were the common goals, tactics, and organizational form of a working-class–Nationalist alliance ever elaborated seriously and in detail.[59]

In the late 1930s Gallastegui fled Francoist Spain and settled in Ireland. There he continued to condemn Bilbao's capitalism and the euskalerríacos until his death in 1973. His writings had become immensely popular among some members of the clandestine organization Basque Homeland and Freedom (ETA), which had formed during the 1950s. What he offered the etarras, which most other Aranaist theorists did not, was a deep concern with the plight of industrial workers combined with admiration for small-scale work sites. Because Gallastegui valued small-scale production, a scholar working within a modernization framework might argue that Gallastegui was a backward-looking populist who wanted to forgo the benefits of large-scale production. But if Gallastegui was a backward-looking populist, his nostalgia included, and was not an alternative to, economic matters. He saw something in older forms of production that was relevant to either solving or understanding current economic problems. To borrow a distinction from political anthropologist James Scott, Gallastegui effectively used the past not as a way to escape the present, but as an "ideological backdrop against which to deplore the present."[60]

INTRAPARTY STRUGGLES AFTER FRANCO

In part because they sought different goals, the Basque nationalists sympathetic to Aranaist thinking and the Basque nationalists sympathetic to euskalerrian thinking have always been uneasy
allies.[61] The Aranaists, in general, have distrusted big capitalism and
have advocated a small-town, communitarian ethos and a regenera-
tion of the authority of the Catholic church. The euskalerríacos, on
the other hand, have enthusiastically advocated industrial development, large firms, and rapid rates of economic growth.

While in exile the two factions lived in relative harmony and saw
their common fate as exiles as more important than their differences
in long-term aims and priorities. The partisans of the two ideological
traditions, however, were not randomly distributed among the party's
officers. The two groups controlled different sectors of the party apparatus. Euskalerríacos predominated in the offices and councils dealing with international relations. They occupied all the offices at the
party's headquarters for the national council in Paris, and they presented most of the party's pronouncements before forums of world
opinion, such as the United Nations. Their interests also usually were
voiced by the highest officer of the party, the Lendakari (party president). The Aranaists, on the other hand, predominated in the clandestine chapters of the Basque Nationalist party within Francoist Spain,
especially along the coast and the French frontier.

The primary means by which the exiled leadership of the party
maintained contact with rank-and-file members and sympathizers
inside Spain was the folkloric batzokis, which were reestablished
during the 1970s, under the Francoist government's "law of associations."[62] Immediately after Franco's death, these cultural centers
became lively meeting places for party activists. In certain respects
they looked politically irrelevant. Their inexpensive bars and restaurants were open to all passersby. They organized bingo games and
hobby clubs. One batzoki in the fishing port of Bermeo functioned as
a hotel for tourists and, at least during 1980, showed a videotape of
Tina Turner for interested male viewers.

Alongside these often good-natured appeals to human foibles, a
second, highly politicized atmosphere existed. The walls of the batzokis often were covered with stern portraits of famous nationalists

and with sayings by Sabino Arana. According to cartoons by Basque social humorist Juan Carlos Eguillor, daily life within a batzoki resembled a tight-knit family, paradoxically combining tolerance and even appreciation of family members' personal eccentricities, with steep, unquestioned lines of authority. A Nationalist newsletter in 1977 told of one batzoki recently opened with "a simple and very emotional" ceremony: a priest read scriptures before the members, who lowered their heads before a picture of Sabino de Arana.[63] Obviously, there was an intense and stern side to the batzokis that the bars and videotapes masked.

Perhaps because of members' highly charged commitment to their local batzoki, the leadership council within each batzoki traditionally has enjoyed considerable autonomy from the decisions of the National Council of the Basque Nationalist party. The batzokis also have enjoyed autonomy because they are largely self-financed through their bars and restaurants. In 1981 alone the two hundred batzokis in the region generated about $1.5 million.[64] With these financial resources, some batzokis printed their own newsletters and political pamphlets and also managed election campaigns for local candidates. For example, during the summer of 1980, small propaganda teams were dispatched on weekends by the batzokis in Bilbao to mount political posters on public walls and to distribute handbills on the streets.

Immediately after the death of Franco, the Aranaists controlled a majority of the batzokis in Vizcaya and Guipúzcoa. Because of the party's election rules, which required that the members of the Buru-Batzars be elected by the municipal chapters of the Basque Nationalist party and *not* by the membership at large, the Aranaists also had an enormous majority within the unusually wealthy and prestigious Bizkai-Buru-Batzar, even though probably a much smaller proportion of the rank-and-file members of the party studied and supported (or even knew about) the ideas of Sabino Arana. At the same time, the euskalerríacos controlled a majority of the new batzokis in Alava and Navarra. Furthermore, a politically adroit euskalerríaco, Carlos Garaikoetxea, was selected by the national council of the party to be the next Lendakari. Thus, on the eve of Spain's new liberal political order, the Aranaists and the euskalerríacos were roughly equal in terms of control of the party's organizational apparatus.

The parity in terms of organizational presence did not lead to a harmony of interests between the two factions. There remained serious disagreements about goals, principles, strategies, and tactics. For instance, offended by the small role that the UCD granted the party during the drafting of the post-Franco Spanish constitution (1978), and troubled by the explicit principle of parliamentary sovereignty contained within it, the Aranaists proposed a boycott of the upcoming referendum on the 1978 Spanish constitution. The euskalerríacos said a boycott was politically unwise because it would exhaust the party's limited funds, would not dissuade voters from ratifying the constitution, and would alienate potential parliamentary allies from other regions of Spain. Rather than burning bridges, the party should cultivate as allies other parties who would be needed later in the legislative battle to gain limited regional self-rule. The Aranaists triumphed in this policy skirmish, and the party, largely through its networks of batzokis and periodicals, officially encouraged Basque residents to sit out the referendum.

In late 1979 the chief judicial organ within the Basque Nationalist party declared that new elections for the Bizkai-Buru-Batzar were required by party bylaws. The outcome of the elections was difficult to predict, in part because party membership had changed considerably between Franco's death in 1975 and 1979, when many uncommitted voters, politicians, and political activists had joined the party after its impressive showings in the 1977 and 1979 elections. In addition, several new municipal chapters and batzokis had been opened in and around Bilbao, and their ideological leanings were unclear. When the ballots were counted, the euskalerríacos had won a slight majority among the municipal chapters; because of the party's system of indirect elections, they now constituted a large majority on Vizcaya's executive council.

The Aranaists immediately denounced the elections as improperly administered and hence illegitimate. They also physically obstructed the euskalerríacos from taking office; a group of Aranaistas surrounded the provincial headquarters of the party in Bilbao and temporarily refused to let the euskalerríacos enter (the standoff in the streets ended when a few euskalerríacos secretly entered the party's headquarters through an unlocked window).[65] The Aranaists who formerly had served on the Bizkai-Buru-Batzar decided not to transfer their electronic equipment for organizing demonstrations— such as walkie-talkies—to the new executive council. Several Aranaists publicly accused the euskalerríacos of "bureaucratic secretism" and of being tied to "oligarchic capitalism, both international and indigenous."[66]

Though the Aranaists in numerous ways tried to retain their once extensive influence within the Vizcayan organization, the euskalerríacos now officially controlled the party's bureaucratic apparatus. They immediately centralized party finances by channeling a larger proportion of members' dues from the municipal chapters to the provincial headquarters. The euskalerríacos also purged from the party perhaps the most vocal and rebellious group of Aranaistas within Vizcaya, the members of the municipal chapter of Bermeo. Finally, they banned dissident publications written by Aranaistas from all batzokis in the province.[67]

At the same time, the euskalerríacos increased their control of the Buru-Batzar of Alava by recruiting charismatic immigrant politicians for leadership posts. Many of these politicians already had gained local reputations for courageously resisting the Franco regime during the late 1960s and early 1970s. They joined the Basque Nationalist party partly because they felt uncomfortable with the local leaders of the UCD, which had been organized primarily as a patricians' clique, and partly because the Spanish Socialist party at the time seemed poorly organized and socially insignificant, especially in rural districts. In addition, the social program of the euskalerríacos seemed attractive to local immigrant politicians, many of whom were the upwardly mobile children of poor farm workers, and who saw further industrialization as good for all classes.

By controlling majorities on the Buru-Batzars of Alava and Vizcaya, the euskalerríacos essentially controlled the Basque Nationalist party at the regional level. The rules governing the indirect election of party leaders insured that the euskalerríacos were overrepresented in regionwide councils, conferences, and caucuses. Consequently, many of the party's regional proclamations and publications after 1979 reflected the concerns and priorities of the euskalerríacos, not the Aranaists. In the words of the president of the regional executive council of the party in 1981, "The present social situation of the country is very different from that which existed in the times of Sabino. The thoughts of the rigid purists do not help us now."[68]

In 1979 the Spanish parliament legalized a regional government for the Basque region, a government with limited economic and cultural powers. Thereupon the Basque Nationalist party won the 1980 elections for the Basque autonomous parliament. In the party's appointments for the cabinet, the new strength of the euskalerría-cos became more evident than ever. No well-known Aranaist was chosen; instead, the cabinet was composed largely of professional businessmen—eight of fourteen members were graduates of the prestigious business school at the University of Deusto.[69] Even the Ministry of Education was given not to a theocratic populist but to a young nuclear physicist who only recently had joined the party, who received his doctorate at Cambridge University, who had been a laboratory consultant at the Universities of Munich, Cambridge, and California at Berkeley, and who stated that his primary goal in creating an autonomous Basque system of higher education was to develop "the scientific infrastructure necessary for industrial growth."[70]

Officials of both the Unión de Centro Democrático and the politically and economically conservative Alianza Popular congratulated the Basque Nationalist party on its selection of "technically qualified" cabinet ministers. They never complained that the cabinet was controlled by rural populists. Leaders of the businessmen's association called ADEGUI offered similar compliments. In contrast, leaders of the Spanish Communist party and the Spanish Socialist party denounced the selection of ministers on the grounds that almost all were enthusiastic supporters of breakneck capitalist growth. According to Roberto Lerchundi, the leader of the Basque chapter of the Communist party, the cabinet was essentially "a conservative government directly linked to business interests, supported by the Jesuits, and tied to the world of big finance."[71]

The Basque regional government, dominated by euskalerrian Nationalists, in fact did try to aid local business interests in several ways. For example, it promoted industrial fairs on the Basque coast for purposes of attracting buyers from Europe and the Americas. It also established a regional labor relations board in the hopes of enhancing communication between industrial unions and employers' associations and peacefully arbitrating any heated conflicts. In 1981 it formed the Society for Industrial Promotion and Reconversion, which was to provide funds to promising private companies for updating machinery. The new agency generated considerable controversy within the regional parliament because several left-opposition leaders believed that the Nationalist government was ignoring reduction of local unemployment as a criterion in the distribution of public funds to private businesses.[72]

By 1980 the euskalerríacos controlled most of the Buru-Batzars and provincial parliaments in the region, the Basque regional government, and the National Council of the Basque Nationalist party. Though of one mind about the desirability of continued economic growth and industrialization, the euskalerríacos were nonetheless divided among themselves about *how* best to use government to promote industrial and economic growth. Coming from the corporate world, Garaikoetxea and his cabinet wanted the newly established regional government to have extensive taxing and budgetary powers and the right to borrow money in order to stimulate specific sectors of the economy. Many euskalerríacos, however, thought that Garaikoetxea and his ministers tended to be too "interventionist" and even "socialistic" in their thinking. Garaikoetxea's critics among the euskalerríacos wanted explicit constitutional restrictions on the powers of the regional government to intervene in the local economy, and they also wanted the economic powers sought by Garaikoetxea to devolve to the provincial governments, where euskalerríacos with more laissez-faire leanings predominated.[73]

In the opinion of Justo de la Cueva, the conflict also partly reflected a dispute among the region's capitalists. The advocates of strong provincial governments vis-à-vis the Basque government represented the interests and wishes of smaller, domestic capitalists, whereas Garaikoetxea's desire for a strong regional government that could selectively aid "progressive sectors" of the economy reflected the interests of bigger businesses tied to the international economy.[74]

This latent feud among the euskalerríacos became more intense during the early 1980s, when the Socialist party took office in Madrid and its leaders initially agreed to cooperate with Garaikoetxea's economic program of industrial reconversion. It appeared to some euskalerríacos that by means of subsidies, taxes, and the issuance of public debt, the Basque regional government was unjustly favoring some business enterprises, particularly in the export sector and electronics industry, at the expense of smaller enterprises, and especially in the declining steel and naval industries. Hoping to win further monies and legislative powers from the new Socialist government in Madrid, Garaikoetxea continued to meet with high-ranking Socialists and discuss possible pacts of legislative cooperation. Many euskalerríacos, particularly from Vizcaya, saw his behavior as willful deviation from the national council's desire for economic liberty and provincial self-rule. Garaikoetxea ceased to attend meetings of the national council, and the president of the council began to accuse him of desiring "despotism."[75]

Hoping to end intraparty animosities and slurs, the national council asked its incumbent president to step down, and nominated another member to the post. However, the nominated successor also was an advocate of provincial self-rule and an opponent of a powerful regional government. Garaikoetxea broke with long-standing party custom and publicly endorsed a different council member, who was more sympathetic toward his plans for an economically active regional government. Garaikoetxea maintained that he was only exercising his right as an ordinary party member in good standing to express his preference. The national council accused him of breaking the party's long-standing principle of separation of powers. During the dispute it was publicized that the national council's candidate could not speak Basque, a fact that infuriated many in the Aranaist minority, who then supported Garaikoetxea. Amid the charges and countercharges, a third candidate, Román Sodupe, was selected and finally confirmed. Sodupe promised to improve "communication" between Garaikoetxea and his regional government, on the one hand, and the national council of the Basque Nationalist party, on the other hand.

Meanwhile Garaikoetxea continued negotiating with the Socialists, and the cabinet issued a statement of support for his goal of a legislatively powerful Basque regional government. Garaikoetxea also met with delegations of Spanish businessmen to assure them that his government desired closer social ties with other parts of Spain: "We do not want to break the commercial unity of Spain, nor its unity in communications, nor any other type of essential unity."[76]

The national council's 1983 decision to form government coalitions with the socially conservative Coalición Popular and Unión del Pueblo Navarro in certain municipalities and in the Navarrese provincial parliament further complicated intraparty cleavages. Basque Nationalist leaders within Navarra balked at the national council's directive to form coalitions with the party's onetime rivals. As a consequence, in May 1974 the council expelled from the party all members of the executive council from Navarra and three elected

members of the Navarrese parliament. Many Nationalists in Guipúzcoa openly objected to what they saw as the national council's heavy-
handedness and proclaimed solidarity with the expelled nationalists
in Navarra.[77]

In fall 1984 the national council decided to call an emergency
national assembly to review Garaikoetxea's behavior and to consider
possible disciplinary actions, justifying the move on grounds that
"whoever intends to divide or weaken the party is committing trea-
son."[78] In the elections for the assembly, Garaikoetxea's supporters
possibly won a majority of all votes cast but only a small minority
of the assembly seats because representation was, once again, determined according to the number of batzokis and municipal chapters
won, not according to total ballots received. For example, Garaikoetxea apparently won 80 percent of the ballots cast in Alava, but
the votes were concentrated in only six of the province's twenty-eight
batzokis; hence a minority of Alava's representatives to the national
assembly were supporters of his position.[79]

On December 4, Garaikoetxea initiated negotiations with the
Socialists sitting in the regional parliament for a piece of fiscal legislation that in the long run would increase the power of the Basque
regional government. Less than two weeks later, the national council,
emboldened by the results of the elections for the national assembly,
asked Garaikoetxea to resign as president of the Basque government.
Facing increasing opposition from Nationalists within the Basque
parliament, Garaikoetxea angrily stepped down. A more laissez-faire
circle of the euskalerríacos momentarily triumphed over a more
interventionist circle.

Less than two years later, Garaikoetxea helped form a new party
out of a complex set of disaffected Nationalists, including Aranaists,
angry former Nationalists from Navarra and Guipúzcoa, prestigious
lawyers, and numerous business leaders.[80] The new party was called
Euzko Alkartasuna-Solidaridad Vasca (or Basque Solidarity). Its electoral platform was a mixture of classical Aranaist ideas and ambitions
(formulated by the party's so-called *bultzagileak* wing), advocacy of
"progressive" corporate capitalism, and social democratic goals, such
as income redistribution and expansion of free social services for the
poor. Partly because of its successful appeals to various interests, the
new party enjoyed enough success during elections in the late 1970s
to reduce considerably the presence of the Basque Nationalist party

both in the regional parliament and in many Guipúzcoan and Alavese municipalities.

CONCLUSION

The Basque Nationalist party, as we have seen, has been an ideologically variegated party. It is an ongoing, yet fragile, alliance of activists with different and often divergent values, goals, and beliefs. In the colorful words of Gregorio Morán, "The Basque Nationalist party includes all: from the radical and progressive to the ancient and troglodytic."[81]

The ideological diversity within the party highlights a difficulty with the current modernization interpretation: it tends to view the interests, issues, and conflicts of Basque nationalist politics too simplistically, as a total rejection of recent modernization.[82] The current modernization interpretation is partly correct, of course. Surely, the rapid transformation of traditional Basque society into an urban, industrial, capitalist, secular, non-Basque-speaking social order was a theme that many Nationalist leaders openly addressed. But the Nationalists thought about, interpreted, analyzed, and judged the process of rapid modernization in many ways (often according to different values) and therefore prescribed a diversity of solutions for the problems they perceived.

Because the phenomenon of rapid modernization was viewed differently by nationalists, the statement that "members of ETA were influenced by earlier traditions of nationalist thought" is by itself less informative than it may first appear. Which, of all the permutations of nationalist thought, did the etarras most loyally follow? Which nationalist traditions were ignored? And how did different etarras modify the nationalist ideas that they chose to inherit? It is to these questions about the specific content of etarras' "nationalist beliefs" that we now turn.

CHAPTER SEVEN

FISSIPAROUS ETA: IDEOLOGICAL EVOLUTION AND ORGANIZATIONAL SUNDERANCE, 1959–1970

*T*he political beliefs of members of ETA during the 1960s and 1970s and those of members of the Basque Nationalist party differ significantly. Scholars, journalists, and politicians sometimes overlook the differences and simply label the beliefs of etarras "nationalist extremism." Such a formulation is partly true. Like most members of the Basque Nationalist party, most members of ETA demanded territorial self-rule for Basques. Moreover, for the etarras, this goal was tied to a belief in the effectiveness of confrontationalist tactics and a distrust of working through established political institutions. In a sense, then, the beliefs typically held by etarras were a more impatient (and therefore "extreme") version of ideas typically found within the Basque Nationalist party.

Still, the beliefs of etarras were not simply a faith in militancy grafted onto traditional nationalist demands for self-rule. Several etarras also often theorized systematically about the dangers of advanced capitalism, the plight of non-Basque workers, the possibilities of a socialist revolution in the region, the possibilities of a proletarian–petite bourgeois alliance, and the value of armed struggle in attaining and protecting a social-political revolution. Some of these ideas, such as the dangers of industrial capitalism, were extensions of themes found in the Aranaist tradition of Basque Nationalist political thought. Some, such as the possibilities for a proletarian–petite bourgeois alliance, were clearly minor themes within the Basque Nationalist party, advanced primarily by mavericks like Gallastegui, but would become central within ETA. Still others, such as the role of armed struggle in political-social change, represented significant breaks with traditional Nationalist thought. In short, like the Basque Nationalist party, ETA was a complex constellation of ideas and aspirations about society and politics. There were some obvious continuities with traditional Nationalist thought, but there were also some important departures.

This chapter describes the early ideological evolution of ETA.[1] Starting with the intellectual and political restlessness of José Luis Alvarez Emparanza, it traces the accretion of ideas within ETA during the 1960s, and summarizes the growing factional rivalries within the movement as advocates of various theoretical traditions vied for control. In its members' explicit opinions on capitalism, workers' political capacities and needs, and guerrilla warfare, ETA was far more than an extension of contemporary Nationalist thought; etarras were constantly and creatively synthesizing Basque and non-Basque traditions of thought.

ORIGINS OF ETA

José Luis Alvarez Emparanza (hereafter referred to as "Txillardegi," his political pseudonym) was arrested in 1950 for being a member of a clandestine student group, Eusko Ikasle Alkartasuna (Society of Basque Students). The society was formally nonpartisan, even though many members were sympathetic to the Basque Nationalist party. It sought to preserve the Basque language through clandestine publication and distribution of magazines, usually written in Basque.

Once released, Txillardegi went to Bilbao for advanced study. With four other youths from the city's two universities, he formed a new illegal student group, this time without a name. All the members were from nationalist households and hence tended to discuss Basque legal and political history during their meetings. They also read and discussed various examples of contemporary European thought, including the writings of French existentialists.

At one meeting in 1953 a copy of *Gudari*, which was a magazine for Basque nationalist soldiers during the Spanish civil war, circulated and inspired a majority within the group (now numbering twelve) to form a secret organization and produce an internal newsletter, to be called *EKIN* (to make). Over the years, other Bilbao students joined the group, including individual members of the local Basque Nationalist party's youth organization, Eusko Gaztedi (Basque Youth), who were attracted by the energy of the new group. As the membership steadily grew, subgroups formed to specialize in such activities as the study of the Basque language and the design and distribution of propaganda.

Although the group remained nameless for several years, some leaders of the Basque Nationalist party, having come across one of the group's newsletters, began to call it the "EKIN group." The Nationalists were aware of the popularity of EKIN among Nationalist youths and soon encouraged the EKIN group to merge with Eusko Gaztedi. The two organizations united in 1956, forming a hybrid that combined the scholarly and urban life-style of the EKIN group with the less intellectualized but highly spirited activism of Eusko Gaztedi, many of whose members participated in dance troupes and worked in semi-illegal *ikastolas* (Basque-language schools) that were sponsored, in part, by the Basque clergy.

From the outset relations between the members of the original EKIN group and the leaders of the Basque Nationalist party were tense. The former admired the Nationalists' efforts to secure a free Basque region during the early twentieth century and shared many of the latter's hopes for national independence. Yet members of the EKIN group also saw the older Nationalists as excessively cautious in their tactics and excessively deferential toward Western powers. The perceptions were not entirely ill-founded. The Nationalist leadership had hoped to work alongside Western democracies for the overthrow of the Franco regime and the return of the autonomous Basque government, which had been created during the Spanish Civil War but now existed in exile. To please Western powers, the Nationalists expelled representatives of the Communist party from the Basque government-in-exile. And after 1947 they generally avoided supporting labor mobilizations, so as to calm United States fears that the overthrow of Franco would either lead to political and economic chaos or, worse yet, renew the spirit of Spanish radicals.[2]

In the opinion of several members of the EKIN group, the Nationalist strategy had failed for more than a decade to increase political freedoms. Repeated demonstrations of self-restraint before Western public opinion had led, ironically, not to the overthrow of the Franco regime but, if anything, to its consolidation. Over time Western powers—the United States in particular—had come to see the regime as well-entrenched and, therefore, as an attractive ally against communism. To the dismay of many advocates of Basque independence (and to members of the Nationalist party in particular) the United States had even begun to provide the regime with economic aid and diplomatic recognition.

Members of the EKIN group were also troubled by what they saw as the Basque Nationalist party leaders' lukewarm commitment to the protection of indigenous Basque culture. Economic growth and industrialization during the 1950s and 1960s had led to a rapid increase in the number of "outsiders," particularly in Bilbao's enormous mining, steel, and naval complex. By the close of the 1970s about half of the region's population was either immigrants or the children of immigrants. At the same time, the Franco regime had prohibited the use of Basque in schools and government institutions, and had tried to prevent its use in public. Members of the EKIN group argued that the indigenous language was on the verge of extinction for both economic-demographic and political reasons, yet the Basque Nationalist party seemed unwilling to resist openly the invading Castilian culture. Instead, many Nationalist leaders used Castilian, *not* Basque, in party meetings, and failed to instruct their children in the use of the local language. In the words of Txillardegi, who had become a leading figure within the EKIN group,

> If I were far from being a Basque patriot, I would smile. But because I am one, I feel shame and disgust. This incessant abandonment of a marvelous national language, and its subordination now happily accepted, to the language of our eternal oppressors, is intolerably painful for true patriots.[3]

Offended by the Nationalists' apparently lukewarm commitment to Euskera and by their restraint, members of the original EKIN group repeatedly made declarations that irritated the Nationalist leadership. For example, they publicly proposed making Euskera the sole official language of an independent Basque republic, and announced that a true Basque patriot should not be content until an independent country combining the southern Basque territory (in Spain) and the northern Basque territory (France) was realized. Most established Nationalist leaders found such expectations utopian, at least in the short run. They also feared that the expectations would alienate potential political allies in Spain and elsewhere.

According to Txillardegi, in 1959 a delegate from the Basque Nationalist party visited him and told him not to use the initials of the Basque Nationalist party's youth organization any more or he would find himself "cast on the rocks" in San Sebastián.[4] Txillardegi and other leaders of the original EKIN group decided that the time was right for a formal separation from the party. They named their breakaway group Euskadi ta Askatasuna (ETA).

The EKIN group's dissatisfaction with the Basque Nationalist party was not idiosyncratic. It was shared by many other youths in auxiliary organizations of the Basque Nationalist party. In fact, in 1957 some young Nationalists wrote anonymously to the leaders of the party, accusing them of indifference toward political freedom within the region and of betraying such local groups as the clandestine trade unions that were actively fighting for liberty. Outraged, the party elders expelled one particularly outspoken young man, Benito del Valle (who also had been one of the founders of the EKIN group). He was alleged to have a "rebellious and undisciplined spirit" and to desire the undermining of authorized leadership. Many in the party's auxiliary organizations resigned in protest. In the end, roughly half of its youth chapters officially separated from the party, many becoming subgroups within the newly founded ETA.[5]

INITIAL ACTIVITIES AND EARLY IDEAS

From its inception ETA lacked a stable and centralized system of authority, partly because of ongoing police repression and partly because of the size and mountainous topography of the region, which impeded regular communication between rural and urban groups. Local groups (not infrequently based on cuadrillas) often acted independently of each other, writing graffiti, distributing small lapel badges of the Basque flag at dances, and defacing government buildings. Meanwhile, hounded by the Spanish police, "generations" of ETA's executive councils were forced to seek refuge in France or Belgium. Thus, two sets of leaders emerged within ETA: (1) battle-hardened and often rhetorically flamboyant leaders and former prisoners who lived abroad and who were generally out of touch with the day-to-day events and organizational problems within the region, and (2) younger, relatively inexperienced resident activists who had belonged to the organization for a few years (at most), who were constantly innovating in response to local problems and events, and who had not yet been caught by the authorities.

During the early 1960s most activities of the etarras were educational. They studied the works of famous nationalist writers like Arana, Eleizalde, and Aranzadi. They also analyzed and judged contemporary events in light of the precapitalist cultures of the region; knowledge of the past society and its politics provided standards against which to consider current trends. Indeed, studying was so important to the organization that before joining ETA, a candidate first had to undertake a six-month reading program on Basque social and political history and on early Nationalist writings, especially those of Arana and Gallastegui.

The first violence by members of ETA occurred in 1961. Although some etarras had previously spoken and written about the advantages of armed struggle, such notions were almost never acted upon. One local cell, however, secretly planned to derail a train carrying Franco supporters to a well-publicized rally. Their purpose was to focus international attention on current injustices of the regime. To minimize possible deaths, the etarras planted a small bomb on the tracks, but it was so weak that it did not even derail the train. The regime was outraged, nonetheless, and arrested more than a hundred suspected etarras, torturing many of them.

Surprised by one cell's unilateral action and confused by the government's repression, the various cells within the ETA organized an assembly of representatives to meet in France in 1962 to clarify the organization's aims and strategies. Assemblies had been planned since 1959 with hopes of coordinating the scattered and varied activities. Periodic arrests had made such gatherings seem imprudent, and therefore they were cancelled. But the 1961 bombing and its aftermath had made such an assembly imperative.

What became known as the First Assembly of ETA momentarily clarified the purpose and goals and internal organization of the diversified collection of local groups. The representatives agreed that ETA was a "Basque Revolutionary Movement of National Liberation," not a party, dedicated to securing the political and cultural liberty of the Basque people from both Spain and France, and to

changing existing society in the region. It would work toward transforming society primarily through grass-roots agitation and popular
mobilizations, not through formal channels of representation within
government institutions. In addition, ETA's executive council would
be internally reorganized into four autonomous "fronts," or types
of activities: mass propaganda, labor activism, internal publications,
and paramilitary preparation. In principle, the executive council was
to coordinate and monitor the activities of all fronts (but it subsequently turned out that over the years the activities of each front were
decided primarily by its own members, with minimal intervention
and oversight by the executive council).[6]

The assembly also set forth the substance of ETA's revolutionary project. In its "Statement of Principles," it proposed creation of
an independent, aconfessional, and democratically elected political
order for the region. The constitutional and procedural details of that
order were to be decided by the people at large, not unilaterally by
any single party or political organization, including ETA. Still, the
etarras at the First Assembly offered some broad recommendations
regarding the future order.

First, there should be guaranteed protection of internationally
recognized human rights, such as freedom of expression, freedom of
assembly, and freedom of religion; this would help prevent emergence of a dictatorial regime ("be it fascist or communist").[7] Protection of the rights of expression and assembly also would help prevent
the predominance of the narrow interests of a particular class or
group (be that group "political, religious, social, or economic, Basque
or non-Basque").[8] The "Statement of Principles" also declared that
unions should have constitutionally protected rights, as should ethnic
and linguistic minorities, so long as they do not actively oppose the
national interests. The future political framework should be as decentralized as possible, with considerable policy-making powers being
reserved for municipalities.

According to the "Statement of Principles," ideally there would
be changes in the region's economy to accompany the protection of
human rights and decentralization of political authority. There would
be "a profound modification in the status of property," a "disappearance of economic liberalism," a "limitation on profits and inherited
wealth," and a "just and dignified social-security legislation."[9] It cannot be concluded from these phrases that the organization was committing itself to a thoroughly planned economy. Most etarras at the

meeting were ambivalent about government planning and centralized power in general, and were deeply suspicious of Soviet communism in particular. Rather, when the phrases are read in context (for
example, alongside other ETA writings), it appears that the etarras
were advocating a modified market economy, in which inequality in
personal wealth and income would be limited, "basic" sectors and
resources would be government owned and/or managed (the identity of these "basic" sectors and resources was never fully specified),
and producer cooperatives would be encouraged.[10]

In terms of cultural policy, the statement proposed that the
Basque language become the sole national language, that it be taught
to all residents, but that no other language be prohibited from public
use. In addition, the statement endorsed a "democratization of culture,"[11] including publicly financed education for all children up to
sixteen, with subsidies for older students pursuing advanced degrees.

To achieve national liberation, guarantee human rights, and initiate limited economic reforms, the etarras at the First Assembly argued
that ETA "must employ the most appropriate methods as dictated by
each historical circumstance" and be open to possible alliances with
other Basque patriotic organizations, so long as the alliances do not
require that ETA be "hypocritical" about its goals.[12] This formulation
is extremely vague—for example, it neither condones nor condemns
violence as a tactic, nor does it clearly endorse or reject an alliance
with the Basque Nationalist party. Viewed in terms of the internal
politics of ETA, the ambiguity is not surprising. At the time there
was no consensus on how to accomplish the group's goals. Some
etarras favored nonviolent resistance and cited Gandhi's actions as
a possible model. On the other hand, some important figures in the
organization, such as Julen K. Madriaga, who was a widely respected
leader within the military front, favored calculated use of defensive
violence. Without consensus on the subject of violence or specific
interparty alliances, an ambiguous statement was inevitable.

Following the First Assembly, ETA's committee for political education (known as its political office) elaborated the group's view
of Basque politics in several pamphlets that stressed the dangerous
growth of Castilian culture and the need for the revitalization of the
indigenous language. According to one publication,

> The Basque-speaking pseudopatriot who does not teach
> Basque to his children is a monster, the ultimate by-product

of national degeneration, a mix of imbecility and northern hysteria, a laughing stock as large as one can find on the step-ladder of politics or society. The Basque patriot who does not speak Basque is a living contradiction, is a constant traitor to his word, is something like an atheist at daily communion. It is a type of idiocy that must disappear.[13]

ETA essays during the early 1960s further suggest that for a significant number of etarras, the farmstead family (as idealized in their imaginations) epitomized a healthy society. According to one publication, "The family is the first among our institutions, not only in economic affairs, but also in civil and political affairs."[14] It appears that many etarras perceived the rural family to be essentially a quasi-egalitarian community infused with a spirit of mutuality, and based on consent and benevolent dominion. Supposedly, paternal authority was exercised for the good of all in the household; and coercion rarely was used to compel cooperation. The father considered the material and spiritual needs of each member of the family and was visible, physically approachable, and respectful toward all family members. The family, in the words of one essayist, was an expression of "natural law."[15]

The pamphlets of the early 1960s also suggest that many etarras believed that sometime in the near future Basque society could be transformed into a collectivity of small, intimate, family-like institutions (such as craft unions and workshops) that would rule themselves with minimal interference from the state. The pamphleteers often called this alternative social order "socialism" but emphasized that they had in mind neither Marxism nor communism but a sort of quasi-feudal estate society, in which municipalities, families, and craft unions would coexist as roughly equal political partners. This vision is partially comparable to the socialist vision of the British Guild Socialists during the early twentieth century. Both sets of radical reformers hoped to construct a world of decentralized authority in which the function of the state was essentially to help resolve occasional conflicts between corporate groups. A sort of harmonious group anarchy would prevail, with little government coercion being used. In the words of the etarras, the translocal state would be "neither politicized nor totalitarian."[16]

During ETA's first decade its writers seldom elaborated on how daily conflicts of interest would be reconciled in such a decentralized political order. They may have expected that intense conflicts would decrease once politics was reconstructed on a smaller scale, for they sometimes suggested that conflicts of interest were artificial problems, products of individuals' underdeveloped feelings of social responsibility, which naturally would improve once more intimate institutions were established. Such thinking, however, seems to have been wishful rather than serious; in an economy as diversified and complex as that of the Basque region, conflicts of interest are structurally inevitable. Consider the likely conflicts of interest between cost-conscious managers and wage-sensitive workers. There also presumably would be conflicts of interest between urban consumers of agricultural products and farmers. Another source of friction could arise between the urban poor, who seek government assistance, and the urban nonpoor, who instinctively oppose taxation for social-welfare services and who may even resent "carrying" the unemployed and other poor. In short, rather than seeing the Basque region in economically plural terms—as having residents with diverse economic needs and priorities—etarras who during the early 1960s wrote on political and social goals seemed to presume homogeneity and consensus within the region. A central question of modern European politics—how to design a political system that can reconcile the diverse interests and aims within an advanced, industrialized, capitalist society—was never seriously addressed.

Despite their avoidance of concrete problems regarding the reconciliation of diverse economic interests, the contributors to ETA publications often confidently predicted that with establishment of their desired political order, certain economic reforms would occur. Such reforms included (1) expansion of communal lands in all rural municipalities, (2) redistribution of farmland so as to reduce inequalities between family farmers, (3) voluntary formation of manufacturing cooperatives, with managers elected by workers, and (4) a system of public education in which all qualified students could develop skills and explore vocational interests, irrespective of their families' social status or income level.[17] Again, the writers never made plain how these reforms would come about, either legally or extralegally, but it is evident that they did not expect the state to impose them.

Many (but not all) early ETA writers contended that their vision of socialism was derived from the ancient Basque customs of family farms and village democracies, which could be realized again. Moreover, they believed that all Europeans could benefit from ancient Basque practices. Hence, these early etarras often insisted that they were "internationalists" in spirit; for they wished to share their indigenous political and social thinking and practices with all peoples. They often cited Yugoslav experiments with a decentralized state and with factory councils, and the 1962 international meeting in Vienna of more than three thousand mayors as evidence that the times were right for creating a "federated Europe" composed of thousands of autonomous workshops, villages, cities, and provinces.[18] One handbill said that the ultimate aim of ETA was to create a novel, federated polity in Europe; however, "this federalism must not be a federalism of monstrous entities, such as modern states. This federalism has to be integrated, in which the individual is a participant within the municipality, the province, the state, and the region."[19]

The early ETA writers commonly contrasted their Continental and radically confederal notion of socialism with another socioeconomic vision that they called "capitalism" and that they associated with current trends in Western Europe. "Capitalism" referred both to a moral and psychological phenomenon and to a political, institutional phenomenon. "Capitalists" were persons with a distinctive set of priorities and commitments, persons inordinately interested in accumulating money for its own sake, misers who indifferently exploited other human beings. Capitalists also were thought so consumed by their passion for accumulating more money that they opposed any collectivity's right to self-government that might impede the quick acquisition of profits, such as a village's traditional right to regulate the use of common lands. Capitalists therefore energetically promoted the formation of large sovereign states that could overrule and even dismantle local governing bodies.

The capitalists' desire for strong states was said to coincide with a "natural" tendency within state bureaucracies to expand their spheres of authority, to increase their resources, and to disregard, violate, and constrain the rights of local groups.[20] In many ETA writers' opinions, a dominant trend in contemporary European politics was the emergence of "totalitarian" states at the expense of local groups.

The early publicists for ETA generally argued that if the organization acted decisively and immediately, it could defeat the rising tide of capitalism and centralized states. They believed that by informing Basques about earlier values and institutions, the organization might inspire them to turn their backs on the Franco regime and the capitalist economic system and to resurrect familial values and institutions. In the words of ETA's newsletter, *Zutik*, the proper goal was to bring back "the 'old' spirit in new forms."[21] Another article read, "Up with folklore! Long live the Basque National Resistance!"[22]

Members of ETA's cultural front and the executive council often argued that popular appreciation of earlier Basque values and institutions was best advanced through resurrection of ancient linguistic habits. Some etarras helped finance and administer ikastolas, or private language schools, in which all subjects were taught in Basque. (There is some controversy over the precise role of ETA within the ikastolas. John Sullivan suggests that they were largely founded and sustained by the local clergy with intermittent assistance from Basque political activists associated with either the Basque Nationalist party or ETA. Txillardegi, in contrast, maintains that most ikastolas were introduced into the Basque region by ETA, and that ETA played a central role in their development throughout the 1960s.)[23] Building upon earlier Nationalist arguments about linguistic determinism, the more linguistically oriented etarras argued that the Basque language encourages distinctive sentiments, values, and beliefs within a person. The triumph of non-Basque languages within the region thus meant the triumph of non-Basque values, life-styles, and social relations, and should be resisted at all costs. "Spanish and French are foreign languages of the occupying armies. We reject them viscerally, vomiting them away!"[24] Through the use of the ancient language, one in principle could begin to break free from the accumulation orientation of capitalism.

Some members of ETA, however, thought that linguistic habits were less central to the moral education of Basque residents in non-capitalist values. Of equal, if not more, importance were constant reminders of earlier values and social arrangements—for example, through written histories, public dances, art expositions, and popular music. Fluency in local dialects was merely one of several methods of reminding residents about earlier ways of life, about alternative moral principles upon which to organize society.

IDEOLOGICAL ACCRETION DURING
THE MIDDLE 1960S

Until 1964 ETA seemed to have a loosely coherent identity. Etarras seldom publicly disagreed over their organization's goals, and they tended to agree on the types of educative projects necessary to improve the world. For example, at the 1962 assembly the participants did not debate goals, principles, or strategies but focused instead on organizational issues concerning the most effective ways to coordinate cell activities. By the middle 1960s, however, it became increasingly obvious that other currents of thought, involving new aims and strategies, were appearing within the movement.

The new patterns of thinking within ETA can be understood in part as responses to suddenly changing social and political conditions within the region. The period 1960–65 was a watershed in Basque economic and political history. The Spanish government permitted formation of factory juries and autonomous neighbors' associations, and relaxed censorship laws. For the first time in almost three decades, there were numerous strikes and proletarian solidarity marches in most parts of the region. The Basque economy grew at breakneck speed: jobs abounded; city populations exploded; and new groups of residents, especially the later arrivals, demanded increased services.

Meanwhile, there began to develop a partial overlap in the memberships of ETA and labor organizations. Several labor activists joined ETA (especially from the radical Catholic organization Juventudes Obrera Católica) and soon held important positions within the economic front and political office—for example, Angel Uresberoeta, who was appointed to the political office and who earlier had been active in a Catholic labor group known as the Frente Liberacíon Popular (FLP).[25] Scores of etarras became active in labor struggles during the 1960s. As early as 1963 etarras were supporting clandestine strike committees in Bilbao.[26] By 1968 approximately two hundred ETA members worked clandestinely in unions on the Left Bank of Bilbao.[27] In Guipúzcoa province, members of ETA helped found a plurality of the clandestine comisiones obreras during the middle and late 1960s.[28]

Because of the constant arrests of established generations of leaders, the newer labor-oriented group of ETA activists soon inherited control of the political office, which was responsible for the organization's newsletters and theoretical pronouncements. University educated and raised in cosmopolitan environments, these etarras were curious about the increasingly militant proletarian movement in the region. Previously, etarras had generally viewed non-Basque workers with disdain because they appeared politically backward and reactionary. One *Zutik* essay had this to say:

> While in Bilbao the Basque proletariat marches demanding free unions, human dignity, Basque independence and liberty in general, . . . in Madrid 10,000 Spanish workers celebrate May 1 with an act of loyalty to the fascist Ministry of Work. . . . Spain, with its feudalism, with its bourgeoisie, and, above all, with its unconscientious proletariat, is a reactionary force.[29]

Now novel and unorthodox questions began to be raised within the organization. Should etarras join forces with the immigrant workers and neighborhood groups? If so, which proletarian demands should they advance? Which, if any, of the multiple proletarian organizations and urban organizations should they join? With which proletarian organizations should ETA cooperate? How might it attract urban workers and residents, many of whom were immigrants, toward the goal of Basque self-determination?

Several of the newer ETA leaders also were curious about political and social theorizing elsewhere in Europe. They read *Cuadernos de Ruedo Ibérico*, a journal edited in Paris that was sympathetic to socialism but hostile to the Soviet Union, especially in wake of the crushed Hungarian uprising of 1956. They were particularly fascinated by the writings of Europe's New Left theoreticians, such as Michel Bosquet ("André Gorz"), Lelio Basso, and Ernest Mandel.[30]

These non-Basque writers argued that a new revolutionary strategy was needed in Western Europe, for postwar capitalism had shown itself capable of continuous growth, of generating comfortable standards of living for almost all industrial workers, and of reducing the material misery of workers. Consumerism, the extension of social welfare, and the ideology of responsible management had given hitherto ruthless capitalism a "human face." It was unreasonable to expect that Western capitalism would soon collapse because of the rapid immiserization of the workers and a consequent insurrection by the have-nots. Likewise, it was ludicrous to expect that a disciplined band of revolutionaries could seize a Western government and then unilaterally impose socialism through tyrannical means upon the populace while foreign powers passively looked on. Neither a dramatic economic collapse nor a coup would lead to socialism. What was needed was a totally new way of thinking about social revolution, a New Left.

The proposed alternative way of thinking about revolution involved an unqualified dismissal of the Russian example of an apocalyptic break with the past. Instead, it was argued, a successful socialist revolution must be viewed as a series of local struggles by workers at work sites, in their neighborhoods, in places of worship, and in local government institutions. The struggles should focus on the right to participate in policy decisions that affect one's life—for example, participation in local school boards' curriculum choices for working-class children. Through patient appropriation of local policy-making centers, workers (in principle) would gradually acquire control over society. New Left theorists acknowledged that cooptation is a risk, but they added that there is no other feasible path to a workable socialist order. The alienation of workers from local positions of authority, not material deprivation per se, therefore should become the issue around which to build a successful revolutionary movement.

Many new etarras (especially those enrolled in universities) found the ideas of the European New Left intriguing and attempted to apply them within the Basque context. They noted that partial experiments in nonhierarchical organization already were being carried out in jurados de empresas and comisiones obreras. So, many new etarras reasoned, successful implementation of a New Left strategy in the Basque region should be possible.

However, New Left thinking was not the only fresh intellectual influence on the youths who were joining ETA during the middle 1960s. Another developed against the backdrop of the anticolonialist struggles in Algeria, Cuba, and Southeast Asia, which many new etarras viewed sympathetically and as possible models. Curious about the ideas that inspired and informed contemporary national liberation movements, a few etarras began reading the works of Franz Fanon, Albert Memmi, Ernesto "Che" Guevara, and Mao Tse Tung. They saw parallels between the cultural aspirations of Algerians and

Cubans and their own cultural worries, and they also found the theories of violence articulated by Algerian and Cuban revolutionaries applicable to their own situation.

Particularly influential was Fanon's *Wretched of the Earth*, which by the mid-1960s was included in the organization's list of recommended readings.[31] Fanon's criticisms of cultural imperialism resonated particularly among etarras who had been raised in the countryside, whose primary language was Basque, and who often had been ridiculed in schools, at work, and by the Spanish police for their indigenous language. Like Fanon, they felt both embarrassed and enraged over the threats to their "parochial" culture. One etarra said,

> When I attended school, I realized that no one talked like me. I felt, then, a feeling of loneliness. They thought that I didn't want to study my lessons, and they punished me. This marked me deeply. And when I grew up I decided to do something for my Basque homeland.[32]

Fanon's book, of course, focused not only on cultural imperialism but also on the psychological benefits of forcefully confronting and resisting one's oppressor, of openly rejecting one's assigned role as a subordinate. Violent resistance against existing authorities, Fanon argued, can generate personal pride, collective confidence, and a willingness to dare to hope. Reading Fanon against the backdrop of the surprisingly successful liberation movements in Algeria and Cuba, some etarras began to speculate whether there was a way to use violent resistance intelligently, so as to cultivate a widespread and energetic national liberation movement.

In this volatile international political context, two writings appeared that would have a long-term impact on the way some members of ETA thought about violence and national liberation. One was *Vasconia*, by Frederico Krutwig, first published in 1962.[33] Analyzing national liberation movements, Krutwig declared that violence can be effectively used to set off widespread popular mobilizations against a government. It is best used once an act of popular protest occurs against a specific injustice by a government and once the authorities attempt to put down the protesters. Trained guerrillas should then inflict physical harm on government personnel—for example, through kidnapping and torture. Not knowing the identity of the guerrillas, the forces of order will themselves often retaliate with indiscriminate beatings, jailings, and even torturing people who had not been involved in the original proscribed protest. This will cause more broadly based protests, which in turn will lead to greater repression, which in its turn will lead to greater popular anger and militancy. Lubricated by occasional calculated violence by the trained guerrillas, a spiral builds until there is a dramatic face-off between the people at large and their far less numerous government adversaries. In the meantime, an informal system of administration will evolve among the growing numbers of rebels and protesters. Serving as a tested model for future policy-making institutions, the alternative administrative system will ease transition to a new, radically decentralized political order.

A few etarras read Krutwig's study (or at least parts of it; it was very long) and subscribed to his ideas, but not all etarras. Txillardegi, for example, was ambivalent. He found the Fanon-like arguments about the importance of preserving indigenous cultures compelling but was dubious about the efficacy of violence in prompting a popular uprising, especially in a highly urban, literate, and economically advanced society, such as Euskadi's. José Luis Zalbide, on the other hand, found Krutwig convincing and helped edit the anonymously written sixty-odd-page *Insurrección en Euskadi* that simplified and to some extent refined Krutwig's argument. Completed in 1963, *Insurrección en Euskadi* was officially endorsed by ETA's Third Assembly in 1964 and thereafter functioned as the organization's primer on guerrilla warfare.

The tone of *Insurrección en Euskadi* was scholarly. References to recent historical examples abounded, and a selected bibliography was included. The authors emphasized the need for guerrillas to control personal emotions. Calculation, not rage, was to be the driving force.[34] The booklet discussed when to move against government forces, how to retreat, how to reimburse civilian owners for confiscated and damaged property, and even how best to use an ancient Basque war call when engaging in night assaults.

Until 1964 ETA had expended few resources on developing a specialized guerrilla unit. This was partly because of financial limitations, partly because of the arrests of leading advocates of guerrilla warfare, and partly because of opposition within the organization to violent tactics. During the first half of the 1960s ETA's energies and resources were devoted primarily to cultural activism (wall daubings and clandestine publications in Basque) and, to a much lesser degree, labor organizing. The military front's activities were limited to periodic bombings of state property and small-group training in firearms in the mountains.

Despite the marginal role of the military front, its existence distinguished ETA from the Basque Nationalist party, which had been endorsing nonviolence and even declaring that Basque people were pacifist by nature. The difference in the thinking of the two groups is illustrated by the following statement published during 1962 in the ETA newsletter, *Zutik*: "Violence is necessary—a contagious, destructive violence that supports our struggle, a good struggle, one that the Israelis, Congolese, and Algerians have taught us."[35] Although the statement expressed what was then a minority viewpoint within ETA, such a clearly militant declaration would not have appeared in an official Nationalist publication.

Violent tactics, hitherto a minor theme in ETA's history, became much more central by 1964, when the growing influence of writings by Fanon, Krutwig, and Zalbide became manifest. In 1964, ETA officially endorsed the spiral theory of violence and began to publicize it. (Largely because of ETA's constant dissemination of the theory, it became widely known in the Basque region, and by the close of the 1970s was even alluded to in the cartoon sections of news dailies; see figure 7.1.) In 1965, armed robberies of bank couriers and factory payrolls began to be used to help finance the purchase of weapons and explosives. Shortly after the first robbery, Zalbide was arrested, removing for a time a key advocate of violence from the ongoing debates over strategy within ETA.

RISE OF THE ECONOMIC FRONT

Meanwhile, members of the economic front increasingly viewed the mobilized workers of the region (regardless of ethnic background) not as potential political threats but as possible allies. They decided in 1963 to support a ten-minute work stoppage by Basque and non-Basque workers in Vizcaya. The editors of *Zutik* also supported the strike: "We ask from all militants in ETA effective, economic, and moral support for the heroic workers of Vizcaya and the highest solidarity with the Spanish workers in Asturias."[36] The

Figure 7.1. Cartoon appearing in *Egin*, June 20, 1980.

stoppage, held in conjunction with a similar action in the neighboring province of Asturias, was intended to secure the release of fifty-two workers arrested the previous year for engaging in illegal labor activities. The government responded quickly and did not overlook members of the economic front. About two dozen etarras were either arrested or detained; several more fled to France. The dreams of an alliance with local workers did not weaken, however; the following year dozens of etarras in and around Bilbao participated for the first time in May Day celebrations, which ETA officially endorsed.

Meanwhile, in Guipúzcoa province, members of the economic front not only assisted established clandestine labor organizations but helped create others, including the first provincewide comisión obrera in 1966. Partly because of ETA's early involvement in Guipúzcoa's labor struggles, the province's labor organizations regularly included nationalist goals, such as regional self-government, in their statements of demands.[37]

In 1966 ETA's economic front made perhaps its most controversial decision of the decade. The Francoist regime had declared a "state of exception" (police could detain Spanish citizens for up to seventy-two hours without notification of friends and family and without formal charges) during a prolonged strike at Laminaciones de Bandas Echevarri, where most workers were immigrants to the region and had been striking for six months—an extraordinary action given the authoritarian political order. Solidarity strikes occurred throughout Spain. During this period of heightened class struggle, elections were scheduled for factory juries and for offices within the government-run labor syndicates. Some labor organizations, in particular the Socialist party and trade union, tried to dissuade workers from participating in the elections, in light of the government's harsh response to the Bandas strike. Some labor organizers, including many activists in the comisiones obreras and the Communist party, argued that it was important for workers to capture as many policy-making offices as possible, even if those offices were established by the Francoist government. The economic front—echoing arguments by the New Left theorists about socialism's being obtainable through a patient, ongoing acquisition of rights of self-determination at the workplace —also urged industrial workers to participate in the government-sponsored elections for factory juries despite the government's harsh response to the strike.

Leaders of the economic front articulated their political position in several pamphlets that were circulated during 1966 among members of the front.[38] In the authors' opinion, participation in local-level institutions, such as factory juries, was not an expression of tacit approval of the regime, but a potentially revolutionary action because of its long-term contribution to workers' institutionalized powers. After all, there is no feasible alternative for achieving socialism in Euskadi (or so leaders of the economic front argued).

The internal documents of the economic front also speculated about the historical significance of the newly emerging asociaciones de vecinos. Although the neighborhood associations had not yet evolved into politically ambitious and tactically militant organizations, leaders of the economic front predicted that they would become important for a future Basque socialist revolution.[39] Specifically, by achieving piecemeal reforms in education, housing, medical care, and sanitation services, and by acquiring quasi-public powers to administer community libraries, day-care centers, and food cooperatives, the asociaciones might inspire people in blue-collar neighborhoods to demand an even greater say in the making of public policy. A Basque socialist political order might thereby be realized. If, however, the asociaciones de vecinos were not organized in a radically democratic manner (such that the great majority of residents can easily attend meetings and participate in policy decisions), or if they proved unsuccessful in influencing the policy decisions of local governments, they might prove catastrophic in terms of realizing a socialist revolution; for they could induce a paralyzing sense of futility in blue-collar workers rather than a sense of political efficacy and a desire for more power.

While etarras in the economic front were advancing theories about proletarian empowerment through factory juries and neighborhood associations, ETA's political office and executive committee (especially during Zalbide's periodic imprisonments) began issuing statements that implied a desire for greater cooperation between ETA and the region's labor movement. In 1964 the Third Assembly declared ETA an "anticapitalist" movement. In 1965, the Fourth Assembly characterized ETA as a "Basque Revolutionary Socialist Movement" (in contrast to the organization's original self-description as a "Basque Revolutionary Movement of National Liberation," which emphasized the theme of cultural and ethnic oppression rather than economic exploitation).[40]

A new vocabulary for discussing politics soon predominated in ETA publications. There were increasing references to economic classes, the proletariat, class struggles, and the miseries of factory production. The following statements from *Zutik* illustrate the new "working-class" style in which some ETA leaders were analyzing and interpreting Basque politics:

> The Basque cause must identify itself with the problems and needs of the actual inhabitants of the country, and above all of the workers.

> In Bilbao there is a population that can save Euskadi—the working class.

> We must convince ourselves that our oppression will not end until we destroy the roots of capitalism.[41]

Between 1965 and 1966 *Zutik* increasingly associated socialism not with precapitalist values and institutions, such as the nuclear families and family farms of the Cantabrian Mountains, but with current experiments with factory juries and strike assemblies.[42] For the first time in its history *Zutik*, in 1966, dedicated an issue to the working-class celebration of May Day. That same year it called for all ETA militants to participate in the elections for factory juries.[43] It also began to endorse strikes by non-Basque workers against employers and factory owners, including factory owners known to be fluent speakers of indigenous Basque dialects. Then, in a handbill entitled

"Por una izquierda socialista revolucionaria vasca" (For the sake of a Basque revolutionary socialist left), members of the ETA political office openly argued for the use of "limited violence" in labor disputes (factory sabotage, plant seizures, and solidarity marches), but denounced "unlimited violence" that "is directed to the destruction of human life."[44]

Like the New Left theorists in France, Belgium, and Germany, the labor-oriented ETA leaders argued that a social revolution in the Basque region would not be provoked by physical misery alone, for the obvious reason that the proletariat in Euskadi, like the proletariat in other advanced capitalist societies, enjoyed secure jobs and decent wages. According to one ETA publication, "Only when there exists a situation of absolute misery do the affected strata of the population fight for socialism without understanding their goal. . . . In Euskadi, that misery does not exist."[45] Another essay cautioned, "We are traveling toward a superdeveloped Western society, where the standard of living is already extremely high. As Basques and Europeans, we must think in terms of the revolutionary possibilities of our continent."[46]

One might think that the above reasoning—that Euskadi has an advanced capitalist economy that meets the material needs of its workers—would lead *Zutik* authors to the conclusion that urban workers in Euskadi would not be an active political force, but they reached a different conclusion, arguing that workers in the Basque region were constantly struggling, but for rights to participate in workplace and government policy-making, not just for material benefits.[47] They were struggling for the freedoms to assemble, to petition, to form unions, to negotiate contracts, to have meaningful factory juries, to publish ideas, and to be protected from arrest for exercising such rights. In short, they were struggling to overthrow the constitutional principles of the Francoist state and therefore were a revolutionary force.

> We must not confuse revolution with taking political power. The socialist Revolution has already commenced. The taking of political power only occurs after different powers (political, economic, social, and cultural) already have been conquered by the popular classes. The culmination of the Revolution is preceded by different types of revolutionary reforms.[48]

Because of their political (and not exclusively economic) goals and militancy, local workers could be valuable allies in Basque patriots' efforts to acquire political independence. To enlist the workers' interest and energies, however, it was first necessary to develop a new political program (a "new nationalism") that would directly address their needs and political aspirations. It also would be necessary to assuage workers' fears, based on the past hostility of the Basque Nationalist party to the demands of immigrant workers, that etarras are unreliable supporters of working-class organizations and demands. Finally, it would be necessary for members of ETA to join working-class organizations and institutions and to have labor activists (including non-Basques) enter ETA, in order to maximize the common identification of the two movements.[49]

Essays favoring an ETA-labor alliance also argued that the most effective method for securing self-rule for the region was through cooperation with other socially progressive groups *outside* the region. By pooling resources and coordinating actions with socialist, communist, and republican unions and parties in Spain, ETA could slowly expand the legal rights of local industrial workers. As the workers began to acquire the rights to assemble, to picket, to sue employers for violation of collective bargaining laws, and to lobby legislators, they would become conscious of their extraordinary numerical strength within the region and then would direct their efforts toward extensive regional autonomy, in order to have even greater influence over public policy.

Articles in *Zutik* also argued that the notion of a "free Euskadi" independent from other parts of Spain should be jettisoned because total isolation is impossible in modern Europe. "Isolationism is neither a workers' program nor a realistic project."[50] Limited autonomy within a broader Iberian or European federation of partly self-governing regions was feasible, however. Such an arrangement would require that ETA be concerned with constitutional changes throughout Spain, not only in Euskadi, and be willing to work with and aid profederalist groups in other parts of Spain. While working for a federated Iberia, etarras should seek no special privileges for the Basque region, but political and economic equality among all regions ("a regime of absolute parity").[51]

Several ETA labor activists and members of the political office saw a major obstacle to a proletarian strategy for attaining autonomy in the persistence of Basque ethnic pride. The problem was muted somewhat in Bilbao, where the working-class culture of the Left Bank had socialized many residents into viewing themselves largely as industrial workers rather than as members of competing ethnic groups. However, in the smaller manufacturing towns of the Cantabrian Mountains, Basque-speaking workers were said to be openly arrogant and hostile toward immigrant workers. Etarras with a proletarian orientation contended that their organization's past celebration of indigenous Basque culture (and its insistence on making the Basque language the sole official language of the region) needlessly exacerbated the hostility between native and immigrant workers. They accordingly entreated other etarras to moderate their praise of Basque folklore and to tone down demands for language revitalization. Some labor-oriented etarras even privately believed that the goal of language revitalization was utopian, for, according to the recollections of one former political office official, Euskera was a "language poorly adapted to modern social and cultural circumstances, [being] divided into dialects and without a written literary tradition."[52]

Finally, according to the essays in *Zutik* in 1965 and 1966, to realize a labor-based nationalist revolution, it was necessary to reinforce workers' intuitive understanding about their personal debasement in the workplace and about the current possibilities for self-rule within workers' councils and factory juries. It was alleged that because of the influence of mass culture, especially television and commercial advertising, workers' natural anger at being bossed had been partly anesthetized, and that their hopes for a better life had been partly narrowed to the pursuit of private pleasures. Basque industrial workers were developing a passive sort of trade-union consciousness, and therefore a culturally active vanguard party (which would include members of ETA) was desperately needed.[53]

ETA LABOR ACTIVISM CHALLENGED

Not surprisingly, the new ideas in *Zutik* troubled many long-standing etarras, some of whom were living in exile in Belgium and France. Some were concerned over *Zutik's* endorsement of participation in the upcoming elections for factory juries and offices in the quasi-governmental syndicates because participation seemed to help legitimate and further secure an oppressive regime. Others found the notion of cooperating with Spanish labor organizations dangerous because of the possibility that closet Marxists might infiltrate ETA. Still others were concerned about *Zutik*'s criticisms of Basque cultural revivalism. After all, the "Statement of Principles," endorsed at ETA's First Assembly, identified among the organization's goals the revitalization of Basque culture and the establishment of Euskera as the sole official language in a self-governing Basque region.

Txillardegi, for one, unhappily reported that "the national language has been swept from our publication," and noted that of the eighty-four pages of *Zutik* published in 1965 and 1966, "91.2 percent have been published in a foreign language [i.e., Castilian]. Of the twelve issues, six do not use Basque words except in the titles." [54] Fearful of the possible influence of the labor agitators on other ETA members in Euskadi and that the organization might lose its distinctive goals and therefore its identity, he wrote an open letter to the membership at large.

> I am terribly disappointed with the present Executive and with certain etarras, for our organization today does not embody the democratic and Basque Euskadi that we want, but a Cantabrian communism that we do not want. [55]

He added in a letter to the executive council:

> One sees only Marxist thinking in the last issues of *Zutik*. What this means is that today Marxism is the Truth of the current editors. Everything is the fault of the bourgeoisie, everything is class. . . . I no longer read in *Zutik* any criticism of the Communist Party. . . . To be progressive and anticapitalist seems to me imperative; but to see in *Capital* the future of Bilbao seems to me a catastrophe. [56]

In yet another letter, he said, "The articles [in *Zutik*] speak of class but not of Spanish oppression." [57]

Quietly meeting with advocates of non–New Left factions within ETA, Txillardegi and other former members of the original EKIN group helped prepare the ground for the Fifth Assembly of ETA, at which they hoped the increasingly variegated ideas of the organization would be pruned and supporters of the "Statement of Principles" would regain control. Txillardegi was especially successful in recruiting as allies some of the advocates of the spiral theory of violence, who saw the New Left etarras as woefully ignorant about the strategic necessity for violence in nurturing a popular uprising, surprisingly utopian in their plans to unify ethnically diverse workers and to form an interethnic labor movement, and obviously insincere "revolutionaries" given their support for existing Francoist workplace agencies (such as factory juries) and their preference for waiting for minor reforms that someday would accumulate into a socialist revolution.

The allies differed in their concerns. Txillardegi was primarily angry at the members of the political office because they seemed to be advocating the sacrifice of Basque cultural liberation for the sake of proletarian liberation. He and his friends used derogatory terms in speaking of members of the political office, unsubtly implying betrayal of the Basque people, such as *"españolistas,"* social chauvinists, and "Felipes" (because of alleged secret connections with the FLP labor group). The advocates of the spiral theory of violence, in contrast, primarily accused members of the political office of being counterrevolutionary "Marxist" reformists rather than genuine Marxist revolutionaries, and cited *Zutik's* recent call for participation in the Spanish syndicate elections as evidence of their nonrevolutionary spirit.

The various opponents of the New Left members of the political office packed the Fifth Assembly, and arrived with dossiers with which to discredit, and subsequently expel, their ideological rivals. Supporters of the New Left tendency were ignorant of most of the machinations. Once they had discovered that Txillardegi's allies wanted to discredit and then expel four leading members of the political office (none of whom was present), approximately a quarter of the etarras present tried to stop the meeting, saying that the significance of the impending decisions demanded advance notice, fuller involvement of the membership, and strict adherence to ETA's bylaws concerning quorums (there were not enough members of the executive committee present at the assembly to make its decisions binding, according to ETA bylaws). There was a vote on whether to suspend the meeting, and Txillardegi's coalition easily won. The dissidents, who tried to walk out, were taken to a nearby room and kept under observation by a security committee. (Whether the dissidents were held captive by armed guards and by threats of violence remains a subject of controversy among members and former members.) Following formal presentations of evidence of the political office's deviations from ETA's original principles, the assembly approved in a near-unanimous vote expulsion of the targeted members of the political office. The assembly ordered all etarras to cease communicating with the expellees, who were denied access to ETA publications.

FURTHER FRAGMENTATION

In the months that followed, supporters and opponents of the former members of the political office made extensive efforts to capture the allegiance of rank-and-file etarras, whose knowledge of the leadership struggle during the Fifth Assembly was sketchy at best. The New Left advocates organized an alternative ETA, called ETA-berri (the New ETA), and persuaded scores of etarras to join. Leaders of ETA-berri insisted that factory workers were the key to regional political and social change.

> The struggle for national liberation runs the risk of being an abstract slogan if it is not closely tied to the struggle for workers' power in the places of production. The great battles for our Homeland must begin in the capitalist firm.

> We affirm that Basque workers are the vanguard of the popular movement of national liberation.[58]

They also insisted that celebration of indigenous Basque culture was counterrevolutionary in its political consequences:

> [It] seems to correspond to certain metaphysical concepts of petite-bourgeois origins about the Basque "spirit" (understood as the "spirit of the community"). These concepts cloak in a pseudoscientific myth about structuralism an often hidden, dangerous orientation resembling racism.

> The union of Basque workers is not a secondary objective; it is a fundamental condition for a national revolution.[59]

Meanwhile, the advocates of the spiral theory of violence took over the leadership of the older ETA (now called ETA-V, because of the significance of the Fifth Assembly). In the elections for president of the assembly, following the expulsion of the New Left members of the political office, Txabi Etxebarrieta, a sympathizer of both armed struggle and labor mobilization, was picked over a representative of the *Branka* group (named after the cultural magazine that Txillardegi had cofounded). In a follow-up meeting of the Fifth Assembly, held in 1967, Etxebarrieta presented a hybrid theory that combined a theory of revolutionary violence with a Marxist-sounding theory of interclass alliances.[60]

According to the ETA-V's new theoretical synthesis, a principal mistake of the expelled members of the political office was their "infantile leftism" that naively romanticized the current revolutionary potential of the working class and overlooked the revolutionary potential of the small bourgeoisie. Industrial workers, though certainly militant, were not yet cognizant of the benefits of Basque self-rule. They needed more political education. The petite bourgeoisie was oppressed culturally (by the imminent disappearance of the Basque language and Basque folkways), politically (by the absence of democratic rights), and economically (by the inroads of big business and multinational corporations into the regional economy). Because of its swelling anger, the petite bourgeoisie could be persuaded to join a radical project for political and social change. It could then, in an alliance with the working class, form a powerful "national front" and set in motion a two-stage political and social revolutionary process: first, achievement of national cultural and political independence from Spain, and second, establishment of a socialist order in which the growing economic and political powers of monopoly capital would be shackled. It followed from this line of strategizing that ETA in the short run should work for a "national front that would combine all patriots, proletarian and bourgeois" behind a three-point program: (1) "total national liberation," (2) the political unification of the Spanish and French Basque provinces and the creation of a Europe-wide federation of self-ruling communities, and (3) the revitalization of the Basque language.[61] At the same time, Etxebarrieta argued, efforts should be made to implant ETA more deeply in the militant labor movement. He envisaged formation of a body within ETA that would specialize in labor organizing, and in 1968 ETA-V added a workers' front to its four organizational subdivisions: cultural front, economic front, military front, and political front.

The members of ETA-V's assembly tried to describe the common ground between urban workers and Basque owners of small commercial property through the acronym PTV (for Pueblo Trabajador Vasco, Basque Working People).[62] PTV referred to all those who labored in the Basque region and also supported the goal of cultural liberation. Owners of small business were included, but owners and managers of larger businesses were not. Immigrant workers were included if they showed clear signs of supporting Basque cultural liberation (for example, by becoming fluent in the Basque language).

Leaders of ETA-V argued that to succeed in mobilizing both the petite bourgeoisie and the working class, ETA must not only participate in such legal institutions as factory juries (which by themselves are "pseudosocialist" and merely a type of economic reformism), but also openly confront economic and political elites (through, say, illegal wildcat strikes), which in principle would intensify repression by the Franquist regime and thus incite a broader uprising. Through carefully planned guerrilla and local strikes ETA would exacerbate the natural distrust between members of the PTV and the Spanish government, induce government repression, and thus indirectly incite broader popular resistance.

The declared strategy and goals of ETA-V troubled members of ETA-berri, who were strongly committed to interethnic unity and the minimization of ethnic distinctions, patient expansion of workplace democracy, and cooperation with non-Basque workers' groups. They viewed ETA-V as, at best, semi-xenophobic and ambivalently proletarian. They also doubted that armed struggle would help modern urban workers. After all, an act of guerrilla violence might lead to the government's suspension of the modicum of rights of association and assembly that had recently been granted and thus make organizing of workers very difficult. What was needed, according to ETA-berri, was a coalition of revolutionary workers' organizations throughout Spain that would coordinate their struggles for the sake of an Iberian federation of free local communities. One ETA-berri pamphlet put it this way:

> The Basque people are not enemies of the Spanish people. The two are friends. All the peoples of the world are friends. Besides being friends they must become allies, because Francoism is the common enemy of the Galician, Catalan, Spanish, and Basque people, and without a common action directed to the liquidation of the powers of the exploiting

bourgeoisie, a Basque National Revolution is pure utopia. . . .
We do not renounce the struggle for independence: we battle
for total independence (economic, political, cultural, and
social) for Euskadi; that is to say, for the total appropriation of the Basque Nation for the Basque people led by the
workers. . . . We maintain a critical posture toward bourgeois nationalism—Spanish or Basque—and we repudiate
exclusivism, national egoism, and all forms of racism, overt
or hidden. . . . The future revolution by the peoples of the
peninsula is for a collaborative future—among them and
with other peoples—with liberty and equality among them
and, of course, independence, each being its own master.[63]

As the years progressed, members of ETA-berri distanced themselves from the cultural issues articulated in ETA's first "Statement of
Principles," merged with local Maoist groups (partly out of loathing
of the Soviet Union, following the invasion of Czechoslovakia), and
changed their name (partly to avoid being identified by the police as a
part of ETA) to Komunistak (Communists) and later to Movimiento
Comunista de España (Spanish Communist movement, MCE).

The ideological synthesis of ETA-V also troubled several of the
original founders of ETA, who had consistently advocated a more
purely cultural path to Basque socialism. In 1966 they had begun
publishing a journal called *Branka* that developed their ideas and encouraged broader use of Euskera. They continued to argue that once
Basques refamiliarized themselves with their own cultural traditions,
a popular movement for a new social and economic order would
spontaneously arise. That future order would be decentralized, small
scale, and libertarian. They also contended that neither workplace
organizing nor guerrilla warfare provided an Archimedean point on
which to elevate a Basque "social humanism." Rather, an alliance of
all nationalist groups, especially with the Basque Nationalist party,
was needed. Repeatedly outvoted in meetings of ETA-V, several members of the *Branka* group (including Txillardegi) resigned, stating that
ETA-V's theories of guerrilla violence and working-class alliances
were impractical and diverted attention from the original goals of
ETA: territorial independence and cultural revitalization.[64]

During the last third of the 1960s, scores of working-class sympathizers temporarily joined some group within the increasingly orga-

nizationally fragmented ETA movement. Moreover, between 1968 and 1970 ETA became considerably more willing to recruit urban immigrant workers, and many non-Basques began to join the organization.[65] They often joined either ETA-berri or ETA-V's workers' front. While working within ETA, they often collaborated with Communists, Maoists, Catholics, anarchists, and other non-ETA labor activists on clandestine strike committees. After leaving ETA-berri or ETA-V, former labor-oriented etarras not uncommonly joined socialist and communist organizations in the region, including the Spanish Communist party, the Trotskyist International Communist League, and the Maoist Workers' Revolutionary Organization.[66]

The influx of new etarras—most of whom were, in ETA parlance, "virgins" because they neither had been arrested nor had police records—fed smoldering debates over goals and strategy. What should ETA's role be vis-à-vis the turbulent labor movement of the time?

One emerging ETA-V faction, variously known as the Células Rojas (Red Cells) or the *Saioak* group (named after the left-leaning journal *Saioak*), argued that as long as nationalists spent their energies helping the Basque middle class, they would be unable to secure the loyalty and support of the working class. Devotion to working-class organizing and attention to working-class needs and demands must be given priority by the organization. Moreover, territorial self-rule would never occur while Spain had a dictatorship. Therefore, ETA-V ought to work with allies in other parts of Spain for the overthrow of the regime.[67]

The Red Cells were composed largely of etarras in exile who formed study groups that analyzed the writings of Marx and Engels. But not all advocates of a proletarian strategy were exiles. The members of ETA-V's new workers' front had become very active in the comisiones obreras, collaborated closely with other Left parties, and in 1970 would sign a pact of cooperation with the Communist party.[68] The members of this ETA subgroup (more than two hundred in Bilbao alone)[69] viewed their task as quietly educative: to work within existing labor organizations and slowly teach others the need for national liberation. Political radicalization of the labor movement would occur through etarras' acquisition of workers' trust through patient, daily, and often dangerous labor organizing, not grand, bold theoretical pronouncements.[70]

Members of the workers' front also developed a novel variant of the spiral theory of violence: through constant confrontation over economic demands, labor activism would provoke the Spanish forces of order into acts of brutality. They "will hit people in the streets, will detain, will torture friends, brothers, loved ones." Then "the fascist Spanish state will show its true face," and all workers in the region—immigrants and native—will be politically radicalized.[71] Although they subscribed to a variant of ETA-V's spiral theory of violence, members of the workers' front, who increasingly viewed themselves as a self-sufficient set of autonomous actors,[72] generally feared armed action, for it brought on levels of repression that made factory organizing nearly impossible.[73]

Because of the arrests of the first generation of leaders of ETA-V, members of the Células Rojas and members of the workers' front soon held a plurality of important decision-making posts within ETA-V. Culturally oriented etarras (who had maintained contact with the *Branka* group) and advocates of armed struggle (some of whom were staunchly anticommunist) watched the rise of these factions with horror. Leaders of ETA-V inside Spain tried to calm critics, in part through theoretical arguments—for example, the publication of "A todos los makos" ("To all the prisons"), which tried to reconcile the different tendencies within ETA-V.[74] The document maintained that ETA-V was making progress in both radicalizing industrial workers and mobilizing a majority of Basque small proprietors around the issue of independence by emphasizing nationalist issues and goals, such as a linguistic-cultural revival. After all, the Spanish Communist party was cooperating with ETA labor activists, and individual members of the youth wing of the Basque Nationalist party and of the party itself were interested in forging much closer ties with ETA-V. By simultaneously building working-class unity and radical consciousness (that could be used to push an independent Basque state in a socialist direction), and establishing an interclass national front that would battle for an independent Basque state, ETA-V was creating the preconditions for a successful, combined nationalist-socialist revolution.

Critics remained uneasy. Culturally oriented etarras, former etarras—such as Txillardegi—and advocates of a rural-based guerrilla war were troubled by ETA-V's increasingly close ties with non-Basque Marxist groups. On the other hand, members of the Red Cells believed that too much attention and energy were being channeled toward cooperation with middle-class constituencies and toward issues of Basque cultural preservation, which hampered organization and education of the largely immigrant working classes.

Perhaps inevitably, the Sixth Assembly of ETA, held in 1970, was a fiasco.[75] The only member of the "milis" (the general title given to advocates of armed struggle) in attendance tried to leave the meeting once the assembly had voted to expel all milis (it had been discovered that the milis were boycotting the meeting and plotting to overthrow it), but he was constrained and held under guard. Then the members of the Células Rojas, frustrated by the current executive council's re-sistance to adoption of a purer program of proletarian organizing, resigned from ETA-V. Contemporaneously, several milis and cultur-alists who were living in exile coauthored a letter stating that they represented the true spirit of the Fifth Assembly and that the Célu-las Rojas and all participants of ETA-V who supported decisions at the Sixth Assembly were henceforth expelled from ETA. Supporters of the authority of the Sixth Assembly responded by accusing the self-styled spokespersons for ETA-V of being racists and "bourgeois" and declared the current leaders of "ETA-VI" (named after the Sixth Assembly) the true leaders of the ETA movement.

Thus etarras were once again dividing their movement. ETA may have theoretically enriched itself during the 1960s by incorporating fresh ideas about working-class struggles and armed struggle, but organizationally it was in shambles.

CONCLUSION

Until the early 1960s, ETA had been ideologically unified; there were few extensive debates about goals and strategies. The Basque Nationalist party's Aranaist tradition had initially provided members with their dominant goals and value orientations. During the middle 1960s, however, two strikingly new ideological currents appeared: one encouraged by West European New Left thinking and interested in enlisting the potential power of the increasingly militant urban workers of the Basque region, and the other encouraged by national liberation movements in nonindustrialized countries and interested in the possible uses of violence in igniting and mobilizing popular protest. By the close of the 1960s the increasing ideological diversity within ETA had crystallized into multiple organizations (ETA-berri, ETA-V, ETA-VI, the workers' front, the Red Cells, and the *Branka* group). Almost all self-described "etarras" desired some form of regional self-rule, and almost all advocated immediate reconstruction of the Basque economy. But they were not united by a common vision of what regional self-rule should look like institutionally, by a common blueprint about what an alternative economic order should look like, or by a common strategy for achieving widespread change. Which ideology (if any) would direct the newly established revolutionary movement was far from clear.

Broadly classified, there are three reasons for ETA's marked divergence from the often gradualist, pacifist, and nonproletarian politics of the Basque Nationalist party. First, members of ETA were exposed to a different set of international political and ideological influences than were the older Nationalists. Having grown up aware of dramatic anticolonial struggles in Cuba and Algeria and the innovations of European New Left theorists, many nationalist youths creatively tried to fuse the general nationalist goal of territorial self-rule with distinctively contemporary ideas about guerrilla warfare or a New Left path to socialism through a series of revolutionary reforms. Second, many Basque youths had decided to explore new goals, theories, and strategies in response to the apparent failure of the Basque Nationalist party's strategy during the 1950s and 1960s. The etarras' spirit of ideological unorthodoxy and restlessness was, in part, an offshoot of a more general sense of political disillusionment with caution and moderation. Finally, the emergence of local social movements, such as the clandestine comisiones obreras and the legalized asociaciones de vecinos, provoked Basques with nationalist sympathies to consider new alliance possibilities. The recent grass-roots political struggles of largely nonnationalist groups nurtured new dreams and therefore new politics.

We have seen that ETA was a profoundly heterogeneous movement by the close of the 1960s. According to one longtime ETA activist, "There has been one constant to ETA. . . . its great dehomogenization [deshomogenización] in matters political and organizational."[76] How did ETA, having so many subgroups not devoted to armed struggle, come to be a movement known primarily for acts of violence? To account for this, one must again look at local history; this time, at the unexpected political problems and opportunities that occurred shortly before and after Franco's death.

CHAPTER EIGHT

A PARTING OF THE WAYS:
ELECTORAL OPPORTUNITIES AND
CHANGING LEVELS OF VIOLENCE

Entering the 1970s, the ETA movement comprised variegated organizations, beliefs, and activities. It would be a gross simplification to describe the ETA of that time as a movement exclusively utilizing tactics of armed struggle. Present in the movement were pacifists, advocates of armed struggle, labor organizers, critics of attempts to organize industrial workers, editors of Basque-language journals, and persons who downgraded celebration of Basque culture. By the close of the 1970s, however, characterization of ETA in terms of armed struggle would be closer to the mark. By then, many individuals within the ETA community who were not advocates of armed violence had either formed or joined other organizations to contest political authorities through less violent means. Most of these groups purposefully eschewed the ETA label, in part because of fears of government reprisals. The ETA acronym soon was almost exclusively used by those who directly engaged in and actively supported the use of arms to achieve their political ends, and they jettisoned the nonviolent proletarian theories that had circulated within ETA during the middle and late 1960s.

By the close of the 1980s, the political behavior of the broader ETA community had changed once more. Many practitioners of armed struggle had laid down their weapons. Approximately 250 members of ETA accepted the government's amnesty programs between 1982 and 1986.[1] Of the ETA cells and organizations actively engaged in armed struggle during the middle and late 1970s, only a handful remained. Most former etarras from the 1970s now either confined themselves to nonviolent political activities or ceased to participate in politics altogether. ETA-organized violence waxed during the 1970s; it now waned.

Focusing on large-scale social changes and populationwide levels of frustration and anomie, most scholars who use the modernization interpretation have not extensively discussed these short-term changes in the political tactics of specific groups within the ETA movement and of individual etarras.[2] This is not surprising. Rapidly changing political behavior at the level of specific organizations and persons is not easily explained in terms of large-scale, long-lasting social change. To account for behavioral metamorphoses, the current modernization interpretation needs to be supplemented with a discussion of more immediate, short-term causes.

This chapter illustrates the usefulness of a more narrowly political interpretation of the ebb and flow of violent behavior in the Basque region. It looks both at the impact of several specific political events on ETA's decisions, and at day-to-day struggles over strategy within the movement. Suarez's reforms and unexpected problems with the spiral theory of violence, in particular, are emphasized as circumstances influencing the conduct of specific etarras and groups within the broader ETA movement.[3]

The greater emphasis on short-term causes in understanding ETA politics does not mean, of course, that the modernization interpretation should be discarded. Obviously, ETA had an emotional, passionate side, and the emotions perhaps were tied to extreme worries and general uneasiness over the disappearance of an indigenous, preurban, prebureaucratic, and precommercial small-town culture. It may be difficult to explain ETA's successful recruitment of members from the countryside—many of whom were unaware of ETA's ideological debates concerning socialism and proletarian alliances—without taking seriously theories of anomie and cultural disorientation.[4] Nonetheless, by itself the modernization interpretation tells only part of the story of ETA, for it minimizes, if not ignores, the extensive role of day-to-day political choice, planning, and predicaments. By itself, then, it limits our understanding of ETA's multifaceted character, which was in certain respects and at times emotional and irrational, yet also utilitarian, calculating, and adjustive.

REGENERATION AND RIVALRIES ON
THE EVE OF FRANCO'S DEATH

As we have seen, since the mid-1960s the ETA movement was pulled in three ideological directions: toward a New Left, proletarian tradition; a guerrilla, National Front tradition; and a nonviolent, ethnically oriented, and culturalist tradition. These tendencies manifested themselves through (and sometimes within) rival organizations, including, ETA-berri, *Branka*, the *Saioak* group, ETA-VI, and ETA-V, all of which sprouted from the original ETA seed planted by Txillardegi and the EKIN group.

Reeling from its internal divisions and continual police harassment, the clandestine ETA movement was greatly weakened and demoralized around 1968 but survived in part because of a series of unanticipated political events known today as the Burgos trial of 1970.[5] On August 2, 1968, Melitón Manzanas, a police commissioner who was reputed to be a torturer of Basque patriots, was killed outside his apartment by a single gunman. The Spanish government imposed a state of exception, and more than two thousand Basque residents were arrested, among them numerous etarras, including "virtually every key leader on the Spanish side of the border."[6] Many ETA prisoners were beaten and tortured, and one suffered a miscarriage. The sixteen etarras and ETA sympathizers charged with complicity in the killing admitted being members of ETA but also pleaded innocent.

The trial in the town of Burgos was carried out by a military tribunal and, being a political trial by an infamous West European authoritarian regime, attracted international press coverage. Foreign journalists reported that the tribunal repeatedly violated internationally recognized principles of procedural due process, and described dramatic actions by the defendants, including their detailed descriptions of police torture in open court. Readers throughout Western Europe were shocked by the government's harshness. Jean-Paul Sartre sympathetically compared the ETA movement to the anti-German resistance movements during World War II. Dockworkers in France and Italy refused to load Spanish ships. After the sentences—which included several orders for execution—were handed down, the Vatican asked the Spanish government to exercise clemency. Within the Basque region, young children soon could recite the names of the convicted (much like children can recite the names of famous athletes); older students occupied churches; and immigrant workers struck. Several Marxist parties successfully called for general strikes. Sociologist Luis Núñez calculated that approximately 55 percent of all industrial workers in the Basque provinces struck at some time during December to protest the trial.[7]

The largely unanticipated outpouring of popular support surprised and reinforced the commitment of many activists within the ETA movement. Members of ETA-VI believed that the demonstrations by immigrant workers and non-Basque labor organizations demonstrated that an alliance of Basque nationalists and the Basque labor movement was hardly a dream. The "Burgos 16," moreover, seemed to endorse openly the leadership and strategy of ETA-VI. Most described themselves as Marxists during the trial. In a letter smuggled from jail, several denounced both the culturalist strategy of the *Branka* group and the lukewarm proletarian commitments of ETA-V. They repeatedly labeled members of both groups "traitors" and "right-wing Basques" who distributed folklore calendars and wrote novels while socially committed patriots relentlessly struggled in factories and worked toward creation of a "Basque Workers' party that assures the proletarian political direction of the Basque Liberation movement and the Basque Revolution and that guarantees the triumph of socialism in Euskadi."[8] The letter also advocated formation of an interethnic proletarian movement that would fight for independence, bilingualism, and nationalization of big business. If, however, the ETA movement tried to nurture rivalries between immigrant and Basque workers, it would become a bourgeois monstrosity, for according to the authors, "Spanish workers [in Granada] are falling struggling against the same oligarchy and the same forces of repression that oppress our country."[9]

ETA-V, in the meantime, kidnapped a West German consul and promised to release him only on condition that the Spanish government treat the convicted defendants in the Burgos trial leniently. The audacious and widely publicized kidnapping attracted many economically aggrieved, culturally proud, and politically frustrated youths from the countryside. Although in the wake of the Manzanas killing ETA had been organizationally decimated by arrests and flights from Spain, scores of new recruits took their places. In 1972 EGI-Batasuna (the youth branch of the Basque Nationalist party) formally joined ETA-V, an organizational transformation involving hundreds of youths, and one that left the Basque Nationalist party severely weakened.

ETA's sociological profile also changed. In the words of Robert Clark,

> the center of gravity of ETA did shift noticeably after 1970, away from Bilbao and other large cities toward the small towns of the mountainous north and central Guipúzcoa, away from students and middle-class professionals and toward workers in the small plants and factories of that region.[10]

Comparing the birthplaces of more than one hundred participants in ETA's assemblies between 1966 and 1970 with the birthplaces of almost two hundred etarras incarcerated in 1980, Patxo Unzueta discovered that over 50 percent of the first sample came from the predominantly urban province of Vizcaya (and the vast majority of the Vizcayan etarras came from either Bilbao or its surrounding industrial towns). Of the 1980 sample, only a minority (30 percent) came from Vizcaya province, and most of the rest came from rural and semirural areas of Alava, Guipúzcoa, and Navarra. Furthermore, of the 1966–70 sample, almost half were students in institutions of higher learning, and less than 5 percent were employed in rural occupations. In the 1980 sample students were far less numerous, and agriculturalists and former agriculturalists had become far more numerous. Unzueta writes, "an obvious conclusion is that between 1965 and 1980 the fundamental social bases of ETA had moved from Vizcaya to Guipúzcoa, and from centers of an industrialized population (in particular Bilbao and the banks of the Nervión) to rural and semirural zones."[11]

The shift in class background seemed to coincide with a growing ideological chasm between the older, largely urban-based etarras, a good number of whom were in ETA-VI and were self-declared "Marxist-Leninists," and the newer recruits, who were attracted primarily by ETA's daring militancy, not its ongoing theoretical debates and agonizing decisions about revolutionary strategy. Basque historian Pedro Ibarra Güell, for example, argues that before 1970 most youths who joined ETA-V or ETA-VI were motivated to do so not only because of its commitment to nationalism "but also, and I would say that after 1968 above all, because it was increasingly socialist and directly Marxist."[12] After 1970 the recruits seemed considerably less interested in Marxist theories and economic socialism. According to John Sullivan, "The new recruits tended to be of more rural origins than those who joined ETA in the late sixties, and their low political level shocked ETA-VI members whom they encountered in prison."[13]

In 1972 ETA-V (greatly strengthened by recruits) carried out its first kidnapping of a major industrialist, Lorenzo Zabala, who had been involved in a drawn-out labor dispute and who also was ethnically and linguistically Basque. ETA-V threatened to execute him unless his company reemployed all striking workers and accepted a proposal for a wage increase. The company capitulated. Spokespersons for ETA-V argued that the kidnapping demonstrated how workers' ongoing struggles and ETA's armed struggle could be constructively combined. Members of the Basque Nationalist party, on the other hand, were dismayed that ETA would conduct such an operation.

ETA-V next "unleashed a wave of violence unlike anything ever seen before in the Basque country."[14] Armed robberies, property bombings, and kidnappings became almost daily events during the early and middle 1970s. Spokespersons for ETA-V defended attacks against the region's wealthy and symbols of wealth—such as the burning of a tourist office in a fashionable resort center—on grounds that the attacks not only helped workers in labor disputes but were necessary first steps toward a popular uprising, as posited by the spiral theory of violence. And a new justification was aired: intense differences of opinion among government officials about how best to respond to ETA's violence would tear apart the current elite coalition of moderate reformers and hard-core Francoists. The attacks thus "intensified the contradictions between liberal and ultra-fascists" and impeded superficial, co-optive, nonsocialist reform of the Spanish state.[15] Many workers' groups (among them, the comisiones obreras and the Maoist ORT), however, increasingly insisted that the acts of ETA-V against factory owners were neither wanted by Basque workers nor needed. Some dissident activists in ETA-V similarly disapproved of the frequency of acts of violence.

Eschewing violence, ETA-VI tried to help local workers by means of more symbolic acts. For example, in 1971 it called for a hunger strike among all Basque political prisoners as a show of support for Basque workers who were about to negotiate new labor contracts.

Leaders of ETA-VI also began to propose a radically decentralized, participatory form of democracy that would eventually replace the current Spanish state once Franco died. They advocated a federated Basque people's government composed of armed councils of workers (a sort of re-creation of the Paris Commune, at least as romantically depicted in Marx's *Civil Wars in France*), socialization of the property of multinational corporations and local big business without compensation, and the development of extensive powers within unions.[16]

A series of organizational setbacks, including the arrests of leaders in Vizcaya during 1971 and laborers' apparent indifference to the etarras' hunger strike, provoked widespread disillusionment within ETA-VI during the early 1970s. Local cells called for wiser translocal leadership and fewer visionary pronouncements. Idealistically committed but discouraged activists began to desert the apparently incompetent organization in droves. Some joined other clandestine groups within the ETA movement, such as ETA-V; some joined outside groups, like the Spanish Communist party; some left political activism altogether. In 1973 a large number of remaining members of ETA-VI, who were Trotskyist in sympathy, agreed to fuse with a Trotskyist organization, the Revolutionary Communist League, and to discard the name ETA-VI. This left ETA-V the sole remaining group within the ETA movement still using "ETA" as part of its title.

As mentioned in chapter 7, ETA-V, under the intellectual leadership of Txabi Etxebarrieta, had advocated development of a multiclass Basque national front that would fight for independence of the Basque region from both France and Spain, for restoration of Basque as the official language of the new state, and for the democratization of industry (apparently through workers' councils). ETA-V's strategy was to be armed struggle supplemented by patient labor organizing, but without alienating the ethnically concerned members of the region's middle classes.[17]

There were growing disagreements within ETA-V over what to emphasize in its hybrid program. Recent recruits and former members of EGI, in particular, tended to favor the emphasis on ethnic liberation and the strong commitment to armed struggle. Violence seemed an effective political tool, especially given the then apparently successful use of violence in other parts of the world—by the Tupamaros in Uruguay and by the Palestinian group Black September, for instance.[18] Others, including some former members of ETA-VI, favored greater stress on labor organizing and were fearful of excessive use of armed actions. A key figure in this circle was Eduardo Moreno Bergareche, whose political pseudonym was "Pertur." [19] Pertur and his cohort argued that the sufferings of the Basque people were primarily the outcome of the worldwide triumph of industrial capitalism, which could be overthrown only by a worldwide proletarian struggle, of which ETA-V must be a part. ETA-V should participate in international conferences in support of national liberation movements in the Third World. Further, it should patiently mobilize urban laborers, including non-Basques. This required that the military front of ETA-V resist reckless violence, which could eventuate in the arrest of ETA-V labor organizers or greater police repression, which would make popular mobilization nearly impossible.

In 1973, after the death of the charismatic leader "Txikia," ETA-V held an organizational assembly. Members of its workers' front agreed to attend on condition that extensive discussions of principles, goals, and strategies be held, and that the decision-making procedure of democratic centralism be adopted to insure that all fronts (especially the military front) comply with the assembly's and, later, the executive council's, decisions. The atmosphere at the assembly was tense, with several members (especially in the military front) indulging in personal attacks rather than discussing policy and organizational questions. The assembly agreed that thenceforth a four-person executive committee would keep a close rein on the commandos' "major" projects, but the military front was otherwise free to choose targets. The meeting concluded without a major split largely because most participants feared an organizational rupture, although some anarchistic members of ETA-V resigned because, they charged, "democratic centralism" had been adopted as the future method of decision making.

The futility of trying to control the military front through an executive committee was revealed less than a year later in the bold assassination of Franco's apparent successor, Admiral Luis Carrero Blanco. The act was committed independently by the military front, without prior notification of other subgroups in ETA-V. A bomb, planted under a Madrid street, flung Carrero Blanco's car high in the air. Carrero Blanco and his driver were immediately killed.

The Spanish government swiftly rounded up all known labor and political dissidents in the Basque region and began a new series of states of exceptions. Many members of the ETA-V's labor front were arrested while organizing workers in factories. Afterward, most clandestine labor organizations in the region refused to cooperate with or accept aid from known etarras, largely because of risks of police repression.

The labor front's leadership held a special meeting to decry openly the assassination of Carrero Blanco, calling it "the greatest error in the history of the ETA."[20] Several angry labor activists also declared themselves free of the discipline of ETA. Supporters of the military front argued that the wave of government repression was, from a revolutionary point of view, functional because it helped reveal the reactionary, nonreformist spirit of the regime. The executive council, siding with the military front, accused leaders of the labor front of "factionalizing" the ETA, and expelled several labor leaders. Additional activists within the labor front then resigned and with some of the former labor leaders founded an independent organization, the Patriotic Revolutionary Workers' party (Langille Abertzale Iraultzalean Alderdia—LAIA).

Again, a proletarian-oriented faction was at odds with a military-oriented faction, and organizational fission took place. To some extent the members of LAIA were simply repeating the actions of their forerunners in ETA-berri and ETA-VI, but in some respects they were ideologically unique. They saw armed action as sometimes needed to achieve workers' aims. Furthermore, they did not want to join forces with revolutionary "Spanish" labor organizations, such as ORT, that worked for proletarian power throughout Spain.

Tensions soon developed within LAIA over the proper form and strategy for a Basque revolutionary proletarian movement. Some activists were inspired in part by the Kropotkin-like anarchist theories of former etarra Emilio López Adán ("Beltza") and favored participatory factory assemblies and a radically democratic evolution of factory juries. Others favored a more traditional social democratic Basque trade union movement. The infighting reduced the effectiveness of LAIA, and in some ways hindered development of widespread support among regional workers.

The assassination of Carrero Blanco created havoc within ETA-V but also gave it increased visibility and prestige among Basque youths, who were joining the organization in ever-increasing numbers. The total number of active etarras in Spain rose to approximately two hundred, from fewer than one hundred in 1970, when the Manzanas killing led to waves of arrests and deportations (immediately prior to the Manzanas killing there had been around six hundred etarras in Spain).[21]

Meanwhile, Franco's imminent death reopened long-standing ideological debates among those veteran etarras who chose to remain in ETA-V. It was unclear whether Franco's death would initiate political reform, which would require a new set of strategies, or whether authoritarianism would continue regnant. Pertur's circle expected a period of liberal-democratic reforms—perhaps including the establishment of an elected Spanish parliament and the legalization of independent trade unions. Reforms would give local radicals new points of leverage from which to change the political and economic condition of Euzkadi. Therefore ETA-V should channel its limited energies and resources into popular mobilization, in order to take advantage of the impending creative movement.

Others, especially members of the military front, doubted that Franco's demise would naturally lead to any liberal-democratic reforms of which ETA-V could take advantage. After all, Arias Navarro, Franco's replacement for Carrero Blanco, had promised in February 1974 to democratize politics but in practice had reduced civil liberties, had cracked down on clandestine union organizing, and had seemed to condone violence by ultraright vigilante groups, which were made up in part of off-duty police officers. If the authoritarian regime was to be overthrown and freedom gained for the Basque region, continued and intensified armed struggle would be needed. To believe otherwise was not realistic.

Gradually the two sides of this debate became associated with the labels "ETA poli-milis" (also known by the acronym ETA-pm), referring to those who wished to subordinate military action to the primary task of nonviolently mobilizing nonelites, and "ETA militar" (or ETA-m), referring to those who believed ETA's first and foremost task was to carry out armed struggle in accordance to the spiral theory of violence.

Each side was distrustful of the other. Suffering from police repression, supporters of the ETA-m line were fearful of security leaks. Further, they tended to view themselves as a specially trained and experienced unit whose views on the proper use of violence should not be constrained by other etarras unfamiliar with the possibilities and problems of armed struggle. They constantly resisted oversight by ETA's executive council and often carried out attacks without advance notification to etarras involved in other forms of popular organizing.

Supporters of the ETA-pm line (especially activists in the labor front) were increasingly annoyed and frustrated by the unpredictable actions of members of the military front, who seemed repeatedly to place field organizers in jeopardy. In September 1974 a bomb in a Madrid café that was frequented by Spanish police killed and wounded more than sixty-five persons, most of whose political preferences and loyalties remain either unknown or unclear. Several members of the Spanish armed forces were among the casualties. Despite ETA-V denials, there was pervasive suspicion that the military front had committed the act. The two factions within ETA-V formally separated. ETA-pm openly declared itself a Marxist organization and sought alliances with other Spanish Marxist counterparts, such as MCE (made up to some extent of former members of ETA-berri) and ORT, the Maoist group that was particularly active in Navarra. ETA-m pursued a nationalist front strategy and sought an alliance of all "patriotic left" groups, such as the *Branka* group, but opposed alliances with "Spanish left" organizations, such as MCE and ORT. Due chiefly to Pertur's prompting, ETA-pm joined with the nonanarchist wing of LAIA to create a new labor organization, the Basque Workers' Committee (Langile Abtaleon Bitaedeak, LAB), whose purpose was to unite native and immigrant workers into a single political force. ETA-pm also tried unsuccessfully to form a revolutionary alliance of Basque and Spanish groups tentatively called Herrihko Batasuna (Popular Unity).

Interestingly, ETA-pm openly criticized the cooperative experiments in Mondragón for being excessively "technocratic," "bureaucratic," and hierarchical. Although members of ETA-pm liked the idea of periodic assemblies in which workers, alongside managers, could help decide plant policies, they believed that in reality the power of the cooperatives' managers over employees was so unchecked that exploitation constantly occurred, as managers (whatever their declared values) sought to remain competitive in a capitalist economy and sought to protect their high income and other workplace privileges from the employees. Cooperatives offered labor activists an opportunity to educate workers about their legal rights and collective power, but cooperatives fell far short as realizations of the ideal of democratic, nonexploitative, egalitarian work.[22]

In the meantime the members of the military front who joined ETA-pm formed a distinctive, specialized subunit known as the Berezi commandos (or the Bereziak), whose charge was to carry out high-risk assaults against representatives of the state. In theory, the attacks would both pressure the Spanish government into negotiations with ETA-pm over political and economic reform and reinforce Basques' will to resist. Between 1975 and 1976, the Bereziak launched an offensive that largely backfired, resulting in widespread arrests. The commandos tried to intimidate their critics within ETA-pm. An angry Pertur wrote that the Bereziak had created within the ETA movement "a police state where everyone suspected his comrades."[23] After the controversial 1976 killing by the Berezi Commandos of a Basque industrialist and sympathizer of the Basque Nationalist party, Pertur resigned. Talked into returning, he agreed to attend a meeting with commando leaders to iron out differences. Pertur was never seen again. That same month, July 1976, a new Spanish president took office—Adolfo Suárez—who would initiate legalization of political parties and trade unions, the types of political reforms that Pertur had anticipated.

Following the presumed killing of Pertur, many members of ETA-pm resigned and formed a new organization known as EIA (Euskao Iraultzale Alderdia, the Basque Revolutionary party) that was explicitly devoted to nonviolent action. Many observers believe that the formal separation of military and nonmilitary wings of ETA-pm on the eve of the post-Franco liberal-democratic reforms had considerable impact on how the ETA movement responded to new political opportunities in Spain, for organizational communication between the two wings was thereby seriously weakened, and intra-organizational debates that might have led to moderation or even a termination of armed struggle never occurred.[24]

EIA's stated goal was to mobilize nonelites and prepare them for seizing institutional opportunities for power. In theory, EIA activists would be involved in citizens' day-to-day struggles for increased powers in the workplace, in the neighborhood, and in the broader political system. Ideological differences between immigrant workers and native Basque workers would be bridged, and a homogenization of political culture would take place.[25]

EIA's leaders insisted that Basque independence could not be achieved in a single stroke, through legislative fiat from Madrid. Instead, independence would require long-term organization and mobilization of the Basque people that would eventuate in partial reforms in economic, cultural, and political life. If the daily struggles were well coordinated, a Basque socialist state could emerge, in which the working classes of the region would be the dominant force.

From the activists' point of view, the success of EIA's project demanded organizational severance from all armed struggle, cooperation and solidarity with socialist parties and unions throughout Spain, and encouragement of all current and former activists in the ETA movement to join EIA and work patiently toward an independent Basque socialist state. The phrase *"izquierda abertzale"* ("the Basque patriotic Left") was coined to refer to all who had ever been part of the ETA movement and who might become part of EIA's socialist-independent coalition. The Basque Nationalist party was explicitly excluded because it seemed too bourgeois in economic and social sentiments and goals, and too ethnically Basque in prejudices to aid in the creation of an interethnic Basque labor movement.

POLITICAL CHANGE AFTER FRANCO

While these ideological and organizational developments were occurring within the ETA movement, Spanish politics was rapidly becoming transformed. Franco's death in 1975 at first appeared to change little. Prime Minister Arias continued to crack down on clandestine labor organizations, and ETA-m and ETA-pm (now, essentially, the Bereziak and its supporters) went on attacking and killing police, civilians (often political officials) with right-wing sympathies, and suspected informants. During a wildcat strike in Vitoria in 1976 the Spanish police shot a group of strikers assembling outside a church, whereupon a regionwide general strike broke out. Some foreign journalists foresaw a new Spanish civil war.[26] ETA-m and ETA-pm announced that the massacre had proved that the authoritarian regime could not be peacefully transformed, that force was necessary. But King Juan Carlos quickly replaced Arias with Adolfo Suárez, who adroitly set in motion several institutional and procedural changes, such as the legalization of oppositional political parties and labor unions.

Once elections for a parliament with constitution-drafting

powers were announced, EIA declared itself a proletarian party and held its first public rally in Gallarta, an immigrant, industrial stronghold in Vizcaya and the birthplace of "La Pasionaria," one of Spain's most famous and militant labor leaders. According to Clark, "In choosing this locale from which to begin its search for votes in the upcoming parliamentary elections, EIA was sending a clear message that it would count primarily on working class support, and only secondarily on the votes of ethnic Basques from the middle class, the professions, small towns, and farming communities."[27] EIA formed an electoral coalition called Euskadiko Ezkerra (Basque Left) with MCE and ORT. Many of EIA's members were primarily concerned, however, with mobilizing working-class populations into grass-roots self-governing bodies, loosely resembling soviets. These radicals, like members of MCE and ORT, hoped that such organizations, often extensions of the asociaciones de vecinos, would eventually become the institutional basis for a radically decentralized, participatory, and proletarian political order.[28]

The culturalist wing of the ETA movement, meanwhile, also tried to take advantage of the new political opportunities that Suárez was creating. Activists within the *Branka* group joined forces with some activists in the Basque cooperative movement and created a new party, known as ESB (Euskadi Sozialista Biltzarrea, the Basque Socialist Convergence). ESB's primary goals were protection and revitalization of the Basque language, encouragement of cooperative production and restrictions on big business, and opposition to communist theory and organizations and to state ownership of the means of production. Unlike EIA, ESB was primarily committed to electoral activism and was willing to work with more socially egalitarian activists and factions within the Basque Nationalist party. Despite its electoral strategy, ESB did poorly whenever it ran candidates by itself and hence had to depend on broader coalitions like the Herri Batasuna (to be described below) for success. Divisions between the more culturally oriented group, led by Txillardegi, and the cooperativists (whom Txillardegi accused of Marxism) further weakened the group and ultimately led to its dissolution.[29]

EIA's electoral coalition, the Euskadiko Ezkerra, did much better, winning enough votes in the 1977 parliamentary elections to capture one seat in the Spanish parliament and one seat in the Basque General Council, a representative body that Suárez's reform coalition was establishing to facilitate the expected limited transfer of powers from Madrid to the Basque region. Partly because it was small and wished not to be excluded from important decisions in either representative body, EIA set about toning down its anarcho-communalist rhetoric. Its leaders began to contend that a more traditional social-democratic strategy of participating constructively in elected representative bodies was necessary, for the Basque proletariat was currently too divided and disorganized to attempt more radical projects—such as a system of directly participatory asociaciones de vecinos that would replace less participatory, elected municipal councils.

The evolving tactical moderation and social-democratic conventionality of EIA disturbed some of its most visible activists, like Francisco Letamendia (whose political pseudonym was "Ortzi"). Members of ORT and MCE soon left the coalition, frustrated by EIA's patient political style and by its refusal to give more power to other groups in the coalition. Many activists in EIA, in addition, were troubled by their leaders' continuous attacks on what they called the "chauvinism" of the Basque Nationalist party and ETA-m.[30]

Finally, complex issues involving violence kept threatening to divide EIA. ETA-pm, which initially wished to subordinate acts of violence to goals of nonviolent popular mobilization, had begun a more culturally oriented series of attacks, such as bombing institutions that it said encouraged exploitative values (such as cinemas showing erotic films) and attacking reputed drug dealers, as well as terrorizing representatives of management during heated labor disputes. At the same time, ETA-m—insisting that Suárez's reform initiatives were a facade hiding a hierarchical and exploitative social, economic, and political system—regularly struck at politicians, journalists, and police officers. Killings carried out by ETA units had never exceeded seventeen a year between 1968 and 1977, but over sixty-five killings occurred each year in 1978, 1979, and 1980.[31]

There are many possible explanations for the escalation of ETA violence, and the explanations are not logically incompatible. Payne believes that acute fear of linguistic-cultural extinction had pushed some members of the Basque nationalist movement into unusually violent action.[32] Clark at one point argues that competition for new recruits and fear of losing rank-and-file members pushed rival armed groups in ETA into "dramatic and shocking action" as a method of sustaining morale in existing organizations.[33] Ibarra Güell and Clark contend that greater violence was primarily strategic: fearing that they were losing ground in the post-Franco reforms and that a unique chance for extensive political and economic change was being squandered, the Bereziak and ETA-m tried to remain central figures by forcing the Spanish government to pay attention to their demands.[34]

The government responded sternly, suspending several civil liberties in the region and detaining suspected etarras without formal charges. At first glance, the government's retaliatory moves seem to be in accordance with the spiral theory of violence, but the theory was not completely vindicated. A popular uprising against the regime did not occur. Instead, police units occasionally rampaged against Basque residents—for example, smashing windows in the working-class district of Renteria and shooting at unarmed spectators in and near a bullring during the Pamplona festival of 1978. Basque youths sometimes reacted by burning automobiles and barricading roads, but a coordinated and sustained resistance never developed.

The absence of a popular uprising is partly explained by the selectivity of the government repression. Spanish courts and police forces were treating etarras much more harshly than other political and economic dissidents. A person convicted of illegal trade-union activism might be incarcerated for a few months; etarras were usually incarcerated for several years. Police frequently tortured etarras, but seldom other dissidents. In short, repression was falling heavily on etarras, who understandably saw no significant difference in the behavior of the police before and after the death of Franco. For most sectors of Basque society, however, the difference was evident, and the felt need for resistance to state repression was therefore small.[35]

EIA was torn apart, however, trying to decide whom to denounce for violence: the police, ETA-m and ETA-pm, Basque youths, all these groups, only some groups? Leaders of EIA, in part because of electoral and political pressure, tried to take the high road of condemning all acts of violence by the Spanish government's police units and by Basque youths and ETA units. Some EIA militants, outraged by the leadership's apparent siding with the government against ETA guerrillas and Basque youths, resigned. Other members thought that EIA's decisions to denounce universally all acts of violence was its only politically prudent option if it wished to maintain support among Basques sympathetic to ETA, yet still work within the existing political order.

Partially in response to the repeated acts of police repression and brutality and to the government's refusal to grant amnesty to all Basque political prisoners, a new coalition of former and current etarras and their sympathizers arose, calling itself Herri Batasuna (People's Unity). The more anarcho-syndicalist and factory-assembly wing of LAIA; HASI (an acronym for a small party that informally spoke for ETA-m); the ever-struggling ESB; local groups lobbying for political amnesty; politically radical members of the asociaciones de vecinos; Askatasuna (an anarcho-communist collective); and some militant members and former members of the Basque Nationalist party were among the early groups constituting the Herri Batasuna. Because the coalition was a loose one, its coordinating board could not make decisions binding on constituent groups. Instead, the groups pledged themselves to a set of demands known as the KAS Alternative, which included immediate withdrawal of all Spanish police forces from the Basque region, release of all Basque political prisoners, and political independence for all four Basque provinces.[36]

The leaders of the coalition also maintained that the political reforms initiated by the Suárez government did not give adequate power to the poor or to the Basque people. Even with new bodies of elected officials, the Spanish political system was basically not democracy, but "fascist democracy" and "reformist Francoism." Therefore, the coalition would not participate in the newly developing political institutions.[37] The coalition, instead, would encourage the development of a popular "counterpower," a set of institutions challenging the Spanish government, among them neighborhood councils that would make public policy for the Basque people. Local coordinating committees were set up to develop political consciousness within factory councils, neighborhood associations, and other "proletarian" organizations (broadly understood). The attempt to create a popular counterpower was short lived. With legalization of parties and unions, popular political forms that had evolved during the Francoist years, such as factory assemblies and neighborhood associations, had lost their social function and begun to disband. Moreover, many of the popular groups that continued did not view the KAS Alternative as a high priority. So by the end of the 1970s, the Herri Batasuna ceased emphasizing the idea of a "popular counterpower" and directing its energies and resources into various forms of social assemblies.[38]

This does not mean that the Herri Batasuna ceased to be politically active. Rather, the nature of its activities changed. Promising not to take their seats in existing parliaments if elected, candidates of the Herri Batasuna in the 1979 general elections did remarkably well, attracting more votes than the Euskadiko Ezkerra and almost as many votes as the Spanish Socialist party. In the municipal elections held in spring 1979, the coalition again did very well, capturing majorities in the governing councils of several working-class communities. The Herri Batasuna also sponsored large demonstrations by the close of the 1970s that succeeded in drawing larger numbers than could any other political organization in the region, including the Basque Nationalist party.

In the summer of 1979 the Suárez government, hoping to stem the rising tides of Basque radical voting and ETA violence, proposed an ambiguous autonomy statute that allowed the provinces of Alava, Guipúzcoa, and Vizcaya to have a regional parliament with limited educational, fiscal, and other policy-making rights. The Euskadiko Ezkerra and the Basque Nationalist party endorsed the proposal and urged Basque citizens to approve the statute through the established referendum process. The Herri Batasuna opposed the statute, saying among other things that the powers of the proposed government were too limited, that the statute did not include Navarra, and that demands for removing the Spanish police and granting amnesty for political prisoners were not yet satisfactorily addressed. The referendum passed, nonetheless, suggesting limits to the Herri Batasuna's appeal, but in the subsequent elections for the regional parliament the coalition again did well and its candidates again refused to take their seats.

After 1979 the Herri Batasuna became organizationally anemic as constituent groups, such as LAIA and ESB, resigned. The reasons for the resignations related partially to dissatisfaction over the continuing boycott of government institutions. Some groups, such as Askatasuna, strongly supported grass-roots activism while opposing expending energy on "bourgeois parliamentarianism."[39] But some members of ESB and LAIA believed that by refusing to take seats in elected legislative bodies, such as the Basque parliament, the Herri Batasuna was becoming politically irrelevant rather than politically powerful. After the 1979 municipal elections, several Herri Batasuna candidates decided to take their seats despite the coalition's declared policy of institutional nonparticipation. This led to considerable disagreement and anger within the coalition and to the above-mentioned resignations of ESB and LAIA the following year.

In addition, the constant endorsement of ETA-m's actions by the coalition's coordinating committee troubled several of the coalition's partners and, again, led to resignations. Finally, there were disputes among constituent groups over whose members should be selected to be on electoral lists, which again led to individuals' abandonment of the coalition.

Ironically, despite the numerous desertions, the Herri Batasuna continued to attract surprisingly large proportions of the Basque electorate throughout the 1980s. It became one of the region's most consistently successful electoral organizations, regularly receiving between 10 and 20 percent of ballots cast in the region.

EIA, ESB, and the Herri Batasuna manifested what might be called the more political side of the ETA movement during the early post-Franco period. Using elections and demonstrations, and entering popular assemblies, these groups sought to create a self-governing, socialist Basque region largely through nonviolent action. But what about the military side of ETA: What did ETA-pm and ETA-m do?

Although there was an escalation of violence during the final years of the 1970s, as early as 1977 some leaders of ETA-pm had wanted to abandon armed struggle and engage in nonviolent political activity. Some of this inclination, undoubtedly, was due to the increasing effectiveness of the Spanish police in capturing ETA cells. Additionally, after the attempted military coup of 1981, leaders of Euskadiko Ezkerra had become much more critical of ETA-pm's attacks on politicians and civilians. The attempted coup reminded all of the fragility of the post-Franco liberal-democratic reforms. Mario Onaindía, a principle theoretician in EIA and formerly one of the "Burgos 16," made a particularly tough criticism of both ETA-m and ETA-pm in 1981, arguing that violence under current political circumstances was counterrevolutionary. A special assembly of EIA soon met and asked both ETA-m and ETA-pm to lay down their arms because continuation of violence encouraged military intervention in politics and thus "favored the position of the right."[40] Exhausted by government repression, frustrated by their failure to ignite popular resistance, and subject to the increasingly strong disfavor of the

Euskadiko Ezkerra, most of the units of ETA-pm self-dissolved in the middle 1980s, following policies of partial amnesty coordinated by the Euskadiko Ezkerra and the Spanish government.

This left a small group of former Berezi Commandos and ETA-m the sole remaining sectors of the ETA community still engaged in armed struggle. Some organizational loyalists tried to discourage desertions through threats of reprisals, especially following the Spanish government's offers during the 1980s of partial amnesty to etarras who would drop their guns. An example of the hard-liners' ruthlessness was former ETA militant María Dolores González Catarain ("Yoyes"), who in 1986, after accepting amnesty, was shot in the back of the head by an ETA commando while walking her child in a park.

Periodic acts of reprisal could not hold back the growing doubts within commando units about the wisdom of violence. The failure of the spiral theory of violence to trigger a mass uprising, the fresh constitutional possibilities of electoral strategies, the Spanish government's increasing effectiveness in battling ETA's armed units and the French government's sudden cooperation with Spain in its efforts to capture suspected etarras jointly had weakened the resolve of many members of ETA-m. In 1984, "Txomin," a key leader in ETA-m, conceded that things were not going well and said "the thing is to look for a way out." Years later he added, "If we don't negotiate now, within a year the French will have dismantled everything; they will have decimated us, seized our weapons and money, and we will not have anything to negotiate."[41]

Pressed by increasingly adverse circumstances and attracted to new legal opportunities to contest governing elites, many veterans decided individually to leave armed struggle during the 1980s and pursue Basque ends through nonviolent means (or, in some cases, to leave politics altogether). The number of ETA fighters dwindled. A partial consequence was that the yearly number of deaths due to ETA attacks halved between 1980 and 1985.[42] By 1989 an unusually violent phase of Basque nationalist politics was apparently drawing to a close. There were still troubling instances of bloodshed, such as the 1987 bomb explosion in a crowded supermarket in Barcelona that killed a score of people. Nonetheless, it appears that a combination of new political circumstances had caused many individuals to reassess their political choices.

CONCLUSION

We began our reflections on the causes and characteristics of Basque political violence by recounting a common view on the subject, what we have called the modernization interpretation. According to this position, the violence was primarily an expression of Basques' intense feelings of cultural dislocation and personal stress brought about by unusually rapid and widespread social changes, including secularization, urbanization, and industrialization. Popular feelings of distress also were reflected in and reinforced by the antimodern ideology propagated by the Basque Nationalist party, which strongly criticized the values and structures of industrial, urban, and commercial society, and celebrated those of preindustrial times. Culturally uprooted, persons from rural and small-town backgrounds lashed out at the agents and symbols of modernity, but without specific grievances in mind and without thoughts of achieving particular goals. Violence principally resulted not from economic concerns and political calculations but from cultural unfamiliarity and acute personal pain. The expressive political violence in turn antagonized Spain's armed forces and thus indirectly endangered Spain's open, pluralistic political system.

This study has presented an alternative interpretation that places greater emphasis on economic problems and grievances, the mediating influence of local social movements and political struggles, and the adaptation and modification of non-Nationalist as well as Nationalist ideologies to a complex political and economic situation. The book has viewed the members of ETA as rational actors who consciously gave meaning to their circumstances, and who adapted, refined, and readjusted ideas according to constantly changing political circumstances. Etarras' ideas, such as the spiral theory of violence, were not simply expressions of rage but attempts to calculate under complex, local circumstances how best to respond to economic crises. Events and institutions, such as general strikes and the asociaciones de vecinos, shaped the strategic calculations of etarras and even their visions of and hopes for a reconstructed Basque society.

Throughout the book historical events and patterns that depart from the modernization interpretation have been discussed. Backward-looking populism, for example, hardly is as hegemonic within the Basque Nationalist party as most users of the current modernization interpretation maintain. The correlation between etarras holding socially nostalgic ideologies and etarras advocating armed action also is far from perfect—as the case of Txillardegi suggests. Similarly, the economic problems of the Basque region have been far more numerous and complex than most modernization interpreters today contend. On the basis of these and other findings, it has been concluded that the common modernization interpretation greatly oversimplifies the social and economic context of Basque politics as well as the motivations and strategic ideas leading to violent acts.

But the finding that the modernization interpretation oversimplifies aspects of political history is, by itself, not very interesting. All systematic theories about politics and society inevitably and inescapably oversimplify and exaggerate. Simplification is one of the purposes (and values) of a coherent theory. More important, are there ways to build upon and extend current theoretical frameworks so as to have a richer, more rounded understanding of political reality? By looking more closely at economic conditions, social movements, and formal ideologies and ideological debates, this book has attempted to do so.

One obvious consequence of interpreting political violence mainly in terms of local nonviolent political struggles, economic difficulties, and overt ideologies is that new characteristics of the region's society and politics suddenly come into focus. As the analyst's theoretical interests broaden, the historical landscape no longer appears quite as barren. No longer is attention inadvertently turned away from nonviolent strikes, petitions, peaceful lobbying, Third World ideologies, and neighborhood assemblies. The structures, processes, interests, and forces of Basque politics appear richer and therefore more intriguing.

In addition to enhancing our perception of the many elements and dynamics of contemporary Basque politics, the modified interpretation presented in this study can lead to a more contingent view about future violence in the region. If short-term political, economic, and intellectual circumstances—such as surges in protest by urban laborers, the government's nonresponsiveness to rural discontent, and the recent publication of Franz Fanon's theories—were significant influences on the decisions of some etarras to launch armed attacks, then the levels and forms of violence should vary as these and other pertinent circumstances change. Indeed, there is growing evidence that after 1980, as armed actions repeatedly failed to ignite a popular rebellion, as legal opportunities to influence government officials altered, and as police surveillance in France and Spain stiffened, many etarras reconsidered their strategy and concluded that armed actions should be abandoned and more institutionalized forms of political participation explored. The yearly number of killings by Basque guerrillas halved between 1980 and 1985. Approximately 250 etarras between 1982 and 1986 gave up armed struggle and accepted the government's amnesty plan. Popular insurgency increasingly appeared a foolish hope to many ETA activists. As one disillusioned etarra concluded after years of struggle, "The people applaud us from the balconies but do not come down into the streets to fight."[1]

The book's portrait of ETA also encourages us to take more seriously the theoretical debates within ETA and its diverse electoral offshoots. If, in fact, the debates were not sociologically epiphenomenal—mere rationalizations for people wanting to vent destructive impulses generated by rapid modernization—but were systematic judgments and deliberations about what a modern industrial society should be like and how an existing industrial society can best be improved, then the substance of the debates has relevance for many non-Basques. The questions the revolutionaries asked are hardly unique to the Basque region. After all, what *should* a modern industrial society be like? Whose short- and long-term economic interests should be protected, advanced, and sacrificed in a competitive economy? Does a particular political system, even a parliamentary system, consistently benefit some interests in society and neglect others? And what should those who believe that their interests are being routinely neglected in the policy-making process do to be sure that their voices are heard? These fundamental issues are addressed in the writings pro and con of current and former etarras. By viewing etarras and former etarras not as abnormally emotional "extremists" but as rational people coping with problems of governance, we might learn more from their exchanges.

Finally, the book's perspective should remind us to look closely at the circumstances surrounding controversial politics and always consider the day-to-day environment in which political actors find themselves, which shapes their consciousness, and with which they cope. Many social arrangements and experiences intervene between personal or social grievances and political recourse. If we ignore the influence of context and its dynamics on activists' thinking and deeds, our understanding of controversial political events will suffer —including events close to home.

NOTES

INTRODUCTION

1. For example, in 1979, fifteen of the nineteen news reports about Basque politics published in the *Christian Science Monitor* focused on acts of political violence. Political violence was a secondary but nonetheless major topic in the four remaining reports. That same year, sixteen of the twenty news reports about Basque politics in the *Washington Post* focused on political violence.

2. Gordon Smith, *Politics in Western Europe: A Comparative Analysis* (New York: Holmes & Meier, 1984), p. 15.

3. Stanley G. Payne, "Terrorism and Democratic Stability in Spain," *Current History* 77 (November 1979): 167, 169.

4. Juan J. Linz, "The Basques in Spain: Nationalism and Political Conflict in a New Democracy," in *Resolving Nationality Conflicts: The Role of Public Opinion Research*, ed. W. Phillips Davison and Leo Gordenker (New York: Praeger, 1980), p. 44.

5. Ibid., p. 43.

6. Stanley G. Payne, *Basque Nationalism* (Reno: University of Nevada Press, 1975); Stanley G. Payne, "Regional Nationalism: The Basques and the Catalans," in *Spain in the 1970s: Economics, Social Structure, Foreign Policy*, ed. William Salisbury and James D. Theberge (New York: Praeger, 1976), pp. 76–102; Stanley G. Payne, "Recent Research on Basque Nationalism: Political, Cultural, and Socioeconomic Dimensions" (1980, mimeographed); Juan J. Linz, "Early state-building and late peripheral nationalisms against the state: The case of Spain," in *Building States and Nations: Models, Analyses, and Data across Three Worlds*, ed. S. N. Eisenstadt and Stein Rokkan (Beverly

Hills: Sage, 1973), 2: 74–83; Juan Pablo Fusi Aizpurua, *El País Vasco: Pluralismo y nacionalidad* (Madrid: Alianza Editorial, 1984); John Sullivan, *ETA and Basque Nationalism: The Fight for Euskadi, 1890–1986* (London: Routledge, 1988). It should be noted that Linz's use of phraseology and logic from modernization theory is less frequent in his post-1973 writings on Basque politics. Still, to the extent that he has a coherent sociological theory about why political violence emerged in the Basque region (in contrast to other areas of Spain), it seems to rely heavily on the psychological themes and tradition-to-modernity framework typical of modernization theory. See Linz, "The Basques in Spain"; Juan J. Linz, "From Primordialism to Nationalism," in *New Nationalisms of the Developed West: Toward Explanation*, ed. Edward A. Tiryakian and Ronald Rogowski (Boston: Allen & Unwin, 1985), pp. 203–53.

7. Linz, "Early state-building and late peripheral nationalisms against the state," p. 79.

8. Ibid., p. 82.

9. Linz, "The Basques in Spain," p. 13; Juan J. Linz, Manuel Reino Gómez, A. Francisco, and Darío Vila, *Conflicto en Euskadi, Estudio sociológico sobre el cambio político en el País Vasco, 1975–1989* (Madrid: Espasa Calpe, 1986), p. 58; Payne, *Basque Nationalism*, pp. 249–52; Vernon Bogdanor, "Ethnic Nationalism in Western Europe," *Political Studies* 30 (June 1982): 287, 290; Walker Connor, "Eco- or ethno-nationalism?" *Ethnic and Racial Studies* 7 (July 1984): 349. Ken Medhurst, it should be noted, is a clear exception to the current tendency among scholars who use the modernization theory to minimize the role of economic conditions and grievances. Ken Medhurst, "Basques and Basque Nationalism," in *National Separatism*, ed. Colin H. Williams (Cardiff: University of Wales Press, 1982), pp. 235–61.

10. For a very brief but provocative discussion of the different ways "pluralism" has been used by scholars in the United States, see Raymond Wolfinger, *The Politics of Progress* (Englewood Cliffs: Prentice-Hall, 1974), pp. 9–10.

11. For illustrations and sympathetic explications of the pluralist viewpoint, see Robert A. Dahl, *A Preface to Democratic Theory* (Chicago: University of Chicago Press, 1956); Robert A. Dahl, *Who Governs?* (New Haven: Yale University Press, 1961); John Plamenatz, "Electoral Studies and Democratic Theory: A British View," *Political Studies* 6(1): 1–9; Nelson W. Polsby, *Community Power and Political Theory: A Further Look at Problems of Evidence and Inference*, second, enlarged edition (New Haven: Yale University Press, 1980). For critiques of pluralist interpretations of politics, see Doug McAdam, *Political Process and the Development of Black Insurgency, 1930–1970* (Chicago: University of Chicago Press, 1982); Theodore Lowi, *The End of Liberalism* (New York: W. W. Norton, 1969); Kenneth Newton, *Second City Politics: Democratic*

Processes and Decision-Making in Birmingham (Oxford: Oxford University Press, 1976); E. E. Schattschneider, *The Semi-Sovereign People: A Realist's View of Democracy in America* (Hinsdale, Ill.: Dryden Press, 1960); Jack L. Walker, "A Critique of the Elitist Theory of Democracy," *American Political Science Review* 60 (June 1966): 285–95.

12. See, for example, Payne, "Terrorism and Democratic Stability in Spain"; Juan J. Linz, "Europe's Southern Frontier: Evolving Trends Toward What?" *Daedalus* 108 (Winter 1979): 175–209; Linz, "The Basques in Spain"; Raymond Carr and Juan Pablo Fusi Aizpurua, *Spain: Dictatorship to Democracy*, 2d ed. (London: Allen & Unwin, 1981).

13. Readers interested in relating what I call the "modernization interpretation" of Basque politics to other trends in contemporary social-science theorizing might consult Michael Paul Rogin, *The Intellectuals and McCarthy: The Radical Specter* (Cambridge: MIT Press, 1967); Sandor Halebsky, *Mass Society and Political Conflict: Towards a Reconstruction of Theory* (Cambridge: Cambridge University Press, 1976); Irene L. Gendzier, *Managing Political Change: Social Scientists and the Third World* (Boulder, Colo.: Westview Press, 1985); Eldon Kenworthy, "The Function of the Little-Known Case in Theory Formation or What Peronism Wasn't," *Comparative Politics* 6 (October 1973): 17–45; J. Craig Jenkins, "Sociopolitical Movements," in *Handbook of Political Behavior*, ed. Samuel L. Long (New York: Plenum Press, 1981), 4: 81–153.

14. McAdam, *Political Process and the Development of Black Insurgency.*

15. William Kornhauser, quoted in McAdam, *Political Process and the Development of Black Insurgency*, pp. 17–18.

16. Aldon Morris and Cedric Herring, "Theory and Research in Social Movements: A Critical Review," in *Annual Review of Political Science*, ed. Samuel Long (New York: Plenum Press, 1981), 2: 171.

17. Rogin, *The Intellectuals and McCarthy*, p. 171.

18. McAdam, *Political Process and the Development of Black Insurgency*; Maurice Pinard, *The Rise of a Third Party: A Study in Crisis Politics* (Englewood Cliffs, N.J.: Prentice-Hall, 1971); Maurice Pinard, "Mass Society and Political Movements: A New Formulation," *American Journal of Sociology* 73 (May 1968): 682–90; Charles Tilly, *From Mobilization to Revolution* (Reading, Mass.: Addison-Wesley, 1978); Halebsky, *Mass Society and Political Conflict.*

19. An obvious exception is John Sullivan's work, which laudably emphasizes the causal significance of local cultural and recreational institutions, such as youth gangs and mountain-climbing clubs. Sullivan, *ETA and Basque Nationalism.*

20. I know of only one serious, systematic attempt to verify the alleged psychological abnormalities of Basque guerrillas, and it reached the opposite conclusion: that etarras who participated in armed attacks were *not* abnor-

mally nonrational but, to the contrary, were psychologically "normal to the point of being mundane." Robert P. Clark, *The Basque Insurgents: ETA, 1952–1980* (Madison: University of Wisconsin Press, 1984), pp. 141–42.

21. Robert P. Clark, *Negotiating with ETA: Obstacles to Peace in the Basque Country 1975–1988* (Reno: University of Nevada Press, 1990).

22. For data on the occupations of victims of armed attacks, see Clark, *The Basque Insurgents*, pp. 134–40.

23. I am indebted to James B. Rule's reflections on social science for reminding me of this important but often forgotten point. James B. Rule, *Theories of Civil Violence* (Berkeley: University of California Press, 1988), chaps. 8–9.

24. Karl Polanyi, *The Great Transformation: The Political and Economic Origins of Our Time* (Boston: Beacon Press, 1957); E. P. Thompson, *The Making of the English Working Class* (New York: Vintage Books, 1963); E. J. Hobsbawm, *The Age of Revolution, 1789–1848* (New York: World Publishing Company, 1962); E. J. Hobsbawm, *The Age of Capital, 1848–1875* (New York: Charles Scribner's Sons, 1975); Hannah Arendt, *The Origins of Totalitarianism* (New York: World Publishing Company, 1951); Charles S. Maier, *Recasting Bourgeois Europe: Stabilization in France, Germany, and Italy in the Decade after World War I* (Princeton: Princeton University Press, 1975); Lawrence Goodwyn, *The Populist Moment: A Short History of the Agrarian Revolt in America* (Oxford: Oxford University Press, 1978); Adam B. Ulam, *The Unfinished Revolution* (New York: Random House, 1960).

25. For a useful summary and critique of this body of theoretical literature, see Rule, *Theories of Civil Violence*, chaps. 6, 8.

26. Rule, *Theories of Civil Violence*, p. 180; Tilly, *From Mobilization to Revolution*, chap. 5.

27. McAdam, *Political Process and the Development of Black Insurgency*; Aldon D. Morris, *The Origins of the Civil Rights Movement: Black Communities Organizing for Change* (New York: Free Press, 1984).

28. McAdam, *Political Process and the Development of Black Insurgency*; Tilly, *From Mobilization to Revolution*, chaps. 4–8.

29. Sidney Tarrow, *Struggle, Politics, and Reform: Collective Action, Social Movements, and Cycles of Protest* (Ithaca: Center for International Studies, Cornell University, 1989), p. 46.

30. McAdam, *Political Process and the Development of Black Insurgency*.

31. I was reminded of this by Pedro Ibarra Güell's comments on the multiple meanings of ETA, as a specific organization and as a more general Left-patriotic "community," and by José Mari Garmendia's insistence that to understand the politics of ETA, one must view it not as a simple organization with agreed upon priorities and a single system of authority, but as a movement with disparate tendencies and interests. Pedro Ibarra Güell, *La Evolución Estratégica de ETA (1963–1987)* (Donostia: Kriselu, 1987), p. 141;

José Mari Garmendia, *Historia de ETA* (San Sebastián: L. Haranburu, 1980), vol. 2, pp. 71–72.

32. In particular, I have been influenced by *The Basque Insurgents; The Basques: The Franco Years and Beyond* (Reno: University of Nevada Press, 1979); "Euzkadi: Basque Nationalism in Spain since the Civil War" in *Nations without a State: Ethnic Minorities in Western Europe*, ed. Charles R. Foster (New York: Praeger, 1980), pp. 75–100.

33. These additional themes seem much more common in books published in Spain. See, for example, Francisco Letamendia (political pseudonym, "Ortzi"), *Historia de Euskadi: El nacionalismo vasco y ETA* (Barcelona: Ruedo Ibérico, 1977); Gurutz Jáuregui Bereciartu, *Ideología y estrategia política de ETA: Análisis de su evolución entre 1959 y 1968* (Madrid: Siglo Veintiuno, 1981); Güell, *La Evolución Estratégica de ETA*. It is possible that these themes are becoming more common in scholarship published in English. The recent work of Clark and Joseba Zulaika come to mind. But such works still seem to be the exception, rather than the rule; in any case, reliable predictions of scholarly trends are always difficult to make, as philosophers of science and social science such as Rule and Thomas Kuhn constantly point out. Joseba Zulaika, *Basque Violence: Metaphor and Sacrament* (Reno: University of Nevada Press, 1988); Rule, *Theories of Civil Violence*, chap. 9; Thomas S. Kuhn, *The Structure of Scientific Revolutions*, second edition, enlarged (Chicago: University of Chicago Press, 1970).

34. My interviews usually lasted an hour or so and were based on four or five open-ended questions. I tried to meet with individuals in semiprivate places and on a one-to-one basis in order to facilitate openness and avoid distractions. To encourage informality and spontaneity, I did not use a tape recorder but openly jotted a few notes on a small pad of paper. I then retired to my hotel room and described the meeting in more detail in my notebooks.

CHAPTER ONE

1. Examples of such statistics can be found in Payne, *Basque Nationalism*, pp. 230, 232; Rafael Ossa Echaburu, *Euzkadi/80* (Madrid: Espasa Calpe, 1982), p. 48.

2. Antonio de Madriaga y Zobaran, *Clases sociales y aspiraciones vascas* (Bilbao: La cámara oficial de comercio, industria, y navegación, 1979), p. 43.

3. Payne, "Regional Nationalism: The Basques and Catalans," pp. 98, 91, 100; Linz, "The Basques in Spain"; Linz, Reino Gómez, Francisco, and Vila, *Conflicto en Euskadi*; Walter Laqueur, *The Age of Terrorism* (Boston: Little, Brown and Company, 1987); Bogdanor, "Ethnic Nationalism in Western Europe," pp. 287, 290; Connor, "Eco- or ethno-nationalism?" p. 349.

4. Linz, Reino Gómez, Francisco, and Vila, *Conflicto en Euskadi*, pp. 57–58; Linz, "The Basques in Spain," p. 13.

5. Laqueur, *The Age of Terrorism*, p. 223.

6. Ignacio Ballester Ros, "La Evolución de la Población del País Vasco en el Periódo 1900–1981," *Revista de Estudios de Vida Local* 42 (January–March 1983): 143–58.

7. Information on the physical geography of the Basque region was gathered from personal observations during the summer of 1980 and from published descriptions by Martin Blinkhorn, "War on two fronts: politics and society in Navarre 1931–6," in *Revolution and War in Spain, 1931–1939*, ed. Paul Preston (London: Methuen, 1984), pp. 60–64; Clark, *The Basque Insurgents*, pp. 8–20, 198–203; William A. Douglass, "Rural Exodus in Two Spanish Villages: A Cultural Explanation," *American Anthropologist* 73 (October 1971); Davydd J. Greenwood, *Unrewarding wealth: The commercialization and collapse of agriculture in a Spanish Basque town* (Cambridge: Cambridge University Press, 1976), pp. 3–11, 27–29, 100; Robert Laxalt and William Albert Allard, "The Land of the Ancient Basques," *National Geographic* 134 (August 1968): 240–77.

8. For descriptions of linguistic habits in the Basque region, see Clark, *The Basques*, chap. 6; Robert P. Clark, "Language and Politics in Spain's Basque Provinces," *West European Politics* 4 (Jan.): 85–103; José María Satrústegui, "La Hora de Navarra," in *Navarra desde Navarra*, ed. J. Bueno Asin et al. (San Sebastián: Ediciones Vascas, 1978), pp. 29–33; Javier Villán and Félix Población, *Culturas en lucha, Euskadi* (Madrid: Editorial Swan, 1980).

9. Illustrations from Herbert Pierrepont Houghton, *An Introduction to the Basque Language: Labourdin Dialect* (Leiden, Netherlands: E. J. Brill, 1961), p. 3.

10. Houghton, *An Introduction to the Basque Language*; Antonio Tovar, *The Basque Language* (Philadelphia: University of Pennsylvania Press, 1957); Antonio Tovar, *El Euskera y sus Parientes* (Madrid: Ediciones Minotauro, 1959).

11. *The Economist* (April 10, 1982): 72.

12. Clark, *The Basques*, p. 219; Clark, *The Basque Insurgents*, pp. 14–15, 200; Demetrio G. Vingileos, "Desarrollo de la industria de Guipúzcoa y ordenación de su territorio," *Información Comercial Española*, special issue, "La metalurgia del Norte," (February 1966): 106; *The Economist*, (April 10, 1982): 106; Milagros García Crespo, Roberto Velasco Barroetabeña, and Arantza Mendizabal Gorostiaga, *La Economía vasca durante el franquismo (Crecimiento y crisis de la economía vasca: 1936–1980)* (Bilbao: Editorial la Gran Enciclopedia Vasca, 1981), p. 152; Departamento de estudios y desarrollo regional de caja laboral popular, *Aproximación a la estructura industrial del País Vasco* (Bilbao: Editorial Vizcaina, 1976), p. 120.

13. Robert Graham, *Spain: Change of a Nation* (London: Michael Joseph, 1984), pp. 70–73.

14. *Business Week* (July 28, 1975): 33–34.

15. *The Economist* (April 10, 1982): 73.

16. *The New York Times* (July 19, 1980): 23.

17. Víctor Urrutia Abaigar, *El Movimiento Vecinal en el Area Metropolitana de Bilbao* (Bilbao: Instituto Vasco de Administración Pública, 1985), p. 137–38.

18. *The New York Times* (July 19, 1980): 23.

19. See, for example, the descriptions of urban life in La Asociación de Familias de Recaldeberri, *El Libro Negro de Recaldeberri* (Barcelona: Editorial Dirosa, 1975), pp. 13–15; Peru Erroteta, "Los que perdieron el sol," *La Calle*, no. 119(July 1–6, 1980): 41–43; Urrutia Abaigar, *El Movimiento Vecinal*.

20. For discussions of the emergence and characteristics of the "oligarquía vasca," see Clark, *The Basque Insurgents*, pp. 15–16; Letamendia, *Historia de Euskadi*; Jesús Arpal and Agustín Minondo, "El Bilbao de la industrialización: una ciudad para una elite," *Saioak*, Año 2, no. 2(1978): 31–68; Graham, *Spain*, pp. 70–73, 90–105.

21. Gerald Meaker, *The Revolutionary Left in Spain, 1914–1923* (Stanford: Stanford University Press, 1974), p. 371.

22. Josu Irigoien, "El desempleo en el País Vasco," *Revista de Fomento Social* 36 (1982): 319–27.

23. For alternative accounts of the origins of the coastal depression of the late 1970s, see Cyrus Ernesto Zirakzadeh, "The Political Thought of Basque Businessmen, 1976–1980," in *Basque Politics: A Case Study in Ethnic Nationalism*, ed. William A. Douglass (Millwood, N.Y.: Associated Faculty Press, 1985); M. C. Gallastegui and J. Urrutia, "La economía del País Vasco ante la crisis y la autonomía. Experiencia y perspectivas," *Información Comercial Española* 598 (June 1983): 33–47; *The Economist*, March 17, August 18, 1979.

24. For discussions and information about the petite bourgeoisie in the Basque region, see Emilio López Adán (political pseudonym, "Beltza"), *Nacionalismo vasco y clases sociales* (San Sebastián: Editorial Txertoa, 1976), pp. 45–56, 98; José Luis Lascurain Argarate, "Grandes Almacenes 'versus' Pequeño Comercio en Bilbao y San Sebastián" in *Información Comercial Española* (July–August 1972): 137–41; Francisco José Llera, "La estructura social del País Vasco," *Revista Internacional de Sociología* (October–December 1982): 589–93.

25. Departamento de estudios y desarrollo regional de caja laboral popular, *Aproximación a la estructura industrial del País Vasco*, p. 120.

26. *Punto y Hora* (October 1–15, 1976): 11; Lascurain Argarate, "Grandes Almacenes 'versus' Pequeño Comercio en Bilbao y San Sebastián."

27. For descriptions and histories of manufacturing in the Cantabrian Mountains, see Fernando García de Cortázar and Manuel Montero, *Histo-*

ria Contemporánea del País Vasco (San Sebastián: Editorial Txertoa, 1980), pp. 75–85, 93–95; Vingileos, "Desarrollo de la industria de Guipúzcoa"; López Adán, *Nacionalismo vasco y clases sociales*, pp. 45–66, 93–94; F. Luengo Teixidor, "La Sociedad Guipuzcoana de la Restauración. Algunas Claves para su Interpretación," in Segundo Congreso Mundial Vasco, *Cultura e Ideologias (Siglos XIX–XX)* (San Sebastián: Editorial Txertoa, 1988), pp. 135–43.

28. For descriptions and histories of the cooperative movement in the Basque region, see William Foote Whyte and Kathleen King Whyte, *Making Mondragon: The Growth and Dynamics of the Worker Cooperative Complex* (Ithaca: Industrial and Labor Relations Press, Cornell University, 1988); Keith Bradley and Alan Gelb, "Cooperative Labour Relations: Mondragon's Response to Recession," *British Journal of Industrial Relations* 25 (March 1987): 77–96; Daniel Talberna, "Alternative Organizations: The Cooperative Society Movement. The Basque Experience," *Journal of Basque Studies in America* 5 (1984): 65–77; Hank Thomas and Chris Logan, *Mondragon: An Economic Analysis* (London: Allen & Unwin, 1982); Ana Gutiérrez Johnson and William Foote Whyte, "The Mondragón System of Worker Production Cooperatives," in *Workplace Democracy and Social Change*, ed. Frank Lindenfeld and Joyce Rothschild-Whitt (Boston: Porter Sargent, 1982); Iñaki Gorroño, *Experiencia cooperativa en el País Vasco* (Durango: Leopoldo Zugaza, 1975); Luis C-Núñez Astrain, *Clases sociales en Euskadi* (San Sebastián: Editorial Txertoa, 1971); José María Arizmendi, "La contribución de las cooperatives industriales al desarrollo economico-social," *Información Comercial Española*, special issue, "La metalurgia del Norte" (February 1966): 129–33. For a somewhat critical view of the Basque cooperative experience, see Edward S. Greenberg, *Workplace Democracy: The Political Effects of Participation* (Ithaca: Cornell University Press, 1986).

29. Bradley and Gelb, "Cooperative Labour Relations," pp. 79, 84; Gorroño, *Experiencia cooperativa en el País Vasco*, p. 162.

30. Thomas and Logan, *Mondragon*, pp. 45, 102–3; C-Núñez Astrain, *Clases sociales en Euskadi*, p. 133; Bradley and Gelb, "Cooperative Labour Relations," p. 79.

31. Vingileos, "Desarrollo de la industria de Guipúzcoa," pp. 105–7.

32. Juan J. Linz, "The Party System of Spain: Past and Future," in *Party Systems and Voter Alignments: Cross-National Perspectives*, ed. Seymour M. Lipset and Stein Rokkan (New York: The Free Press, 1967), p. 220.

33. Luengo Teixidor, "La Sociedad Guipuzcoana de la Restauración," pp. 138, 140–41.

34. See chapter 3 on strikes in general. On labor unrest in the cooperatives, see Whyte and Whyte, *Making Mondragon*, chaps. 9–10; Greenberg, *Workplace Democracy*, pp. 103–4, 107–8.

35. On the support that Basque clergy, churches, and seminaries gave to diverse popular movements, see Luengo Teixidor, "La Sociedad Guipuzcoana de la Restauración"; V. Urrutia, "Socialización Política e Iglesia Vasca,"

in Alfonso Perez-Agote, *Sociología del Nacionalismo* (Vitoria: Universidad del País Vasco, 1989); Fernando García de Cortázar, "Iglesia Vasca, Religión y Nacionalismo en el Siglo XX," in *Congreso de Historia de Euskal Herria* (Vitoria: Publicaciones del Gobierno Vasco, 1988), vol. 4, pp. 193–217; Zulaika, *Basque Violence*.

36. García de Cortázar, "Iglesia Vasca, Religión y Nacionalismo en el Siglo XX," p. 213.

37. Zulaika, *Basque Violence*, p. 78.

38. For discussions of some political functions of the Basque cuadrillas, see Jesús Arpal, "Solidaridades elementales y organizaciones colectivas en el País Vasco (cuadrillas, txokos, asociaciones)," *Cuaderno de Formación de IPES* 3(1982): 51–60; Eugenia Ramírez Goicoechea, "Cuadrillas en el País Vasco: Identidad Local y Revitalización Etnica," *Revista Española de Investigaciones Sociológicas* 25(Jan.–March 1984):213–20.

39. "La Crisis de la Maquina Herramienta," *Berriak*, March 30, 1977; *Deia*, July 2, 18, 24, 1980.

40. Bradley and Gelb, "Cooperative Labour Relations," p. 88. For a discussion of how the cooperatives coped with this unexpected recession, see Whyte and Whyte, *Making Mondragon*, chaps. 12–15.

41. For some detailed descriptions of mountain farming, see William A. Douglass, *Echalar and Murelaga: Opportunity and Rural Exodus in Two Spanish Basque Villages* (New York: St. Martin's Press, 1975); Zulaika, *Basque Violence*.

42. Douglass, *Echalar and Murelaga*, p. 161.

43. Cortázar and Montero, *Historia Contemporánea del País Vasco*, p. 94; C-Núñez Astrain, *Clases sociales en Euskadi*, p. 58; *Anuario estadístico de España, 1980* (Madrid: Ministerio de Estadística).

44. José Andrés-Gallego, *Historia Contemporánea de Navarra* (Pamplona: Dario de Navarra, 1982), p. 202.

45. Mario Gabiria et al., *Navarra: Abundancia* (Donostia: Hordago, 1978), p. 26.

46. See chapter 2, "Agrarian Protest in the Cantabrian Mountains."

47. Andrés-Gallego, *Historia Contemporánea de Navarra*, p. 202. See also chapter 2, "Agrarian Capitalism and Popular Protest on the Southern Plains."

48. Vicente Huici Urmeneta et al., *Historia contemporánea de Navarra* (San Sebastián: Editorial Txertoa, 1982), p. 249.

49. García Crespo, Velasco Barroetabeña, and Mendizabal Gorostiaga, *La Economía vasca durante el franquismo*, p. 152; C-Núñez Astrain, *Clases sociales en Euskadi*, p. 58; Llera, "La estructura social del País Vasco," p. 583.

50. Anthony Giddens, *The Class Structure of Advanced Societies* (New York: Harper & Row, 1973), pp. 211–14.

51. See chapter 2, "Agrarian Capitalism and Popular Protest on the Southern Plains."

52. For discussions of some of these obstacles, see James C. Scott, *The*

Moral Economy of the Peasant: Rebellion and Subsistence in Southeast Asia (New Haven: Yale University Press, 1976); John Gaventa, *Power and Powerlessness: Quiescence and Rebellion in an Appalachian Valley* (Urbana: University of Illinois Press, 1980).

CHAPTER TWO

1. For useful reviews of this literature, see J. Craig Jenkins, "Resource Mobilization Theory and the Study of Social Movements," *Annual Review of Sociology* 9 (1983): 527–53; McAdam, *Political Process and the Development of Black Insurgency*, chaps. 1–3; Morris and Herring, "Theory and Research in Social Movements."

2. Morris, *The Origins of the Civil Rights Movement*, p. 20.

3. McAdam, *Political Process and the Development of Black Insurgency*; Morris, *The Origins of the Civil Rights Movement*.

4. Zulaika, *Basque Violence*, pp. 103–36; Patxo Unzueta, *Los Nietos de la IRA: Nacionalismo y violencia en el País Vasco* (Madrid: El País, 1988), pp. 173–85; Clark, *The Basque Insurgents*, chap. 8; Garmendia, *Historia de ETA*.

5. For information about commercial fishing in Spain and particularly in the Basque region, see José Ignacio Saterain, "Problemática específica de la región marítima vasca," *Información Comercial Española* 546(February 1979): 50–61; Joseba Zulaika, *Terranova: The Ethos and Luck of Deep-Sea Fishermen* (Philadelphia: Institute for the Study of Human Issues, 1981); López Adán, *Nacionalismo vasco y clases sociales*, 1976), p. 90; Thomas and Logan, *Mondragon*, pp. 31–32; "Nos quedamos sin pesca," *La Calle*, August 29, 1978; "La mar militarizada," *Berriak*, February 7, 1977; *The Economist*, March 10, 1979, p. 86; Sarah Keene Meltzoff and Edward LiPuma, "The Troubled Seas of Spanish Fishermen: Marine Policy and the Economy of Change," *American Ethnologist* 13 (November 1986): 681–99.

6. Zulaika, *Terranova*, pp. 29, 55, 57, 61, 105.

7. The first recorded major strike by Basque fishermen since the end of the Spanish civil war occurred in the port of Ondarroa and lasted for more than a month. *Punto y Hora*, nos. 20 and 24 (1976).

8. Zulaika, *Terranova*, pp. 7, 14, 29, 87, 107.

9. Zulaika, *Terranova*, pp. 12–16; "La mar militarizada," *Berriak*, February 7, 1977.

10. Salterain, "Problemática específica de la región marítima vasca," pp. 56–59; Thomas and Logan, *Mondragon*, p. 31.

11. Zulaika, *Terranova*, p. xi; Saterain, "Problemática específica de la región marítima vasca," pp. 56–59; "Nos quedamos sin pesca," *La Calle*, August 29, 1978.

12. "Nos quedamos sin pesca," *La Calle*, August 29, 1978, p. 6; *The Times*, August 22, 24, September 26, 1978; *The Economist*, March 10, 1979, March 17, 1984; *St. Louis Post Dispatch*, October 21, 1984.

13. For discussions about Cantabrian and coastal farm life, see Greenwood, *Unrewarding wealth*; Davydd J. Greenwood, "The Demise of Agriculture in Fuenterrabia," in *The Changing Faces of Rural Spain*, ed. Joseph B. Aceves and William A. Douglass (Cambridge: Schenkman, 1976); William A. Douglass, "Serving Girls and Sheepherders: Emigration and Continuity in a Spanish Basque Village," in *The Changing Faces of Rural Spain*, ed. Joseph B. Aceves and William A. Douglass (Cambridge: Schenkman, 1976); Douglass, "Rural Exodus in Two Spanish Basque Villages"; Douglass, *Echalar and Murelaga*; Zulaika, *Basque Violence*; Miguel Olza Zubiri, *Psicosociología de una población rural vasca* (Pamplona: Diputación Foral de Navarra, 1979); C-Núñez, *Clases sociales en Euskadi*, pp. 136–56; Laxalt and Allard, "Land of the Ancient Basques"; Joxerramon Rengoetxea, "Uztaetaburu: Social Anthropology in a Basque Rural Community," *Journal of Basque Studies* 6(1985): 4–7.

14. Greenwood, *Unrewarding wealth*, p. 17; Douglass, *Echalar and Murelaga*, pp. 139, 142; Zulaika, *Basque Violence*, p. 113.

15. C-Núñez Astrain, *Clases sociales en Euskadi*, p. 147.

16. Greenwood, *Unrewarding wealth*, p. 8.

17. Douglass, "Serving Girls and Sheepherders," pp. 47–48. See also Douglass, *Echalar and Murelaga*, pp. 85–135, 154–91.

18. Greenwood, *Unrewarding wealth*, pp. 2, 17; Douglass, "Serving Girls and Sheepherders," p. 52; Douglass, *Echalar and Murelaga*, pp. 180–91.

19. Greenwood, *Unrewarding wealth*.

20. Douglass, "Serving Girls and Sheepherders," p. 53; See also Douglass, *Echalar and Murelaga*, pp. 163–191. Greenwood, *Unrewarding wealth*, pp. 37, 71, 123.

21. Greenwood, *Unrewarding wealth*, pp. 112–113, 169, 201, 213.

22. Douglass, *Echalar and Murelaga*, pp. 132–33, 182–91.

23. Greenwood, *Unrewarding wealth*, pp. 68–69, 72, 77–78, 100–101, 169–70; Letamendia, *Historia de Euskadi*, p. 288; V. L. Alonso, J. Calzada, J. R. Herta, A. Langreo, and J. S. Vina, *Crisis agririas y luchas campesinas (1970–1976)* (Madrid: Editorial Ayuso, 1976), pp. 85–120.

24. Zulaika, *Basque Violence*, chaps. 3, 5.

25. Louis Wirth, "Urbanism as a Way of Life," *American Journal of Sociology* 44(July 1938): 1–24; Thomas Bender, *Community and Social Change in America* (Baltimore: Johns Hopkins University Press, 1982); Antonio García Tabuenca, Mario Gabiria, and Patxi Tuñón, *El Espacio de la fiesta y la subversión: Análisis socioeconómico del Casco Viejo de Pamplona* (Donostia: Hordago, 1979); Arpal, "Solidaridades elementales y organizaciones colectivas en el País Vasco"; Ramírez Goicoechea, "Cuadrillas en el País Vasco."

26. Zubiri, *Psicosociología de una población rural vasca*, pp. 138–39, 141–44, 150.

27. Douglass, *Echalar and Murelaga*, pp. 85, 176–77.

28. For sociopolitical histories of farming and the southern plains, see Huici Urmeneta et al., *Historia contemporánea de Navarra*; Andrés-Gallego, *Historia Contemporánea de Navarra*; J. Bueno Asin et al., *Navarra desde Navarra* (Bilbao: Editorial Vizcaina, 1978).

29. Huici Urmeneta et al., *Historia contemporánea de Navarra*, p. 243.

30. Andrés-Gallego, *Historia Contemporánea de Navarra*, p. 202; Ballester Ros, "La evolución de la población del País Vasco en el Periódo 1900–1981," p. 154.

31. Tony Judt, *Socialism in Provence 1871–1914: A study in the origins of the modern French Left* (Cambridge: Cambridge University Press, 1979); Seymour Martin Lipset, *Political Man: The Social Bases of Politics*, exp., updated ed. (Baltimore: Johns Hopkins University Press, 1981), pp. 104–5, 262–67.

32. Huici Urmeneta et al., *Historia contemporánea de Navarra*, pp. 227–28, 260–61; Paulo Iztueta Armendariz, *Sociología del fenomeno contestatario del clero vasco: 1940–1975* (San Sebastián: Eklar, 1981), pp. 168–69; Alonso, Calzada, Herta, Langreo, and Viñas, *Crisis agrarias y luchas campesinas*, pp. 55–120. For a discussion on the relatively low priority given to the desires of small farmers by the Franco regime, see Joseph B. Aceves, " 'Forgotten in Madrid': Notes on Rural Development Planning in Spain," in *The Changing Faces of Rural Spain*, ed. Joseph B. Aceves and William A. Douglass (Cambridge: Schenkman, 1976). In the same volume, in "Serving Girls and Sheepherders," Douglass writes,

> At the level of government planning, Spain is committed to a program of industrialization and tourism. The small portion of the national budget (a scant 0.5% between 1957 and 1962) which enters the agricultural sector of the economy as a subsidy is concentrated upon such modern reclamation projects as the Plan Badajoz [p. 48].

33. *¡Queremos vivir en la tierra! Primer Congreso de la Unión de Agricultores y Ganaderos de Rioja* (Donostia: Hordago, 1978), pp. 21, 54, 184, 185.

34. *Punto y Hora*, March 3–9, 1977, pp. 10–12.

35. For examples of the myth of the rural oligarchy, see Bueno Asin et al., *Navarra desde Navarra*; *¡Queremos vivir en la tierra! Primer Congreso de la Unión de Agricultores y Ganaderos de Rioja*. For analyses of the constitutional arrangements and social interests informing Navarrese politics, see Huici Urmeneta et al., *Historia contemporánea de Navarra*; Andrés-Gallego, *Historia Contemporánea de Navarra*; Mirentxu Purroy, "Navarra ya no es 'foral'," in *Navarra desde Navarra*, ed. Bueno Asin et al.; *ERE*, November 19–25, 1980;

Mario Onaindia, *La lucha de clases en Euskadi (1939–1980)* (Donostia: Hordago, 1979), pp. 189–98; Jaime Ignacio del Burgo, *Navarra en Navarra* (Pamplona: Gráficas Irujo, 1979).

36. Huici Urmeneta et al., *Historia Contemporánea de Navarra*, pp. 227, 235; Andrés-Gallego, *Historia Contemporánea de Navarra*, p. 201; Letamendia, *Historia de Euskadi*, pp. 290, 294, 374; Jon Amsden, *Collective Bargaining and Class Conflict in Spain* (London: London School of Economics and Political Science, 1972), chap. 5.

37. For discussions about the complex ideological and organizational evolution of Carlism during the twentieth century, see Martin Blinkhorn, "Carlism and the Spanish Crisis of the 1930s," *Journal of Contemporary History* 7(July–October 1972): 65–88; Martin Blinkhorn, " 'The Basque Ulster': Navarre and the Basque Autonomy Question under the Spanish Second Republic," *Historical Journal* 17(Sept. 1974): 595–613; Blinkhorn, "War on two fronts"; Colin M. Winston, "The Proletarian Carlist Road to Fascism: Sindicalismo Libre," *Journal of Contemporary History* 17(Oct. 1982): 557–85; Huici Urmeneta et al., *Historia Contemporánea de Navarra*, pp. 221, 236–37; Mari Cruz Mina, "Introducción a la historia contemporánea de Navarra," in *Navarra desde Navarra*, ed. Bueno Asin et al., pp. 135–39. On current Carlist ideas, see Alberto Pérez Calvo, *Los partidos politicos en el País Vasco* (San Sebastián: L. Haranburu, 1977), pp. 88–92; TALDE, *Euskadi, ante las elecciones municipales* (San Sebastián: Ediciones Vascas, 1979), pp. 160–68. For scattered information about the Carlists in the Basque region during the late 1970s, see Letamendia, *Historia de Euskadi*, pp. 374–76; Pérez Calvo, *Los partidos politicos*, pp. 88–92; José Ignacio Ruiz Olabuenaga and Víctor Urrutia, "Elecciones generales en Navarra," in *Navarra desde Navarra*, ed. Bueno Asin et al., p. 159; Robert Fishman, "The Labor Movement in Spain: From Authoritarianism to Democracy," *Comparative Politics* 14 (April 1982): 286.

38. C-Núñez Astrain, *Clases sociales en Euskadi*, p. 202.

39. Huici Urmeneta et al., *Historia Contemporánea de Navarra*, pp. 255–71.

40. Zulaika, *Basque Violence*, pp. 118, 121. See also Garmendia, *Historia de ETA*, vol. 2, p. 72.

41. Clark, *The Basque Insurgents*, pp. 155, 200–203.

42. Zulaika, *Basque Violence*, pp. 61–62; Sullivan, *ETA and Basque Nationalism*, chap. 4.

CHAPTER THREE

1. Letamendia, *Historia de Euskadi*, pp. 294–95.

2. For statistics on the distributions of different classes within the Bilbao metropolitan area, see Víctor Urrutia, "Estructura socio-económica del

Bilbao," in *Comun 2: Bilbao* (Bilbao: Instituto de Arte y Humanidades de la Fundación Faustino Orbegozon, 1979), pp. 10–14.

3. Interview in Bilbao, July 18, 1980.

4. For discussions about Bilbao's labor organizations and activism during the nineteenth century, see Letamendia, *Historia de Euskadi*, pp. 114–19; Emilio López Adán (political pseudonym, "Beltza"), *El nacionalismo vasco (de 1876 a 1936)* (Hendaye: Ediciones Mugalde, 1974), chap. 8; Dolores Ibárruri, *They Shall Not Pass: The Autobiography of La Pasionaria* (New York: International Publishers, 1976), chaps. 1–6.

5. Ibárruri, *They Shall Not Pass*, pp. 26–28.

6. Meaker, *The Revolutionary Left in Spain*, pp. 351–52.

7. For analyses and descriptions of the split between Basque Socialists and Communists, see Letamendia, *Historia de Euskadi*, pp. 156, 165–66; Ibárruri, *They Shall Not Pass*, chap. 9; López Adán, *El nacionalismo vasco*, pp. 161–65; Meaker, *The Revolutionary Left in Spain*, chap. 9; Antonio Elorza, "Movimiento obrero y cuestión nacional en Euskadi (1930–1936)," in *Estudios de Historia Contemporánea del País Vasco*, ed. Juan Carlos Jiménez de Aberasturi (San Sebastián: L. Haranburu, 1982), pp. 173, 177–78.

8. Ibárruri, *They Shall Not Pass*, p. 69; see also chap. 11 and p. 131.

9. Elorza, "Movimiento obrero y cuestión nacional," pp. 144–45, 180.

10. Meaker, *The Revolutionary Left in Spain*, pp. 13, 429, 352; Gerald Brenan, *The Spanish Labyrinth: An Account of the Social and Political Background of the Spanish Civil War* (Cambridge: Cambridge University Press, 1969), p. 219. See also Paul Preston, *The Coming of the Spanish Civil War: Reform, Reaction and Revolution in the Second Republic, 1931–1936* (New York: Harper & Row, 1978), p. 3.

11. For descriptions of Basque Socialist politics and Socialist ideology before the rise of Franco, see Meaker, *The Revolutionary Left in Spain*; Preston, *The Coming of the Spanish Civil War*; Letamendia, *Historia de Euskadi*; "UGT: 88 años de historia," *Berriak*, October 21, 1976.

12. Ibárruri describes this dispute from a pro-Communist perspective in *They Shall Not Pass*, chaps. 9, 11, 12, 15–16.

13. Ibid., pp. 93, 72; Meaker, *The Revolutionary Left in Spain*, pp. 428–31.

14. For historical analyses of the SOV and ELA-STV, see J. A. Sasgardoy Bengoechea and David León Blanco, *El poder sindical en España* (Barcelona: Editorial Planeta, 1982), pp. 190–98; Policarpo de Larrañaga, *Contribución a la historia obrera de Euskalerria* (San Sebastián: Editorial Aunamendi Argitaldaria, 1977), vol. 2; Juan Pablo Landa Zapirain, *Sindicalismo y crisis* (Bilbao: Universidad del País Vasco, 1983), pp. 176–206; López Adán, *El nacionalismo vasco; Berriak*, October 21, 1976.

15. For descriptions of the syndicate and its roles in representing labor within the policy-making process, see Charles W. Anderson, *The Political*

Economy of Modern Spain: Policy-Making in an Authoritarian Regime (Madison: University of Wisconsin Press, 1970), pp. 48–51, 60–64, 66–73, 95–96; Richard Gunther, *Public Policy in a No-Party State: Spanish Planning and Budgeting in the Twilight of the Franquist Era* (Berkeley: University of California Press, 1980), pp. 26–29, 33, 271–72, 312, 341; Joseph W. Foweraker, "The Role of Labor Organizations in the Transition to Democracy in Spain," in *Spain in the 1980s: The Democratic Transition and a New International Role*, ed. Robert P. Clark and Michael H. Haltzel (Cambridge, Mass.: Ballinger, 1987), pp. 97–122; Sheelagh Ellwood, "The Working Class under the Franco Régime," in *Spain in Crisis: The Evolution and Decline of the Franco Régime*, ed. Paul Preston (London: Harvester Press, 1976), pp. 159–62.

16. Anderson, *The Political Economy of Modern Spain*, p. 49. See also Foweraker, "The Role of Labor Organizations," pp. 100–101.

17. Sima Lieberman, *The Contemporary Spanish Economy: A Historical Perspective* (London: George Allen & Unwin, 1982), p. 49. See also Gunther, *Public Policy in a No-Party State*, pp. 273, 342; José Mari Garmendia, "El Moviemiento Obrero en el País Vasco bajo la Dictadura Franquista," in Segunda Congreso Mundial Vasco, *Cultura e Ideologias (Siglos XIX–XX)* (San Sebastián: Editorial Txertoa, 1988), pp. 86–88.

18. For descriptions of the 1947 strike, see Max Gallo, *Spain Under Franco: A History* (New York: E. P. Dutton, 1974), pp. 169, 176–77; Emilio López Adán (political pseudonym, "Beltza"), *El Nacionalismo Vasco en el Exilio, 1937–1960* (San Sebastián: Editorial Txertoa, 1977), pp. 35–43; Garmendia, "El Movimiento Obrero en el País Vasco," pp. 82–86.

19. Vingileos, "Desarrollo de la industria de Guipúzcoa," p. 107.

20. José Maria Aboitiz Saenz, "La industria química y de derivados del petroleo en la región vasco-navarra-riojana," *Información Comercial Española*, nos. 467–468 (July–August 1972): 182.

21. Clark, *The Basques*, p. 236.

22. Amando de Miguel, "Estructura social e inmigración en el País Vasco-navarro," *Papers: Revista de sociología*, no. 3 (1974): 262.

23. José Maravall, *Dictatorship and Political Dissent: Workers and Students in Franco's Spain* (London: Tavistock, 1978), chap. 2; López Adán, *El Nacionalismo Vasco en el Exilio*, pp. 84–91.

24. For discussions of the evolution of factory juries in Spain, see Amsden, *Collective Bargaining and Class Conflict in Spain*. See also Fishman, "The Labor Movement in Spain," pp. 282–83; Foweraker, "Role of Labor Organizations," pp. 102–7; Ellwood, "The Working Class under the Franco Régime," pp. 162–66. For references to the Basque region, see Pedro Ibarra Güell, "El Movimiento Obrero en el País Vasco durante el Franquismo, 1960–1977," Segundo Congreso Mundial Vasco, *Cultura e Ideologias (Siglos XIX–XX)* (San Sebastián: Editorial Txertoa, 1988), pp. 96–97, 194; Koldo San Sebastián,

"El Renacer del Movimiento Obrero Vasco y la Crisis de las Organizaciones Historicas," *Muga* 30(March 1984): 38.

25. Amsden, *Collective Bargaining and Class Conflict in Spain*, chap. 4.

26. *Berriak*, October 14, 1976, pp. 34–35; Landa Zapirain, *Sindicalismo y crisis*, pp. 155–60; Amsden, *Collective Bargaining and Class Conflict in Spain*, chap. 5; Carr and Fusi, *Spain: Dictatorship to Democracy*, pp. 143–44; López Adán, *El nacionalismo vasco en el exilio*, p. 55; Letamendia, *Historia de Euskadi*, p. 294.

27. C-Núñez Astrain, *Clases sociales en Euskadi*, p. 198; Maravall, *Dictatorship and Political Dissent*, pp. 29–41, 54–56.

28. Maravall, *Dictatorship and Political Dissent*, pp. 54, 36–39; Amsden, *Collective Bargaining and Class Conflict in Spain*, chaps. 5, 7; Carr and Fusi, *Spain*, p. 141.

29. For discussions of the assembly, see Amsden, *Collective Bargaining and Class Conflict in Spain*, chap. 5.

30. One Communist labor organizer from Madrid explained to me that his party scrupulously observed democratic procedures and norms in the assemblies because authoritarian and excessively partisan behavior would have angered the workers at the plant, discouraged attendance at the assemblies, and weakened the moral authority of all decisions made in the assemblies. Interviews held in Berkeley, California, in May 1981 and November 1982.

31. Amsden, *Collective Bargaining and Class Conflict in Spain*, chap. 5; Carr and Fusi, *Spain*, pp. 143–44; Letamendia, *Historia de Euskadi*, pp. 292–93, 354.

32. Amsden, *Collective Bargaining and Class Conflict in Spain*, pp. 116–17. In Pamplona several members of the Spanish Communist party told me that they believed that employers in coastal provinces are generally more willing to talk to delegations from factory assemblies than are employers in inland provinces. They speculated that the latter are often first-generation capitalists with no knowledge of past strikes. In contrast, employers on the coast, having lived in a long-established capitalist enclave with a history of almost a hundred years of labor violence and general strikes, have learned that interclass compromise is better than interclass war. Interviews on June 30 and July 1, 1980.

33. Amsden, *Collective Bargaining and Class Conflict in Spain*, chap. 3 and p. 83; Maravall, *Dictatorship and Political Dissent*, pp. 40–41.

34. Maravall, *Dictatorship and Political Dissent*, p. 33; Amsden, *Collective Bargaining and Class Conflict in Spain*, introduction and chaps. 4, 8; Carr and Fusi, *Spain*, pp. 145–46; Ellwood, "The Working Class under the Franco Régime," pp. 176–79.

35. Maravall, *Dictatorship and Political Dissent*, pp. 33–34; *Berriak*, October 14, 1976; Landa Zapirain, *Sindicalismo y crisis*, pp. 155–76. For informa-

tion about the Communist movement, see Iosu Perea, Fernando Etxebarría, and Iosu Aldama, *¿Por Qué Ocupamos el Parlamento Vasco?* (Madrid: Editorial Revolución, 1980); *Punto y Hora*, May 26–June 1, 1977, pp. 22–25; Ortzi, *Historia de Euskadi*, pp. 350–53, 364, 414–16; Ibarra, "El Movimiento Obrero en el País Vasco," p. 102.

36. For examples of, and information about, debates within the labor movements in the Basque region and in Spain in general, see Fishman, "The Labor Movement in Spain"; Foweraker, "The Role of Labor Organizations," pp. 108–18; Beate Kohler, *Political Forces in Spain, Greece, and Portugal* (London: Butterworth Scientific, 1982), pp. 55–59; "El sindicalismo de Euskadi contra el Estatuto CEOE-UGT," *ERE*, December 6–13, 1979; "Ley básica del empleo," *ERE*, April 17–24, 1980; *Libro blanco sobre el paro y economía en Euskadi* (Bilbao: Consejería de Trabajo del Consejo General Vasco, n.d.), pp. 133–63; Graham, *Spain: Change of a Nation*, pp. 116–31.

37. Llera, "La estructura social del País Vasco," p. 585; Gallastegui and Urrutia, "La economía del País Vasco ante la crisis y la autonomía," p. 36; *Berriak*, March 30, 1977, p. 18; *ERE*, July 16, 1980, p. 34; Clark, *The Basque Insurgents*, p. 19.

38. *Euskadi 1982* (Donostia: Egin, 1983), p. 169; *ERE*, May 5, 1980.

39. *Punto y Hora*, June 1–7, 1979, pp. 19–20. See also Robert Pastor, *Euskadi ante el futuro* (Bilbao: L. Haranburu, 1977), p. 52. For further information about ELA-STV(a), see its various publications (which sometimes include English translations); Landa Zapirain, *Syndicalismo y crisis*, p. 83; *Deia*, December 31, 1978, p. 22.

40. Pastor, *Euskadi ante el futuro*, p. 58. In the words of labor historian Juan Pablo Landa Zapirain, "The maximum autonomy among the organizations which compose the confederation was the 'leitmotif' of its organizational policy" (*Sindicalismo y crisis*, p. 184).

41. Pastor, *Euskadi ante el futuro*, p. 59.

42. For example, Bonifacio Rojo of Bilbao. See also "Navarra: De CC.OO. a U.G.T.," *Berriak*, October 7, 1986; Landa Zapirain, *Sindicalismo y crisis*, p. 137.

43. Landa Zapirain, *Sindicalismo y crisis*, pp. 138–43.

44. For descriptions of the U.G.T. congresses during the late 1970s, see ibid., pp. 139–55.

45. Landa Zapirain, *Sindicalismo y crisis*, pp. 152–53; *Askatasuna*, no. 6 (January 1980): 30–31; *Blanco y Negro*, March 19–25, 1980, pp. 18–20.

46. Landa Zapirain, *Sindicalismo y crisis*, pp. 144–45, 150–52.

47. Ibid., pp. 155–60.

48. Ibid., pp. 162–63, 168–69, 172–76.

49. *Punto y Hora*, November 1–8, 1979, p. 28.

50. Ibid., 1979, pp. 28–39; *Euzkadi*, May 28, 1980; *ERE*, September 5,

1980. Naturally, the presence of a few former Communists in the ELA-STV created new cleavages within this largely anti-Communist labor organization. For casual observations about the entry of individual Communists into the ELA-STV, see Landa Zapirain, *Sindicalismo y crisis*, pp. 191–92; *Euzkadi*, November 13, 1981.

51. Letamendia, *Historia de Euskadi*, p. 353.

52. Jáuregui Bereciartu, *Ideología y estrategia política de ETA*, pp. 169–83, 282–83; Garmendia, *Historia de ETA*, vol. 2, pp. 23–37, 75–88; Letamendia, *Historia de ETA*, pp. 353–63; Pedro Ibarra Güell, *El Movimiento Obrero en Vizcaya: 1967–1977* (Bilbao: Universidad del País Vasco, 1987), pp. 82–89; Ibarra Güell, "El Movimiento Obrero en el País Vasco," pp. 110–11; San Sebastián, "El Renacer del Movimiento Vasco," p. 41.

53. Pedro Ibarra Güell, "Movimiento obrero en Bizkaia, 1962 a 1977," *Cuaderno de Formación de IPES* 4(1983): 181–86.

54. Letamendia, *Historia de Euskadi*, p. 353; Ibarra Güell, "Movimiento obrero en Bizkaia, 1962 a 1977," pp. 185–87.

CHAPTER FOUR

1. Frente Obrero de ETA, "Acción Democrática en el Barrio," *Documentos Y* (Donostia: Hordago, 1979), vol. 5, pp. 94–101.

2. See, for example, ETA, *Documentos Y*, vol. 17, pp. 256–57, 408–10.

3. Interviews with Javier Markiegi of Euskadiko Ezkerra (July 22, 1980) and with two members of TALDE, a group of Basque sociologists and activists, in San Sebastián (July 30, 1980).

4. Juanjo de Andrés and José Antonio Maisuetxe, *El movimiento ciudadano en Euskadi* (San Sebastián: Editorial Txertoa, 1980), p. 52; Colectivo IPES, *Euskadi: Herri batzarrea-asamblea de pueblo-y política municipal* (Bilbao: Zero, 1978), pp. 146, 148; "Asociaciones de vecinos: Un cuerpo viva y en lucha," *Punto y Hora*, December 13–20, 1979.

5. De Andrés and Maisuetxe, *El movimiento ciudadano en Euskadi*, chap. 3; interviews with Bonifacio Rojo (July 22, 1980) and David Morín (July 24, 1980).

6. Llera, "La estructura social del País Vasco," p. 578; *Anuario Estadístico de España*, vols. for 1968, 1983 (Madrid, Instituto Nacional de Estadística); Alfonso Pérez-Agote, "Racionalidad urbana y relaciones sociales. El Gran Bilbao, 1945–1975," *Saioak* 3(1979):16.

7. Martin Wynn, "Spain," in *Housing in Europe*, ed. Martin Wynn (New York: St. Martin's Press, 1984), p. 125; Clark, *The Basques*, pp. 212–18, 227–31, 238–45; de Madriaga y Zobaran, *Clases sociales y aspiraciones vascas*, p. 43; *Berriak*, October 28, 1976.

8. Interviews with David Morín (July 24, 1980), Bonifacio Rojo (July 22, 1980), two anonymous members of the asociación de vecinos in the

Casco Viejo district of Bilbao (July 22 and 25, 1980), two anonymous former members of the Asociación de Familias de Recaldeberri (July 16, 1980), an anonymous member of the asociación de vecinos in the Casco Viejo district of Pamplona (June 28, 1980); Eugenio Ibarzabal, *Euskadi: Diálogos en torno a las elecciones* (Zarauz: Editorial Itxaropena, 1977), p. 134; de Andrés y Maisuetxe, *El movimiento ciudadano en Euskadi*, chap. 3; Juan Emilio Pujol, "En turno al movimiento ciudadano," *Askatasuna*, segunda época, no. 2, 1979: 20–26; Colectivo IPES, *Euskadi: Herri batzarrea—asamblea de pueblo— y política municipal*, pp. 138–50.

9. *La Calle*, May 1–7, 1979. See also *Punto y Hora*, July 16–31 and November 1–15, 1976; La Asociación de Familias de Recaldeberri, *El libro negro de Recaldeberri; Cuadernos para el Diálogo*, segunda época, no. 262, May 1–7, 1979; Jesús Omeñaca, *Movimiento ciudadano: crisis* (Bilbao: Gráficas Ellacuría, 1977), pp. 11–12, 76–77.

10. *Berriak*, October 7, November 4, 1976.

11. For information about this event, see La Asociación de Familias de Recaldeberri, *El libro negro de Recaldeberri*, pp. 9–10, 45–279; *La Vanguardia*, April 10, 15, 16, 1975; de Andrés and Maisuetxe, *El movimiento ciudadano en Euskadi*, pp. 35–37.

12. *Berriak*, January 5, 19, March 16, 1977; *Punto y Hora*, June 1–15, 1976.

13. "Mesa Redonda," in *Hauzolan*, May 1978; *Askatasuna*, n. 18, (October 1977); interview with Mikel "Tar" Orrantia (July 16, 1980).

14. Interviews with Ignacio Zabaleta (December 1982) and Bonifacio Rojo (July 22, 1980); *Punto y Hora*, July 16–31, 1976; *13 Preguntas a 150 vitorianos* (Vitoria: El Correo Español—El Pueblo Vasco, 1978), pp. 203–4; *Berriak*, April 30, 1977; *Punto y Hora*, January 17–24, 1980; *Combate*, July 16, 1980; *Egin*, July 17, 1980; *Deia*, July 18, 1980.

15. Interviews with Juan Goicolea and Ignacio Zabaleta (December 1978); Ibarzabal, *Euskadi: Diálogos en torno a las elecciones*, p. 131; *13 Preguntas a 150 vitorianos*, pp. 13, 69, 111, 147, 193, 203, 239; "Recaldeberri: La lucha une," *La Calle*, May 1–7, 1979. Every asociación with which I am familiar organized youth programs, and most of the asociaciones lobbied for additional schools. For discussions about the importance of education to urban middle classes, see Arno J. Mayer, "The Lower Middle Class as Historical Problem," *Journal of Modern History* 47 (September 1975): 430–31; Albert Soboul, *The Sans Culottes: The Popular Movement and Revolutionary Government, 1793–1794* (Garden City, N.Y.: Anchor Books, 1972), pp. 85–92.

16. La Asociación de Familias de Recaldeberri, *El libro negro de Recaldeberri*, p. 13.

17. From interviews with Juan Goicolea and Ignacio Zabaleta (December 1982).

18. Omeñaca, *Movimiento ciudadano*, p. 82.

19. *Berriak*, March 2, 1977.

20. I am greatly indebted to Juan Goicolea and Ignacio Zabaleta for describing in detail the legal and extralegal procedures for making decisions within the associations (interviews with Goicolea and Zabaleta, December 1982). Accounts of the decision-making processes within the associations also can be found in de Andrés and Maisuetxe, *El movimiento ciudadano en Euskadi*, chap. 4; Omeñaca, *Movimiento ciudadano*, pp. 87–95.

21. This general description is based on information from interviews with an anonymous member of the asociación de vecinos in the Casco Viejo district of Bilbao on July 22, 1980, an anonymous member of the asociación de vecinos in the Basurto district of Bilbao on July 23, 1980, an anonymous member of the asociación de vecinos in the Casco Viejo district of Pamplona on June 28, 1980, Ignacio Zabaleta of Pamplona in December 1980; and from comments about asambleas in *Askatasuna*, June 1979, and in *Berriak*, September 23, 1976.

22. Interviews with an anonymous member of the asociación de vecinos in the Casco Viejo district of Bilbao (July 22, 1980), an anonymous member of the asociación de vecinos in the Casco Viejo district of Pamplona (June 28, 1980), Ignacio Zabaleta (December 1982), David Morín (July 24, 1980), Bonifacio Rojo (July 22, 1980), two anonymous former members of the Asociación de Familias de Recaldeberri (July 16, 1980), and two members of the TALDE research team active in the neighborhood associations of San Sebastián (July 30, 1980).

23. *Deia*, July 25, 1979; *Berriak*, September 23, 30, December 29, 1976.

24. On the relationship between the associations and political parties see Omeñaca, *Movimiento ciudadano*, pp. 104–5; "Los partidos y las asociaciones," *Berriak*, April 13, 1977; *13 Preguntas a 150 vitorianos*, pp. 13–14, 68–70, 111–12, 147–48, 193–94, 239–40.

25. Ibid. (All sources in note 24.) Also, interviews with Javier Markiegi of Euskadiko Ezkerra (July 22, 1980) and with members of TALDE (July 30, 1980).

26. De Andrés and Maisuetxe, *El movimiento ciudadano en Euskadi*, pp. 36–37, 95–96; *Berriak*, November 11, 1976. For information about the Lemoniz controversy, see *El País*, April 5, 1981.

27. *Berriak*, October 7, 14, 1976.

28. Ibid., September 23, 1976; La Asociación de Familias de Recaldeberri, *El libro negro de Recaldeberri*; *Berriak*, October 14, 1976; *Punto y Hora*, July 16–31, 1976.

29. *Blanco y Negro*, July 12–18, 1978; La Comisión Investigadora de las Peñas de Mozos de Pamplona, *San Fermin 78: Así fue* (Pamplona: Gráficas Irujo, 1978); *The Times* (London), July 10, 11, 12, 14, 15, 1978.

30. La Asociación de Familias de Recaldeberri, *El libro negro de Recaldeberri*; *Berriak*, September 23, October 14, November 11, December 29, 1976;

Punto y Hora, July 16–31, 1976; "Las Asociaciones de Vecinos de la zona minera piden centros de salud," *Deia*, July 12, 1979; interviews with two members of the asociación de vecinos in the Casco Viejo district of Bilbao (July 22 and 25, 1980).

31. *Berriak*, March 30, 1977; *Punto y Hora*, October 15–31, 1976, November 10–16, 24–30, December 1–7, 1977, July 19–26, November 1–8, 1979; *Egin*, June 13, 1979; Colectivo IPES, *Euskadi: Herri batzarrea—asamblea de pueblo—y política municipal*, pp. 159–89. In Pamplona the relationship between the city hall and the associations was more complex and contradictory; the mayors and many of the council members refused to meet and discuss grievances with the delegations from local asociaciones. However, the relations between lower-level municipal administrators and the associations were close and cordial, involving many exchanges of aid and information. For information on the associations and the municipal government in Pamplona, see *Berriak*, December 1, 1976, March 30, 1977; *Punto y Hora*, March 27–April 10, 1980; interviews with Ignacio Zabaleta (December 1982).

32. La Asociación de Familias de Recaldeberri, *El libro negro de Recaldeberri*, pp. 9–10, 45–279; *La Vanguardia*, April 10, 15, 16, 1975; de Andrés and Maisuetxe, *El movimiento ciudadano en Euskadi*, pp. 35–37.

33. On the difficulties of measuring and generalizing about power in urban politics, see Matthew A. Crenson, *Neighborhood Politics* (Cambridge: Harvard University Press, 1983), pp. 280–82; Polsby, *Community Power and Political Theory*. For a discussion of the fluctuating power of nonelite groups, see McAdam, *Political Process and the Development of Black Insurgency*.

34. *Business Week*, July 28, 1975, pp. 32–34.

35. On the unavoidable difficulties in using police, government, and press accounts as sources of information about social movements and antigovernment protest, see Richard Cobb, *The Police and the People: French Popular Protest, 1789–1890* (Oxford: Oxford University Press, 1970), pt. 1; James C. Scott, "Resistance without Protest and without Organization: Peasant Opposition to the Islamic *Zakat* and the Christian Tithe," *Comparative Studies in Society and History* 29 (July 1987): 422; David Apter and Nagayo Sawa, *Against the State: Politics and Social Protest in Japan* (Cambridge: Harvard University Press, 1984), chap. 9; Lynn Hunt, "Charles Tilly's Collective Action," in *Vision and Method in Historical Sociology*, ed. Theda Skocpol (Cambridge: Cambridge University Press, 1984), pp. 256–57; Todd Gitlin, *The Whole World Is Watching: mass media in the making & unmaking of the new left* (Berkeley: University of California Press, 1980).

36. Urrutia Abaigar, *El Movimiento Vecinal en la Area Metropolitana de Bilbao*, p. 119.

37. Frente Obrero de ETA, "Acción Democrática en el Barrio," *Documentos Y*, vol. 5, pp. 94–101.

38. ETA, *Documentos Y*, vol. 17, pp. 256–57, 408–10.

39. Ibid., p. 408.

40. Urrutia Abaigar, *El Movimiento Vecinal en la Area Metropolitana de Bilbao*, pp. 210, 245.

41. Ibid., pp. 119, 133, 143, 156, 165, 245.

42. Ibid., pp. 186, 230–33.

43. ETA, *Documentos Y*, vol. 17, pp. 408–10.

44. Frente Obrero de ETA, "Acción Democrática en el Barrio," *Documentos Y*, vol. 5, p. 101.

CHAPTER FIVE

1. Fusi Aizpurua, *El país vasco. Pluralism y nacionalidad*; Payne, *Basque Nationalism*, pp. 239–42; Payne, "Regional Nationalism," pp. 87–88, 91; Payne, "Recent Research on Basque Nationalism," pp. 6–9, 12, 15; Linz, "Early state-building and late peripheral nationalisms against the state," pp. 78–83.

2. Jean-Claude Larronde, *El Nacionalismo Vasco: Su origen y su ideología en la obra de Sabino Arana-Goiri* (San Sebastián: Editorial Txertoa, 1977), pp. 279, 361.

3. Joseph Harrison, "Big Business and the Rise of Basque Nationalism," *European Studies Review* 7(October 1977): 378, 379.

4. Antonio Elorza, *Ideologias de Nacionalismo Vasco, 1876–1937* (San Sebastián: L. Haranburu, 1978), pp. 252–53.

5. The information used in this chapter comes primarily from the collection of Basque newspapers and newsmagazines that are available at the Basque Studies Program, University of Nevada, Reno, and also from publications by business organizations in the Basque region (also available at the Basque Studies Program). About 300 pages of political declarations by Basque business leaders were examined.

6. For examples of business leaders' endorsements, see *Deia*, June 17, October 19, 1977, December 16, 1978, July 5, 12, 1979; *Libro blanco sobre el paro y economía en Euskadi*, pp. 166–210; Departamento de Estudios y Estadística, Cámara Oficial de Comercio, Industria, y Navegación de Bilbao, *Avance económico de Vizcaya—1978* (Bilbao: Cámara Oficial de Comercio, Industria, y Navegación de Bilbao, n.d.), pp. 3–8. A good example of business leaders' changes in party affiliation is the steel magnate, Luís Olarra, who in 1977 was elected to the Spanish parliament but not as a member of the Basque Nationalist party, and who afterwards joined the party.

7. *Deia* (April 8, 1980): 27.

8. Ibid., August 1, 1980.

9. *La Calle* (June 20–26, 1978): 62.

10. *Deia*, July 18, 1980; Jesús Lobo Aleu, "Política industrial en la

Comunidad Autónoma del País Vasco," in *Información Comercial Española*, no. 598 (June 1983): 66.

11. *Deia*, August 1, 1980; Clark, *The Basque Insurgents*, p. 19.

12. *ERE* (March 18–24, 1981): 39.

13. *Deia*, August 6, 1977; Clark, *The Basque Insurgents*, p. 19.

14. *Deia*, October 16, 1977.

15. Ibid., July 11, 12, 1979.

16. Ibid., June 17, 1977.

17. *Avance económico de Vizcaya—1978*, pp. 3, 7.

18. *Libro blanco sobre el paro y economía en Euskadi*, pp. 199–201; Pastor, *Euskadi ante el futuro*, pp. 64–66.

19. *Libro blanco sobre el paro y economía en Euskadi*, p. 186.

20. *ERE* (October 29–November 4, 1980): 28.

21. Departamento de Estudios y Desarrollo Regional de Caja Laboral Popular, *Aproximación a la estructura industrial del País Vasco*, p. 15.

22. *Libro blanco sobre el paro y economía en Euskadi*, p. 169.

23. Clark, *The Basques*, p. 222.

24. Robert Pastor, *Autonomía, año cero* (Bilbao: Editorial Iparraguirre, 1980), p. 317.

25. Luis C-Núñez Astrain, *La sociedad vasca actual* (San Sebastián: Editorial Txertoa, 1977), p. 26.

26. For declarations about economic principles by the UCD's economic ministers and descriptions of their policies, see *Blanco y Negro* (October 4–10, 1978): 4–7; *Cambio 16*, August 19, December 30, 1979; preface to Luis Gámir, ed., *Política Económica de España* (Madrid: Alianza Editorial, 1980), pp. 9–25; *The Economist* (February 11, 1978): 90, (September 23, 1978): 100, (September 13, 1980): 53, 81–82.

27. *Quarterly Economic Review of Spain: 4th Quarter 1977*, p. 3.

28. *Blanco y Negro*, February 8–14, 1978; *The Economist* (February 11, 1978): 90; *Quarterly Economic Review of Spain: 2nd Quarter 1978*, p. 10.

29. *The Economist* (October 10, 1981): 83–84; Kohler, *Political Forces in Spain, Greece, and Portugal*, p. 59.

30. *The Economist* (October 10, 1981): 83–84.

31. *Deia*, September 28, 1977.

32. Ibid., July 11, 1979.

33. Ibid., July 11, 12, 21, 1979; *Cambio 16* (July 22, 1979): 39–41; *The Economist* (August 18, 1979): 64.

34. *Deia*, October 6, 1977.

CHAPTER SIX

1. Payne, *Basque Nationalism*, p. 61; Letamendia, *Historia de Euskadi*, p. 112.

2. Pérez-Agote, "Racionalidad urbana y relaciones sociales," *Saioak,* p. 17; Juan Pablo Fusi Aizpurua, "The Basque Question, 1931–1937," in *Revolution and War in Spain, 1931–1939,* ed. Paul Preston (London: Methuen, 1984), p. 187.

3. For journalistic and scholarly analyses of the Euskalerrian tradition, see Elorza, *Ideologías del País Vasco,* chap. 4; Larronde, *El Nacionalismo Vasco,* pt. 2; Ramón Zallo, "La crisis del PNV y los intereses de clase," *Egin,* January 19, 1980, p. 8; Harrison, "Big Business and the Rise of Basque Nationalism"; Sira García Casado and Jesús M. Abad Ruiz, "Evolución ideologica del Partido Nacionalista Vasco: 1913–1918," *Cuadernos de Alzate* 4(1986): 81–87.

4. Joseph Harrison, "Heavy Industry, the State, and Economic Development in the Basque Region, 1876–1936," *Economic History Review* 36(November): 535–51.

5. For information about Aranzadi, see Letamendia, *Historia de Euskadi,* pp. 153, 158, 164; Jáuregui Bereciartu, *Ideología y estrategia política de ETA,* pp. 36–37; García Casado and Abad Ruiz, "Evolución ideologica del Partido Nacionalista Vasco."

6. García Casado and Abad Ruiz, "Evolución ideologica del Partido Nacionalista Vasco," p. 86.

7. Ibid.

8. For information about Sarriá, see Letamendia, *Historia de Euskadi,* pp. 164–65; Larronde, *El Nacionalismo Vasco,* pp. 370–71; Elorza, *Ideologías del País Vasco,* pp. 244–55.

9. Elorza, *Ideologías del País Vasco,* p. 252.

10. Ibid., pp. 252–53.

11. Ibid., p. 247.

12. Ibid., pp. 251, 253.

13. Letamendia, *Historia de Euskadi,* p. 159. For information about Sota, see ibid., pp. 153, 158–64; Larronde, *El Nacionalismo Vasco,* pp. 266–69, 272–73, 278–80; Elorza, *Ideologías del País Vasco,* pp. 236–37, 241, 256.

14. Payne, *Basque Nationalism,* p. 78.

15. Quoted in Elorza, *Ideologías del País Vasco,* p. 235.

16. Ibid., p. 235.

17. Ibid., pp. 237–43; Harrison, "Big Business and the Rise of Basque Nationalism," pp. 379–83.

18. Javier Tusell Gómez, *Historia de la Democracia Cristiana en España, Tomo II: Los nacionalismos Vasco y Catalan. Los solitarios* (Madrid: Cuadernos para el Diálogo, 1974), pp. 14, 22, and chap. 1, passim.

19. For further historical information, see López Adán, *El Nacionalismo Vasco en el exilio,* pp. 7–84; Clark, *The Basques,* pp. 80–87, 111–16; Clark, *The Basque Insurgents,* pp. 20–24. For an illustration of their dreams (even in exile) concerning rapid economic development, see Jesús María de Leizaola,

Líneas generales de la formación de la economía vasca en la historia hasta hoy: Constantes y variables para la economía vasca (Caracas, Venezuela: publisher unknown, 1962).

20. Beitia, by the way, still denies that these charges are true. For a sample of journalists' views of Beitia, see *Punto y Hora*, May 3–10, and December 13–20, 1979; *ERE*, December 6–13, 1980; *Cambio 16*, December 23–29, 1979. My own understanding of Beitia is based in part on a two-hour interview with him in Bilbao on July 26, 1980.

21. For information about Egocheaga, Uriarte, and Imaz, see Pastor, *Autonomía, año cero*, pp. 323–27, 334–38, and 342–46; *ERE*, May 1, 1980; *Cambio 16*, June 22, 1980; Javier García Egocheaga, "Política industrial," *Boletín de estudios económicos* 37 (August 1982).

22. For information about Garaikoetxea, see Ibarzabal, *Euskadi: Diálogos en torno a las elecciones*, pp. 13–26; Pastor, *Autonomía, año cero*, pp. 286–307, and passim; Zallo, "La crisis del PNV y los intereses de clase"; *La Calle*, October 3–9, 1978; *Euzkadi*, September 25, 1981.

23. Gregorio Morán, *Testamento Vasco: Un ensayo de interpretación* (Madrid: Espasa Calpe, 1988), p. 33.

24. Pastor, *Autonomía, año cero*, pp. 293, 297.

25. Zallo, "La crisis del PNV y los intereses de clases." See also Larronde, *El Nacionalismo Vasco*, pp. 275–79, 363–71; Antonio Elorza, "La herencia sabiniana hasta 1936," *Cuaderno de Formación de IPES* 4(1983): 107–22.

26. For brief reviews of current interpretations of Arana's changing thought, see Jáuregui Bereciartu, *Ideología y estrategia política de ETA*, pp. 33–34; Larronde, *El Nacionalismo Vasco*, pp. 343–61.

27. For biographical information, see Larronde, *El Nacionalismo Vasco*; Letamendia, *Historia de Euskadi*, pp. 124–25, 130–41; Payne, *Basque Nationalism*, chap. 3; Clark, *The Basques*, pp. 40–47; Gorka Aulestia, "The Nationalism of Sabino de Arana y Goiri," *Journal of Basque Studies in America* 6 (1985): 3–25.

28. For a more complete and detailed set of speculations about how the psychological strains of growing up can condition a person's creation of a new political viewpoint, see Hanna Fenichel Pitkin, *Fortune Is a Woman: Gender and Politics in the Thought of Niccolò Machiavelli* (Berkeley: University of California Press, 1984); Erik H. Erikson, *Young Man Luther: A Study in Psychoanalysis and History* (New York: W. W. Norton & Company, 1958).

29. For discussions of some of the complexities of the language issue, see Payne, *Basque Nationalism*, pp. 68–69, 74–75; Clark, *The Basques*, chap. 6; Villán and Población, *Culturas en lucha, Euskadi*.

30. The following interpretation of Arana's political and social thought has been influenced by the analyses of several other intellectual and political historians, including Larronde, *El Nacionalismo Vasco*; Elorza, "La herencia

sabiniana hasta 1936"; Letamendia, *Historia de Euskadi*, pp. 124–25, 130–41; Payne, *Basque Nationalism*, chap. 3; Jáuregui Bereciartu, *Ideología y estrategia política de ETA*, chap. 1; Aulestia, "The Nationalism of Sabino de Arana y Goiri."

31. Larronde, *El Nacionalismo Vasco*, p. 86.

32. Ibid., p. 88.

33. Ibid., p. 94.

34. Ibid., p. 95.

35. Jáuregui Bereciartu, *Ideología y estrategia política de ETA*, p. 19.

36. Letamendia, *Historia de Euskadi*, p. 135; Payne, *Basque Nationalism*, p. 74.

37. Letamendia, *Historia de Euskadi*, p. 133.

38. Larronde, *El Nacionalismo Vasco*, p. 253.

39. Ibid.

40. Ibid., p. 258.

41. Jáuregui Bereciartu, *Ideología y estrategia política de ETA*, p. 25.

42. Payne, *Basque Nationalism*, p. 80.

43. For alternative interpretations of Arana's changing political thought, see note 23.

44. Letamendia, *Historia de Euskadi*, pp. 141, 152; Larronde, *El Nacionalismo Vasco*, pp. 323–24; José Luis Granja, "The Basque Nationalist Community during the Second Spanish Republic (1931–1936)," in *Basque Politics: A Case Study in Ethnic Nationalism*, ed. William A. Douglass (Millwood, N.Y.: Associated Faculty Press, 1985), pp. 164–65.

45. Clark, *The Basques*, p. 44.

46. Jáuregui Bereciartu, *Ideología y estrategia política de ETA*, p. 18.

47. Letamendia, *Historia de Euskadi*, p. 151.

48. Letamendia, *Historia de Euskadi*, pp. 151–52; Frederico Krutwig, *La Nueva Vasconia* (San Sebastián: Ediciones Vascas, 1979); José Luis Alvarez Emparanza (political pseudonym, "Txillardegi"), "Euskarari Bai," *Punto y Hora*, June 29–July 5, 1978, pp. 20–21; José María Sánchez Carrión, "Lengua y Pueblo," *Punto y Hora*, March 10–16, 17–23, 24–30, 1977; Granja, "The Basque Nationalist Community," pp. 166–68.

49. For information about Luis Arana, see "D. Luis Arana Goiri y el Partido Nacionalista Vasco," *Cuadernos de formación, Larrazabal* 1 (June 1980): 14–21; Letamendia, *Historia de Euskadi*, pp. 135–36, 153, 158, 161, 168–69, 185, 218, 227.

50. Letamendia, *Historia de Euskadi*, p. 153.

51. Zallo, "La crisis del PNV y los intereses de clase"; Pastor, *Autonomía, año cero*, pp. 143–57; *Deia*, December 22, 1979; *Cambio 16*, June 29, 1980; *Euskadi*, October 9, 1981.

52. For information about Gallastegui, see Antonio Elorza, "En el tercer aniversario de 'Gudari'," *Berriak*, March 2, 9, 1977; Jáuregui Bereciartu,

Ideología y estrategia política de ETA, chap. 1; Letamendia, *Historia de Euskadi*, pp. 166–71, 177, 188–89, 218.

53. Elorza, *Ideologías del País Vasco*, p. 235.

54. Elorza, "En el tercer aniversario de 'Gudari'," *Berriak*, March 9, 1977.

55. Letamendia, *Historia de Euskadi*, p. 169.

56. Elorza, "En el tercer aniversario de 'Gudari'," *Berriak*, March 9, 1977.

57. Ibid.

58. Ibid.

59. Elorza, "En el tercer aniversario de 'Gudari'," *Berriak*, March 2, 9, 1977; Elorza, "La herencia sabiniana hasta 1931," p. 119.

60. James C. Scott, *Weapons of the Weak: Everyday Forms of Peasant Resistance* (New Haven: Yale University Press, 1985), p. 178.

61. For historical analyses of the relationship between the euskalerríacos and the Aranaists immediately after Franco's death, see Pastor, *Autonomía, año cero*, pp. 143–57; *Cambio 16*, December 23–29, 1979, June 6, 1980; Zallo, "La crisis del PNV y los intereses de clase"; Colectivo IRRINTZI, "La otra cara del PNV," *Punto y Hora*, May 3–10, May 10–17, May 18–25, May 25–June 1, 1979; *ERE*, December 29–January 6, 1980.

62. Thus far, there has been no systematic scholarly research on the batzokis. The present portrait is based on my personal visits to three batzokis in Bilbao and Bermeo during the summer of 1980; on informal discussions with about a half dozen Nationalists about the batzokis; and on two journalistic accounts: "El batzoki, primer centro político de Euzkadi," *Euzkadi*, January 8, 1982, p. 19; "Bares y bibliotecas," *Euzkadi*, September 4, 1980, p. 9.

63. *Euzkadi*, no. 32, June, 1977.

64. *Euzkadi*, January 8, 1982, p. 19.

65. Pastor, *Autonomía, año cero*, pp. 145, 150.

66. Zallo, "La crisis del PNV y los intereses de clase"; *Cambio 16*, December 23, 1979, June 29, 1980; *ERE*, December 6–13, 1979, December 29–January 6, 1980; *Euzkadi*, September 25, October 9, 1981; interview with Xabier Arzallus in San Sebastián on August 2, 1980.

67. *Cambio 16*, June 29, 1980; *Euzkadi*, September 25, October 9, 1981; Pastor, *Autonomía, año cero*, p. 151; *Punto y Hora*, July 28, 1980; *ERE*, May 1, 1980.

68. *ERE*, December 6–13, 1980; *Cambio 16*, April 20, 1980; Pastor, *Autonomía, año cero*, pp. 154–57; *Deia*, July 31, 1980.

69. For journalists' analyses of the political composition of the cabinet of the Basque regional government, see *Punto y Hora*, May 1–7, 1980; *ERE*, April 17–24, May 1, 1980; *Cambio 16*, June 22, 1980; Pastor, *Autonomía, año cero*, chap. 2.

70. Pastor, *Autonomía, año cero*, pp. 316–19.

71. *ERE*, May 1, 1980, pp. 6–8.

72. For journalists' reports on the early economic policies of the Basque regional government, see *ERE* and *Euzkadi*, 1980–1981.

73. During my stay in the Basque region in 1980, several Nationalists told me in private conversations that they feared that certain leaders in the party, such as Garaikoetxea and Marcos Vizcaya, were dangerously "socialistic." For journalists' accounts of the emerging conflict between the regionalist and provincialist members of the party, see *ERE*, March 13, June 3–9, 1981.

74. Justo de la Cueva, *La Escisión del PNV: EA, HB, ETA y la deslegitimación del Estado español en Euskadi Sur* (Bilbao: Txalaparta Argitaldaria, 1988), p. 194.

75. *El País (Edición Internacional)*, April 8, 1984.

76. Ibid., May 14, 1984. For a somewhat different view of the relationship between Garaikoetxea and the Spanish Socialist party, see de la Cueva, *La Escisión del PNV*. De la Cueva perceives the Garaikoetxea government as engaged in far fewer efforts at cooperation with the Socialist government in Madrid than I do, partly because he self-consciously and creatively uses a "world-system" theoretical framework to interpret Basque party politics. The subject of the origins and characteristics of the split within the Basque Nationalist party (and of the role of the Spanish Socialist party) is clearly complex, and further rival interpretations are bound to develop in the near future. For a recent elaboration of world-system theory, see Giovanni Arrighi, Terence K. Hopkins, and Immanuel Wallerstein, *Antisystemic Movements* (London: Verso, 1989). For an interesting and insightful critique of world-system theorizing from a Marxist perspective, see Maurice Zeitlin, *The Civil Wars in Chile (or the bourgeois revolutions that never were)* (Princeton: Princeton University Press, 1984).

77. For discussions of these intraparty battles, see Morán, *Testamento Vasco*; Yolanda Muñoz Castro, "La Crisis del PNV: Historia de una Escisión," *Cuadernos de Alzate* 6(April–September 1987): 31–46.

78. Ibid., October 8, 1984; *Cambio 16*, September 1, 1984.

79. *El País (Edición Internacional)*, October 15, 1984.

80. For discussions about the founding and programs of Basque Solidarity, see Morán, *Testamento Vasco*, pp. 23–47; Muñoz Castro, "La Crisis del PNV"; de la Cueva, *La Escisión del PNV*, chap. 9.

81. Morán, *Testamento Vasco*, p. 27.

82. Among works in English, the writings of Stanley Payne probably best illustrate this tendency. In Spanish, the essays of Ludolfo Paramio come immediately to mind. See, for example, Ludolfo Paramio, "La crisis del nacionalismo y el futuro de la nación," *Cuadernos de Alzate* 4(1986):39–43.

CHAPTER SEVEN

1. The account draws upon several primary and secondary sources, including Angel Amigo, *Pertur: ETA 71–76* (Donostia: Hordago, 1978); Clark, *The Basque Insurgents*; Jáuregui Bereciartu, *Ideología y estrategia política de ETA*; Garmendia, *Historia de ETA*; Letamendia, *Historia de Euskadi*; Sullivan, *ETA and Basque Nationalism*; José Luis Unzueta, "La Vª Asamblea de ETA," *Saioak* 4, no. 4 (1980): 3–52; Unzueta, *Los Nietos de la IRA*. Additional sources are listed below.

2. Representatives of the Basque Nationalist party sometimes contend that the party initiated the extensive 1951 strike wave, but scholars are dubious. See Jáuregui Bereciartu, *Ideología y estrategia política de ETA*, p. 58.

3. Unzueta, *Los Nietos de la IRA*, p. 95.

4. José Luis Alvarez Emparanza (political pseudonym, "Txillardegi"), "Testimonios personales de la crisis teórico política que motive mi salida de ETA," *Cuaderno de Formación de IPES*, 1(1980):37.

5. For descriptions of the intergenerational conflict within the Basque Nationalist party, see Letamendia, *Historia de Euskadi*, pp. 279–80, 297–98; Jáuregui Bereciartu, *Ideología y estrategia política de ETA*, pp. 75–83; López Adán, *El Nacionalismo Vasco en Exilio*, pp. 91–104.

6. For a summary of the formal organization of the ETA, see Clark, *The Basque Insurgents*, chaps. 2, 9. For a variety of anecdotes about the disorganization within the ETA, see Amigo, *Pertur*.

7. ETA, *Documentos Y* (San Sebastián: Hordago, 1979), vol. 1, p. 532.

8. Ibid.

9. Ibid., p. 533.

10. Jáuregui Bereciartu, *Ideología y estrategia política de ETA*, p. 146; ETA, *Documentos Y*, vol. 1, p. 533.

11. ETA, *Documentos Y*, vol. 1, p. 533.

12. Ibid., pp. 532–33.

13. Unzueta, *Los Nietos de la IRA*, p. 96.

14. Garmendia, *Historia de ETA*, vol. 1, p. 48.

15. Ibid., pp. 25, 298.

16. Ibid., p. 65.

17. Ibid., pp. 29, 64–65, 79–85.

18. Ibid., p. 52.

19. Ibid., p. 50.

20. Ibid., p. 47.

21. Ibid., p. 31.

22. Ibid., p. 87.

23. Sullivan, *ETA and Basque Nationalism*, pp. 34–35; Txillardegi, "Testimonios Personales," p. 40.

24. Garmendia, *Historia de ETA*, vol. 1, p. 89.

25. Jáuregui Bereciartu, *Ideología y estrategia política de ETA*, p. 172; Unzueta, *Los Nietos de la IRA*, p. 106.

26. Letamendia, *Historia de Euskadi*, p. 307.

27. Garmendia, *Historia de ETA*, vol. 2, p. 25.

28. Garmendia, *Historia de ETA*, vol. 1, p. 185; Jáuregui Bereciartu, *Ideología y estrategia política de ETA*, pp. 282–83.

29. Patxi Iturrioz, "ETA en el año 1966. Divergencias internas que lleva a la aparición de ETA-berri. Algunas aportaciones teórico-políticas a la causa revolucionaria vasca," *Cuaderno de Formación de IPES* 1(1980):4.

30. Several observers have stressed the influence of European New Left writings on the thinking of this set of etarras. Letamendia, *Historia de Euskadi*, pp. 314–15; Unzueta, "La Vª Asamblea de ETA," p. 6; Unzueta, *Los Nietos de la IRA*, pp. 106–7. For examples of European New Left thought, see Ernest Mandel, "The Lessons of May 1968," *New Left Review*, no. 52 (November–December 1968): 9–31; André Gorz, *Socialism and Revolution* (Garden City: Anchor, 1973); André Gorz, *Strategy for Labor* (Boston: Beacon Press, 1967).

31. Unzueta, *Los Nietos de la IRA*, pp. 65, 106; Letamendia, *Historia de Euskadi*, pp. 309–10.

32. Clark, *The Basque Insurgents*, p. 153. This etarra apparently was not unique; for similar stories, see Garmendia, *Historia de ETA*, vol. 2, pp. 81–82; Unzueta, *Los Nietos de la IRA*, p. 65.

33. For discussions of *Vasconia* and its influence on ETA, see Letamendia, *Historia de Euskadi*, pp. 301–6; Jáuregui Bereciartu, *Ideología y estrategia política de ETA*, pp. 203–25.

34. The pamphlet's recurrent emphasis on dispassionate, calculated violence is remarkable. For example, on page 14 it is stated as a general rule that "euphoria precedes disaster"; and on page 6 the author maintains that "we reject all forms of adventurism and stupid heroics." ETA, "La insurrección en Euskadi," *Documentos Y*, vol. 3, pp. 2–47.

35. Letamendia, *Historia de Euskadi*, p. 300.

36. Jáuregui Bereciartu, *Ideología y estrategia política de ETA*, p. 173.

37. Ibid., pp. 282–83.

38. Frente Obrero, "Catecismo de la Acción Sindical" and "La Acción en la Empresa," *Documentos Y*, vol. 5, pp. 86–93.

39. Frente Obrero, "Acción en el barrio," *Documentos Y*, vol. 5, pp. 94–101.

40. Iturrioz, "ETA en el año 1966," p. 7.

41. Jáuregui Bereciartu, *Ideología y estrategia política de ETA*, pp. 177, 178, 179.

42. See ETA, *Zutik 42* and *Zutik 43*, in *Documentos Y*, vol. 5, pp. 34–61.

43. Ibid., pp. 59–60.

44. Garmendia, *Historia de ETA*, vol. 1, pp. 196–97; Iturrioz, "ETA en el año 1966," p. 7.

45. Garmendia, *Historia de ETA*, vol. 1, p. 195.

46. Jáuregui Bereciartu, *Ideología y estrategia política de ETA*, p. 317.

47. See, for example, ETA, *Zutik 42* and *Zutik 43*, in *Documentos Y*, vol. 5, pp. 34–61; Unzueta, *Los Nietos de la IRA*, pp. 106–16.

48. Garmendia, *Historia de ETA*, vol. 1, p. 195.

49. Sullivan, *ETA and Basque Nationalism*, pp. 47–48.

50. Unzueta, *Los Nietos de la IRA*, p. 114.

51. Ibid.

52. Iturrioz, "ETA en el año 1966," p. 3; Garmendia, *Historia de ETA*, vol. 1, pp. 194–95.

53. ETA, *Documentos Y*, vol. 5, pp. 49, 51; Jáuregui Bereciartu, *Ideología y estrategia política de ETA*, pp. 314–15.

54. Jáuregui Bereciartu, *Ideología y estrategia política de ETA*, p. 356.

55. Ibid., p. 301.

56. Garmendia, *Historia de ETA*, vol. 1, pp. 206–7.

57. Unzueta, *Los Nietos de la IRA*, p. 121.

58. Jáuregui Bereciartu, *Ideología y estrategia política de ETA*, pp. 348, 357.

59. Ibid., pp. 330, 348.

60. For a sympathetic presentation of Etxebarrieta's ideas, see Unzueta, *Los Nietos de la IRA*, pp. 147–71.

61. Ibid., p. 154.

62. On the ambiguities inherent in the idea of "PTV" see Sullivan, *ETA and Basque Nationalism*, pp. 55–56, 61, 75, 77, 79.

63. Iturrioz, "ETA en el año 1966," p. 7.

64. On the *Branka* group, see Unzueta, *Los Nietos de la IRA*, 117–36; Ortzi, *Historia de Euskadi*, pp. 317–19, 360; Jáuregui Bereciartu, *Ideología y estrategia política de ETA*, pp. 359–410.

65. Letamendia, *Historia de Euskadi*, p. 353.

66. Unzueta, *Los Nietos de la IRA*, p. 104.

67. On the Red Cells, see Garmendia, *Historia de ETA*, vol. 2, pp. 87–98; Sullivan, *ETA and Basque Nationalism*, pp. 80–87, 116–17.

68. On the politics of the Workers' Front of the late 1960s, see Ibarra Güell, *El Movimiento Obrero en Vizcaya*, pp. 82–89; Sullivan, *ETA and Basque Nationalism*, pp. 66–67, 69; Garmendia, *Historia de ETA*, vol. 2, pp. 23–37, 61–63.

69. Sullivan, *ETA and Basque Nationalism*, p. 67; Garmendia, *Historia de ETA*, vol. 2, p. 25.

70. Ibarra Güell, *El Movimiento Obrero en Vizcaya*, pp. 83–84.

71. Ibid., p. 86.

72. Ibid., pp. 84–85.

73. Ibid., p. 88.

74. For discussions and interpretations of this document, see Garmendia, *Historia de ETA*, vol. 2, pp. 60–69; Sullivan, *ETA and Basque Nationalism*, pp. 78–80, 85–86; Letamendia, *Historia de Euskadi*, pp. 358–59.

75. For discussions of the VI Assembly and its legacy, see José María Iriarte (political pseudonym, "Bikila"), "La crisis ideológica en 1970. El Proceso de Burgos. Aportaciones del Marxismo revolucionario ante el problema nacional," *Cuaderno de Formación de IPES* 1(1980): 24–30, 54–56; Sullivan, *ETA and Basque Nationalism*, pp. 54–55, 61–88.

76. Bikila, "La crisis ideológica en 1970," p. 24.

CHAPTER EIGHT

1. *The New York Times*, August 24, 1986.

2. An obvious exception is the work of John Sullivan, *ETA and Basque Nationalism*.

3. The following account draws upon several primary and secondary sources, including Clark, *The Basque Insurgents*; Ibarra Güell, *La Evolución Estratégica de ETA*; Sullivan, *ETA and Basque Nationalism*; Unzueta, *Los Nietos de la IRA*. Additional sources of information and interpretation are listed below.

· 4. For insightful descriptions of the noncalculating aspects of ETA, especially among members from the countryside, see Zulaika, *Basque Violence*; Unzueta, *Los Nietos de la IRA*.

5. Most histories of ETA discuss the Burgos trial. For convenient summaries in English, see Clark, *The Basques*, pp. 181–87; Sullivan, *ETA and Basque Nationalism*, chap. 4. For a novelist's interpretation of the trial, see Margaret Shedd, *A Silence in Bilbao* (Garden City: Doubleday & Company, 1974).

6. Clark, *The Basque Insurgents*, p. 51.

7. C-Núñez Astrain, *Clases sociales en Euskadi*, pp. 206–9.

8. Garmendia, *Historia de ETA*, vol. 2, pp. 114–16.

9. Ibid., p. 117.

10. Clark, *The Basque Insurgents*, p. 60.

11. Unzueta, *Los Nietos de la IRA*, pp. 183, 173–85.

12. Ibarra Güell, *La Evolución Estratégica de ETA*, p. 81.

13. Sullivan, *ETA and Basque Nationalism*, p. 134.

14. Clark, *The Basque Insurgents*, p. 68.

15. Ibarra Güell, *La Evolución Estratégica de ETA*, pp. 95–97.

16. For descriptions of the various revolutionary themes and theories within ETA-VI, see Sullivan, *ETA and Basque Nationalism*, pp. 113–27; Clark,

The Basque Insurgents, pp. 57–61; Garmendia, *Historia de ETA*, vol. 2, pp. 119–40; Letamendia, *Historia de Euskadi*, pp. 386–89.

17. For a sympathetic exposition of the central tenets of, and tensions within, Etxebarrita's position, see Unzueta, *Los Nietos de la IRA*, pp. 161–72.

18. Clark discusses ETA's use of the Tupamaros movement as a model for imitation in *The Basque Insurgents*, pp. 62–63, 65, 80. See also Letamendia, *Historia de Euskadi*, pp. 381–82.

19. Pertur was an unusually influential figure in the ETA movement. For information on his life, political activities, and political thought, see Amigo, *Pertur*.

20. Clark, *The Basque Insurgents*, p. 78; Garmendia, *Historia de ETA*, vol. 2, pp. 173–79.

21. Clark, *The Basque Insurgents*, pp. 219–22.

22. ETA-pm, "El Movimiento Cooperativista," *Documentos Y* (San Sebastián: Hordago, 1981), vol. 17, pp. 461–66.

23. Sullivan, *ETA and Basque Nationalism*, p. 169.

24. See, for example, Clark, *The Basque Insurgents*, pp. 77–78, 93.

25. For summaries of EIA's evolving ideology, see J. Garaialde (political pseudonym, "Erreka"), "VII Asamblea y el nacimiento de EIA. Una estrategia para el socialismo en Euskadi," *Cuaderno de Formación de IPES* 1(1980): 31–36; Alberto Ortega, "Informe sobre Euskadi," *Mientras Tanto* 3(1980): 51–76; Sullivan, *ETA and Basque Nationalism*, pp. 190–206, 240. In addition, see the *Aransa* series of booklets published by EIA in the late 1970s.

26. See, for example, the descriptions of workers in Bilbao being "in control of the city's industrial complex" and of Bilbao being "an armed camp" in *The Washington Post*, March 6, 9, 14, 1976; *The Los Angeles Times*, March 9, 1976.

27. Clark, *The Basque Insurgents*, p. 97.

28. See note 22 for sources on EIA's early emphasis on popular mobilizing. For illustrations of the political orientation of ORT and MCE, see the interviews in *Punto y Hora*, April 14–20, 1977, pp. 14–15; May 26–June 1, 1977, pp. 22–25.

29. For information on ESB, see *ESB: Un programa socialista para la autonomía de Euskadi* (Bilbao: Gráficas Ellacuría, 1977); *Punto y Hora*, May 19–25, 1977, pp. 22–25; July 6–12, 1978, pp. 43–44; Pastor, *Euskadi ante el futuro*, pp. 123–34. For data on the ESB's electoral performance before becoming part of the Herri Batasuna, see Clark, *The Basques*, pp. 333–36.

30. On dissent within EIA, see Ortega, "Informe sobre Euskadi"; Sullivan, *ETA and Basque Nationalism*, pp. 105–6, 216–17, 227.

31. Clark, *The Basque Insurgents*, p. 133.

32. Payne, "Terrorism and Democratic Stability in Spain," pp. 167, 169.

33. Clark, *The Basque Insurgents*, p. 93.

34. Clark, *The Basque Insurgents*, p. 106; Ibarra Güell, *La Evolución Estratégica de ETA*, pp. 107, 116–22.

35. For an expanded discussion of the impact of selected state repression on ETA's strategic options, see Ibarra Güell, *La Evolución Estratégica de ETA*, pp. 78–79, 132–33, 149–55; Ibarra Güell, *El Movimiento Obrero en Vizcaya*, pp. 85–88.

36. On the origins of Herri Batasuna, see Ortega, "Informe sobre Euskadi"; Ibarra Güell, *La Evolución Estratégica de ETA*, pp. 111–30.

37. For illustrations of the Herri Batasuna's statements that post-Franco reforms are "fascistic" and nondemocratic, see Ibarra Güell, *La Evolución Estratégica de ETA*, p. 127.

38. On Herri Batasuna's early "assemblyist" or "counter-power" strategy, see Ibarra Güell, *La Evolución Estratégica de ETA*, pp. 167–73; Ortega, "Informe sobre Euskadi"; "Los Origenes de la Alternativa KAS," *Askatasuna* 1(June 1979): 24–30.

39. See, for example, the magazine *Askatasuna*, which was published by the Askatasuna group in Bilbao during the late 1970s, in which the group regularly criticized parliamentary politics and urged the Herri Batasuna coalition to desist from all electoral politics.

40. *Deia*, February 18, 1981.

41. Unzueta, *Los Nietos de la IRA*, pp. 196–97. This, by the way, was not the first time a major advocate of armed action within ETA changed views concerning the usefulness of violence. The well-known case of José María Escubi comes immediately to mind. See Sullivan, *ETA and Basque Nationalism*, p. 74.

42. *The New York Times*, August 24, 1986.

CONCLUSION

1. *The New York Times*, August 24, 1986; Garmendia, *Historia de ETA*, vol. 2, p. 53.

SELECTED BIBLIOGRAPHY

NEWSPAPERS, NEWSMAGAZINES, AND
POLITICAL PERIODICALS

Askatasuna, Bilbao, monthly and bimonthly
Berriak, San Sebastián, weekly
Blanco y Negro, Madrid, weekly
Business Week, New York, weekly
La Calle, Madrid, weekly
Cambio 16, Madrid, weekly
Christian Science Monitor, Boston, daily
Combate, Madrid, weekly
Cuadernos para el Diálogo, Madrid, monthly
Deia, Bilbao, daily
The Economist, London, weekly
Egin, San Sebastián, daily
ERE, San Sebastián, weekly
Euskadi, Bilbao, weekly
Euskadi (Egin), San Sebastián, annual
Euzkadi, Bilbao, weekly
Hauzolan, Bilbao, bimonthly
The Los Angeles Times, Los Angeles, daily
Muga, Bilbao, monthly
The New York Times, New York, daily
El País, Madrid, daily
El País (International Edition), Madrid, weekly
Punto y Hora, San Sebastián, weekly

Quarterly Economic Review of Spain, London
Saioak, San Sebastián, quarterly
St. Louis Post Dispatch, St. Louis, daily
The Times, London, daily
La Vanguardia, Barcelona, daily
Washington Post, Washington, D.C., daily

BOOKS AND ARTICLES

Aboitiz Saenz, José Maria. 1972. "La industria quimica y de derivados del petroleo en la región vasco-navarra-riojana." *Información Comercial Española* 467–468 (July–August): 181–86.

Aceves, Joseph B. 1976. " 'Forgotten in Madrid': Notes on Rural Development Planning in Spain." In *The Changing Faces of Rural Spain*, ed. Joseph B. Aceves and William A. Douglass. Cambridge: Schenkman.

Alonso, V. L., J. Calzada, J. R. Herta, A. Langreo, and J. S. Vina. 1976. *Crisis agririas y luchas campesinas (1970–1976)*. Madrid: Editorial Ayuso.

Alvarez Emparanza, José Luis (political pseudonym, "Txillardegi"). 1978. "Euskarari Bai." *Punto y Hora* June 29–July 5: 20–21.

Alvarez Emparanza, José Luis (political pseudonym, "Txillardegi"). 1980. "Testimonios personales de la crisis teórico política que motive mi salida de ETA." *Cuaderno de Formación de IPES* 1:37–44.

Amigo, Angel. 1978. *Pertur: ETA 71–76*. Donostia: Hordago.

Amsden, Jon. 1972. *Collective Bargaining and Class Conflict in Spain*. London: London School of Economics and Political Science.

Anderson, Charles W. 1970. *The Political Economy of Modern Spain: Policy-Making in an Authoritarian Regime*. Madison: University of Wisconsin Press.

De Andrés, Juanjo, and José Antonio Maisuetxe. 1980. *El movimiento ciudadano en Euskadi*. San Sebastián: Editorial Txertoa.

Andrés-Gallego, José. 1982. *Historia Contemporánea de Navarra*. Pamplona: Dario de Navarra.

Anonymous. 1978. *¡Queremos vivir en la tierra! Primer Congreso de la Union de Agricultores y Ganaderos de Rioja*. Donostia: Hordago.

Anonymous. 1978. *13 Preguntas a 150 vitorianos*. Vitoria: El Correo Española—El Pueblo Vasco.

Anonymous. 1980. "D. Luis Arana Goiri y el Partido Nacionalista Vasco." *Cuadernos de formación, Larrazabal* 1 (June): 14–21.

Anonymous. N.d. *Libro blanco sobre el paro y economía en Euskadi*. Bilbao: Consejería de Trabajo del Consejo General Vasco.

Anuario estadístico de España, 1980. Madrid: Ministerio de Estadística.

Apter, David, and Nagayo Sawa. 1984. *Against the State: Politics and Social Protest in Japan*. Cambridge: Harvard University Press.

Arendt, Hannah. 1951. *The Origins of Totalitarianism*. New York: World Publishing Company.

Arizmendi, José María. 1966. "La contribución de las cooperativas industriales al desarrollo economico-social." *Información Comercial Española*, special issue, "La metalurgia del Norte," 390 (February): 129–33.

Arpal, Jesús (1982) "Solidaridades elementales y organizaciones colectivas en el País Vasco (cuadrillas, txokos, asociaciones)." *Cuaderno de Formación de IPES* 3:51–60.

Arpal, Jesús, and Agustín Minondo. 1978 "El Bilbao de la industrialización: una ciudad para una elite." *Saioak* 2(2): 31–68.

Arrighi, Giovanni, Terence K. Hopkins, and Immanuel Wallerstein. 1988. *Antisystemic Movements*. London: Verso.

Asociación de Familias de Recaldeberri. 1975. *El Libro Negro de Recaldeberri*. Barcelona: Editorial Dirosa.

Aulestia, Gorka. 1985. "The Nationalism of Sabino de Arana y Goiri." *Journal of Basque Studies in America* 6:3–25.

Ballester Ros, Ignacio. 1983. "La Evolución de la Población del País Vasco en el Periódo 1900–1981." *Revista de Estudios de Vida Local* 42(January–March): 143–58.

Bender, Thomas. 1982. *Community and Social Change in America*. Baltimore: Johns Hopkins University Press.

Bengoetxea, Joxerramon. 1985. "Uztaetaburu: Social Anthropology in a Basque Rural Community." *Journal of Basque Studies* 6(1): 4–7.

Blinkhorn, Martin. 1972. "Carlism and the Spanish Crisis of the 1930s." *Journal of Contemporary History* 7(3 & 4): 65–88.

Blinkhorn, Martin. 1974. " 'The Basque Ulster': Navarre and the Basque Autonomy Question under the Spanish Second Republic." *Historical Journal* 17(3): 595–613.

Blinkhorn, Martin. 1984. "War on two fronts: politics and society in Navarre 1931–6." In *Revolution and War in Spain, 1931–1939*, ed. Paul Preston. London: Methuen.

Bogdanor, Vernon. 1982. "Ethnic Nationalism in Western Europe." *Political Studies* 30(2): 284–91.

Bradley, Keith, and Alan Gelb. 1987. "Cooperative Labour Relations: Mondragon's Response to Recession." *British Journal of Industrial Relations* 25(1): 77–96.

Brenan, Gerald. 1969. *The Spanish Labyrinth: An Account of the Social and Political Background of the Spanish Civil War*. Cambridge: Cambridge University Press.

Bueno Asin, J., et al. 1978. *Navarra desde Navarra*. Bilbao: Editorial Vizcaina.

Del Burgo, Jaime Ignacio. 1979. *Navarra en Navarra.* Pamplona: Gráficas Irujo.

Carr, Raymond, and Juan Pablo Fusi Aizpurua. 1981. *Spain: Dictatorship to Democracy,* 2d ed. London: Allen & Unwin.

Clark, Robert P. 1979. *The Basques: The Franco Years and Beyond.* Reno: University of Nevada Press.

Clark, Robert P. 1980. "Euzkadi: Basque Nationalism in Spain since the Civil War." In *Nations without a State: Ethnic Minorities in Western Europe,* ed. Charles R. Foster. New York: Praeger.

Clark, Robert P. 1981. "Language and Politics in Spain's Basque Provinces." *West European Politics* 4(1): 85–103.

Clark, Robert P. 1984. *The Basque Insurgents: ETA, 1952–1980.* Madison: University of Wisconsin Press.

Clark, Robert P. 1990. *Negotiating with Euzkadi ta Askatasuna (ETA): Obstacles to Peace in the Basque Country.* Reno: University of Nevada Press.

C-Núñez Astrain, Luis. 1971. *Clases sociales en Euskadi.* San Sebastián: Editorial Txertoa.

C-Núñez Astrain, Luis. 1977. *La sociedad vasca actual.* San Sebastián: Editorial Txertoa.

Cobb, Richard. 1970. *The Police and the People: French Popular Protest, 1789–1890.* Oxford: Oxford University Press.

Colectivo IPES. 1978. *Euskadi: Herri batzarrea—asamblea de pueblo—y política municipal.* Bilbao: Zero.

Colectivo IRRINTZI. 1979. "La otra cara del PNV." *Punto y Hora* May 3–10, May 10–17, May 18–25, May 25–June 1.

La Comisión Investigadora de las Peñas de Mozos de Pamplona. 1978. *San Fermin 78: Así fue.* Pamplona: Gráficas Irujo.

Connor, Walker. 1984. "Eco- or etho-nationalism?" *Ethnic and Racial Studies* 7(3): 342–59.

Crenson, Matthew A. 1983. *Neighborhood Politics.* Cambridge: Harvard University Press.

Cruz Mina, Mari. 1978. "Introducion a la historia contemporánea de Navarra." In *Navarra desde Navarra,* ed. J. Bueno Asin et al. Bilbao: Editorial Vizcaina.

De la Cueva, Justo. 1988. *La Escisión del PNV: EA, HB, ETA y la deslegitimación del Estado español en Euskadi Sur.* Bilbao: Txalaparta Argitaldaria.

Dahl, Robert A. 1956. *A Preface to Democratic Theory.* Chicago: University of Chicago Press.

Dahl, Robert A. 1961. *Who Governs?* New Haven: Yale University Press.

Departamento de Estudios y Desarrollo Regional de Caja Laboral Popular. 1976. *Aproximación a la estructura industrial del País Vasco.* Bilbao: Editorial Vizcaina.

Departamento de Estudios y Estadística, Cámara Oficial de Comercio, Industria, y Navegación de Bilbao. 1978. *Avance económico de Vizcaya—1978.* Bilbao: Cámara Oficial de Comercio, Industria, y Navegación de Bilbao.

Douglass, William A. 1971. "Rural Exodus in Two Spanish Villages: A Cultural Explanation." *American Anthropologist* 73(5): 1100–14.

Douglass, William A. 1975. *Echalar and Murelaga: Opportunity and Rural Exodus in Two Spanish Basque Villages.* New York: St. Martin's Press.

Douglass, William A. 1976. "Serving Girls and Sheepherders: Emigration and Continuity in a Spanish Basque Village." In *The Changing Faces of Rural Spain,* ed. Joseph B. Aceves and William A. Douglass. Cambridge: Schenkman.

EIA ("Euskao Iraultzale Alderdia"). Late 1970s. *Aransa.*

Ellwood, Sheelagh. 1976. "The Working Class under the Franco Régime." In *Spain in Crisis: The Evolution and Decline of the Franco Régime,* ed. Paul Preston. London: Harvester Press.

Elorza, Antonio. 1977. "En el tercer aniversario de 'Gudari'." *Berriak* March 2 and 9, 1977.

Elorza, Antonio. 1978. *Ideologias de Nacionalismo Vasco, 1876–1937.* San Sebastián: L. Haranburu.

Elorza, Antonio. 1982. "Movimiento obrero y cuestión nacional en Euskadi (1930–1936)." In *Estudios de Historia Contemporánea del País Vasco,* ed. Juan Carlos Jiménez de Aberasturi. San Sebastián: L. Haranburu.

Elorza, Antonio. 1983. "La herencia sabiniana hasta 1936." *Cuaderno de Formación de IPES* 4(1983): 107–22.

Emilio Pujol, Juan. 1979. "En turno al movimiento ciudadano." *Askatasuna* 2: 20–26.

Erikson, Erik H. 1958. *Young Man Luther: A Study in Psychoanalysis and History.* New York: W. W. Norton & Company.

Erroteta, Peru. 1980. "Los que perdieron el sol." *La Calle* 119(July): 41–43.

ESB ("Euskadi Sozialista Biltzarrea"). 1977. *ESB: Un programa socialista para la autonomía de Euskadi.* Bilbao: Gráficas Ellacuría.

ETA ("Euzkadi ta Askatasuna"). 1979–81. *Documentos Y,* 18 vols. San Sebastián: Hordago.

Fishman, Robert. 1982. "The Labor Movement in Spain: From Authoritarianism to Democracy." *Comparative Politics* 14(3): 281–305.

Foweraker, Joseph W. 1987. "The Role of Labor Organizations in the Transition to Democracy in Spain." In *Spain in the 1980s: The Democratic Transition and a New International Role,* ed. Robert P. Clark and Michael H. Haltzel. Cambridge: Ballinger.

Fusi Aizpurua, Juan Pablo. 1984. "The Basque Question, 1931–1937." In *Revolution and War in Spain, 1931–1939,* ed. Paul Preston. London: Methuen.

Fusi Aizpurua, Juan Pablo. 1984. *El País Vasco: Pluralismo y nacionalidad*. Madrid: Alianza Editorial.

Gabiria, Mario, et al. 1978. *Navarra: Abundancia*. Donostia: Hordago.

Gallastegui, M. C., and J. Urrutia. 1983. "La economía del País Vasco ante la crisis y la autonomía. Experiencia y perspectivas." *Información Comercial Española* 598 (June): 33–47.

Gallo, Max. 1974. *Spain Under Franco: A History*. New York: E. P. Dutton.

Gámir, Luis, ed. 1980. *Política Económica de España*. Madrid: Alianza Editorial.

Garaialde, J. (political pseudonym, "Erreka"). 1980. "VII Asamblea y el nacimiento de E.I.A. Una estrategia para el socialismo en Euskadi." *Cuaderno de Formación de IPES* 1(1980): 31–36.

García Casado, Sira, and Jesús M. Abad Ruiz. 1986. "Evolución ideológica del Partido Nacionalista Vasco: 1913–1918." *Cuadernos de Alzate* 4: 81–87.

García Crespo, Milagros, Roberto Velasco Barroetabeña, and Arantza Mendizabal Gorostiaga. 1981. *La Economía vasca durante el franquismo (Crecimiento y crisis de la economía vasca: 1936–1980)*. Bilbao: Editorial la Gran-Enciclopedia Vasca.

García de Cortazar, Fernando. 1988. "Iglesia Vasca, Religión y Nacionalismo en el Siglo XX." In *Congreso de Historia de Euskal Herria*, vol. 4. Vitoria: Publicaciones del Gobierno Vasco.

García de Cortázar, Fernando, and Manuel Montero. 1980. *Historia Contemporánea del País Vasco*. San Sebastián: Editorial Txertoa.

García Egocheaga, Javier. 1982. "Política industrial." *Boletín de estudios económicos* 37(August).

García Tabuenca, Antonio, Mario Gabiria, and Patxi Tuñón. 1979. *El Espacio de la fiesta y la subversión: Análisis socioeconómico del Casco Viejo de Pamplona*. Donostia: Hordago.

Garmendia, José Mari. 1980. *Historia de ETA*, 2 vols. San Sebastián: L. Haranburu.

Garmendia, José Mari. 1986. "El Movimiento Obrero en el País Vasco bajo la Dictadura Franquista." In *Cultura e Ideologias (Siglos XIX–XX)*, ed. Segunda Congreso Mundial Vasco. San Sebastián: Editorial Txertoa.

Gaventa, John. 1980. *Power and Powerlessness: Quiescence and Rebellion in an Appalachian Valley*. Urbana: University of Illinois Press.

Gendzier, Irene L. 1985. *Managing Political Change: Social Scientists and the Third World*. Boulder: Westview Press.

Giddens, Anthony. 1973. *The Class Structure of Advanced Societies*. New York: Harper & Row.

Gitlin, Todd. 1980. *The Whole World Is Watching: mass media in the making & unmaking of the new left*. Berkeley: University of California Press.

Goodwyn, Lawrence. 1978. *The Populist Moment: A Short History of the Agrarian Revolt in America*. Oxford: Oxford University Press.

Gorroño, Iñaka. 1975. *Experiencia cooperativa en el País Vasco.* Durango: Leopoldo Zugaza.

Gorz, André. 1967. *Strategy for Labor.* Boston: Beacon Press.

Gorz, André. 1973. *Socialism and Revolution.* Garden City: Anchor.

Graham, Robert. 1984. *Spain: Change of a Nation.* London: Michael Joseph.

Granja, José Luis. 1985. "The Basque Nationalist Community during the Second Spanish Republic (1931–1936)." In *Basque Politics: A Case Study in Ethnic Nationalism,* ed. William A. Douglass. Millwood: Associated Faculty Press.

Greenberg, Edward S. 1986. *Workplace Democracy: The Political Effects of Participation.* Ithaca: Cornell University Press.

Greenwood, Davydd J. 1976. *Unrewarding wealth: The commercialization and collapse of agriculture in a Spanish Basque town.* Cambridge: Cambridge University Press.

Greenwood, Davydd J. 1976. "The Demise of Agriculture in Fuenterrabia." In *The Changing Faces of Rural Spain,* ed. Joseph B. Aceves and William A. Douglass. Cambridge: Schenkman.

Gunther, Richard. 1980. *Public Policy in a No-Party State: Spanish Planning and Budgeting in the Twilight of the Franquist Era.* Berkeley: University of California Press.

Gutiérrez Johnson, Ana, and William Foote Whyte. 1982. "The Mondragón System of Worker Production Cooperatives." In *Workplace Democracy and Social Change,* ed. Frank Lindenfeld and Joyce Rothschild-Whitt. Boston: Porter Sargent.

Halebsky, Sandor. 1976. *Mass Society and Political Conflict: Towards a Reconstruction of Theory.* Cambridge: Cambridge University Press.

Harrison, Joseph. 1977. "Big Business and the Rise of Basque Nationalism." *European Studies Review* 7(4): 371–91.

Harrison, Joseph. 1983. "Heavy Industry, the State, and Economic Development in the Basque Region, 1876–1936." *Economic History Review* 36(4): 535–51.

Hobsbawm, E. J. 1962. *The Age of Revolution, 1789–1848.* New York: World Publishing Company.

Hobsbawm, E. J. 1975. *The Age of Capital, 1848–1875.* New York: Charles Scribner's Sons.

Houghton, Herbert Pierrepont. 1961. *An Introduction to the Basque Language: Labourdin Dialect.* Leiden: E. J. Brill.

Huici Urmeneta, Vicente, et al. 1982. *Historia contemporánea de Navarra.* San Sebastián: Editorial Txertoa.

Hunt, Lynn. 1984. "Charles Tilly's Collective Action." In *Vision and Method in Historical Sociology,* ed. Theda Skocpol. Cambridge: Cambridge University Press.

Ibarra Güell, Pedro. 1983. "Movimiento obrero en Bizcaya, 1962 a 1977." *Cuaderno de Formación de IPSE* 4: 181–88.

Ibarra Güell, Pedro. 1987. *El Movimiento Obrero en Vizcaya: 1967–1977*. Bilbao: Universidad del País Vasco.

Ibarra Güell, Pedro. 1987. *La Evolución Estratégica de ETA (1963–1987)*. Donostia: Kriselu.

Ibarra Güell, Pedro. 1988. "El Movimiento Obrero en el País Vasco durante el Franquismo, 1960–1977." In *Cultura e Ideologias (Siglos XIX–XX)*, ed. Segundo Congreso Mundial Vasco. San Sebastián: Editorial Txertoa.

Ibárruri, Dolores. 1976. *They Shall Not Pass: The Autobiography of La Pasionaria*. New York: International Publishers.

Ibarzabal, Eugenio. 1977. *Euskadi: Diálogos en torno a las elecciones*. Zarauz: Editorial Itxaropena.

Iriarte, José María (political pseudonym, "Bikila"). "La crisis ideológica en 1980. El Proceso de Burgos. Aportaciones del Marxismo revolucionario ante el problema nacional." *Cuaderno de Formación de IPES* 1: 24–30, 54–56.

Irigoien, Josu. 1982. "El desempleo en el País Vasco." *Revista de Fomento Social* 36: 319–27.

Iturrioz, Patxi. 1980. "ETA en el año 1966. Divergencias internas que lleva a la aparición de ETA-berri. Algunas aportaciones teórico-políticas a la causa revolucionaria vasca." *Cuaderno de Formación de IPES* 1: 3–9.

Iztueta Armendariz, Paulo. 1981. *Sociología del fenomeno contestatario del clero vasco: 1940–1975*. San Sebastián: Eklar.

Jáuregui Bereciartu, Gurutz. 1981. *Ideología y estrategia política de ETA: Análisis de su evolución entre 1959 y 1968*. Madrid: Siglo Veintiuno.

Jenkins, J. Craig. 1981. "Sociopolitical Movements." In *Handbook of Political Behavior*, vol. 4, ed. Samuel L. Long. New York: Plenum Press.

Jenkins, J. Craig. 1983. "Resource Mobilization Theory and the Study of Social Movements." *Annual Review of Sociology* 9:527–53.

Judt, Tony. 1979. *Socialism in Provence 1871–1914: A study in the origins of the modern French Left*. Cambridge: Cambridge University Press.

Kenworthy, Eldon. 1973. "The Function of the Little-Known Case in Theory Formation or What Peronism Wasn't." *Comparative Politics* 6(1): 17–45.

Kohler, Beate. 1982. *Political Forces in Spain, Greece, and Portugal*. London: Butterworth Scientific.

Krutwig, Frederico. 1979. *La Nueva Vasconia*. San Sebastián: Ediciones Vascas.

Kuhn, Thomas S. 1970. *The Structure of Scientific Revolutions*, second edition, enlarged. Chicago: University of Chicago Press.

Landa Zapirain, Juan Pablo. 1983. *Sindicalismo y crisis*. Bilbao: Universidad del País Vasco.

Laqueur, Walter. 1987. *The Age of Terrorism*. Boston: Little, Brown and Company.

De Larrañaga, Policarpo. 1977. *Contribución a la historia obrera de Euskalerria,* 2 vols. San Sebastián: Editorial Aunamendi Argitaldaria.

Larronde, Jean-Claude. 1977. *El Nacionalismo Vasco: Su origen y su ideología en la obra de Sabino Arana-Goiri.* San Sebastián: Editorial Txertoa.

Lascurain Argarate, José Luis. 1972. "Grandes Almacenes 'versus' Pequeño Comercio en Bilbao y San Sebastián." *Información Comercial Española* 467–468(July–August): 137–41.

Laxalt, Robert, and William Albert Allard. 1968. "The Land of the Ancient Basques." *National Geographic* 134(2): 240–77.

De Leizaloa, Jesús María. 1962. *Líneas generales de la formación de la economía vasca en la historia hasta hoy: Constantes y variables para la economía vasca.* Caracas: publisher unknown.

Letamendia, Francisco (political pseudonym, "Ortzi"). 1977. *Historia de Euskadi: El nacionalismo vasco y ETA.* Barcelona: Ruedo Ibérico.

Lieberman, Sima. 1982. *The Contemporary Spanish Economy: A Historical Perspective.* London: George Allen & Unwin.

Linz, Juan J. 1967. "The Party System of Spain: Past and Future." In *Party Systems and Voter Alignments: Cross-National Perspectives,* ed. Seymour M. Lipset and Stein Rokkan. New York: The Free Press.

Linz, Juan J. 1973. "Early state-building and late peripheral nationalisms against the state: The case of Spain." In *Building States and Nations: Models, Analyses, and Data across Three Worlds,* ed. S. N. Eisenstadt and Stein Rokkan. Beverly Hills: Sage.

Linz, Juan J. 1979. "Europe's Southern Frontier: Evolving Trends Toward What?" *Daedalus* 108(1): 175–209.

Linz, Juan J. 1980. "The Basques in Spain: Nationalism and Political Conflict in a New Democracy." In *Resolving Nationality Conflicts: The Role of Public Opinion Research,* ed. W. Phillips Davison and Leo Gordenker. New York: Praeger.

Linz, Juan J. 1985. "From Primordialism to Nationalism." In *New Nationalisms of the Developed West: Toward Explanation,* ed. Edward A. Tiryakian and Ronald Rogowski. Boston: Allen & Unwin.

Linz, Juan J., Manuel Reino Gómez, A. Francisco, and Darío Vila. 1986. *Conflicto en Euskadi, Estudio sociológico sobre el cambio político en el País Vasco, 1975–1989.* Madrid: Espasa Calpe.

Lipset, Seymour Martin. 1981. *Political Man: The Social Bases of Politics,* exp., updated ed. Baltimore: Johns Hopkins University Press.

Llera, Francisco José. 1982. "La estructura social del País Vasco." *Revista Internacional de Sociología* 44(October–December): 577–93.

Lobo Aleu, Jesús. 1983. "Política industrial en la Comunidad Autónoma del País Vasco." *Información Comercial Española,* no. 598(June): 48–72.

López Adán, Emilio (political pseudonym, "Beltza"). 1974. *El nacionalismo vasco (de 1876 a 1936).* Hendaye: Ediciones Mugalde.

López Adán, Emilio (political pseudonym, "Beltza"). 1976. *Nacionalismo vasco y clases sociales*. San Sebastián: Editorial Txertoa.

López Adán, Emilio (political pseudonym, "Beltza"). 1977. *El Nacionalismo Vasco en el Exilio, 1937–1960*. San Sebastián: Editorial Txertoa.

Lowi, Theodore. 1969. *The End of Liberalism*. New York: W. W. Norton.

Luengo Teixidor, F. 1988. "La Sociedad Guipuzcoana de la Restauración. Algunas Claves para su Interpretación." In *Cultura e Ideologias (Siglos XIX–XX)*, ed. Segundo Congreso Mundial Vasco. San Sebastián: Editorial Txertoa.

De Madriaga y Zobaran, Antonio. 1979. *Clases sociales y aspiraciones vascas*. Bilbao: La cámara oficial de comercio, industria, y navegación.

Maier, Charles S. 1975. *Recasting Bourgeois Europe: Stabilization in France, Germany, and Italy in the Decade after World War I*. Princeton: Princeton University Press.

Mandel, Ernest. 1968. "The Lessons of May 1968." *New Left Review* 52(November–December): 9–31.

Maravall, José. 1978. *Dictatorship and Political Dissent: Workers and Students in Franco's Spain*. London: Tavistock.

Mayer, Arno J. 1975. "The Lower Middle Class as Historical Problem." *Journal of Modern History* 47(4): 409–36.

McAdam, Doug. 1982. *Political Process and the Development of Black Insurgency, 1930–1970*. Chicago: University of Chicago Press.

Meaker, Gerald. 1974. *The Revolutionary Left in Spain, 1914–1923*. Stanford: Stanford University Press.

Medhurst, Ken. 1982. "Basques and Basque Nationalism." In *National Separatism*, ed. Colin H. Williams. Cardiff: University of Wales Press.

Meltzoff, Sarah Keene, and Edward LiPuma. 1986. "The Troubled Seas of Spanish Fishermen: Marine Policy and the Economy of Change." *American Ethnologist* 13(4): 681–99.

De Miguel, Amando. 1974. "Estructura social e inmigración en el País Vasconavarro." *Papers: Revista de sociología* 3: 249–73.

Morán, Gregorio. 1988. *Testamento Vasco: Un ensayo de interpretación*. Madrid: Espasa Calpe.

Morris, Aldon. 1984. *The Origins of the Civil Rights Movement: Black Communities Organizing for Change*. New York: Free Press.

Morris, Aldon, and Cedric Herring. 1981. "Theory and Research in Social Movements: A Critical Review." In *Annual Review of Political Science*, vol. 2, ed. Samuel L. Long. New York: Plenum Press.

Muñoz Castro, Yolanda. 1987. "La Crisis del PNV: Historia de una Escisión." *Cuadernos de Alzate* 6(April–September): 31–46.

Newton, Kenneth. 1976. *Second City Politics: Democratic Processes and Decision-Making in Birmingham*. Oxford: Oxford University Press.

Olza Zubiri, Miguel. 1979. *Psicosociología de una población rural vasca.* Pamplona: Díputación Foral de Navarra.

Omeñaca, Jesús. 1977. *Movimiento ciudadano: crisis.* Bilbao: Gráficas Ellacuría.

Onaindía, Mario. 1979. *La lucha de clases en Euskadi (1939–1980).* Donostia: Hordago.

Ortega, Alberto. 1980. "Informe sobre Euskadi." *Mientras Tanto* 3: 51–76.

Ossa Echaburu, Rafael. 1982. *Euzkadi/80.* Madrid: Espasa Calpe.

Paramio, Ludolfo. 1986. "La crisis del nacionalismo y el futuro de la nación." *Cuadernos de Alzate* 4: 39–43.

Pastor, Robert. 1977. *Euskadi ante el futuro.* Bilbao: L. Haranburu.

Pastor, Robert. 1980. *Autonomía, año cero.* Bilbao: Editorial Iparraguirre.

Payne, Stanley G. 1975. *Basque Nationalism.* Reno: University of Nevada Press.

Payne, Stanley G. 1976. "Regional Nationalism: The Basques and the Catalans." In *Spain in the 1970s: Economics, Social Structure, and Foreign Policy,* ed. William Salisbury and James D. Theberge. New York: Praeger.

Payne, Stanley G. 1979. "Terrorism and Democratic Stability in Spain." *Current History* 77(November): 167–71, 182–83.

Payne, Stanley G. 1980. "Recent Research on Basque Nationalism: Political, Cultural, and Socioeconomic Dimensions." Mimeographed paper.

Perea, Iosu, Fernando Etxebarría, and Iosu Aldama. 1980. *¿Por Qué Ocupamos el Parlamento Vasco?* Madrid: Editorial Revolución.

Pérez Calvo, Alberto. 1977. *Los partidos políticos en el País Vasco.* San Sebastián: L. Haranburu.

Pérez-Agote, Alfonso. 1979. "Racionalidad urbana y relaciones sociales. El Gran Bilbao, 1945–75." *Saioak* 3: 3–57.

Pinard, Maurice. 1968. "Mass Society and Political Movements: A New Formulation." *American Journal of Sociology* 73(6): 682–90.

Pinard, Maurice. 1971. *The Rise of a Third Party: A Study in Crisis Politics.* Englewood Cliffs: Prentice-Hall.

Pitkin, Hanna Fenichel. 1984. *Fortune Is a Woman: Gender and Politics in the Thought of Niccoló Machiavelli.* Berkeley: University of California Press.

Plamenatz, John. 1958. "Electoral Studies and Democratic Theory: A British View." *Political Studies* 6(1): 1–9.

Polanyi, Karl. 1957. *The Great Transformation: The Political and Economic Origins of Our Time.* Boston: Beacon Press.

Polsby, Nelson W. 1980. *Community Power and Political Theory: A Further Look at Problems of Evidence and Inference,* second, enlarged edition. New Haven: Yale University Press.

Preston, Paul. 1978. *The Coming of the Spanish Civil War: Reform, Reaction and Revolution in the Second Republic, 1931–1936.* New York: Harper & Row.

Purroy, Mirentxu. 1978. "Navarra ya no es 'foral'." In *Navarra desde Navarra,* ed. J. Bueno Asin et al. Bilbao: Editorial Vizcaina.

Ramírez Goicoechea, Eugenia. 1984. "Cuadrillas en el País Vasco: Identidad Local y Revitalización Etnica." *Revista Española de Investigaciones Sociológicas* 25(January–March): 213–20.

Rogin, Michael Paul. 1967. *The Intellectuals and McCarthy: The Radical Specter.* Cambridge: MIT Press.

Rule, James B. 1988. *Theories of Civil Violence.* Berkeley: University of California Press.

Ruiz Olabuenaga, José Ignacio, and Víctor Urrutia. 1978. "Elecciones generales en Navarra." In *Navarra desde Navarra*, ed. J. Bueno Asin et al. Bilbao: Editorial Vizcaina.

San Sebastián, Koldo. 1984. "El Renacer del Movimiento Obrero Vasco y la Crisis de las Organizaciones Historicas." *Muga* 30(March): 24–41.

Sánchez Carrión, José María. 1977. "Lengua y Pueblo." *Punto y Hora* March 10–16, 17–23, 24–30.

Sasgardoy Bengoechea, J. A., and David León Blanco. 1982. *El poder sindical en España.* Barcelona: Editorial Planeta.

Saterain, José Ignacio. 1979. "Problemática específica de la región marítima vasca." *Información Comercial Española* 546(February): 50–61.

Satrústegui, José María. 1978. "La Hora de Navarra." In *Navarra desde Navarra*, ed. J. Bueno Asin et al. San Sebastián: Ediciones Vascas.

Schattschneider, E. E. 1960. *The Semi-Sovereign People: A Realist's View of Democracy in America.* Hinsdale: Dryden Press.

Scott, James C. 1976. *The Moral Economy of the Peasant: Rebellion and Subsistence in Southeast Asia.* New Haven: Yale University Press.

Scott, James C. 1985. *Weapons of the Weak: Everyday Forms of Peasant Resistance.* New Haven: Yale University Press.

Scott, James C. 1987. "Resistance without Protest and without Organization: Peasant Opposition to the Islamic *Zakat* and the Christian Tithe." *Comparative Studies in Society and History* 29(3): 417–52.

Shedd, Margaret. 1974. *A Silence in Bilbao.* Garden City: Doubleday & Company.

Smith, Gordon. 1984. *Politics in Western Europe: A Comparative Analysis.* New York: Holmes & Meier.

Soboul, Albert. 1972. *The Sans Culottes: The Popular Movement and Revolutionary Government, 1793–1794.* Garden City: Anchor Books.

Sullivan, John. 1988. *ETA and Basque Nationalism: The Fight for Euskadi, 1890–1986.* London: Routledge.

Talberna, Daniel. 1984. "Alternative Organizations: The Cooperative Society Movement. The Basque Experience." *Journal of Basque Studies in America* 5: 65–77.

TALDE. 1979. *Euskadi, ante las elecciones municipales.* San Sebastián: Ediciones Vascas.

Tarrow, Sidney. 1989. *Struggle, Politics, and Reform: Collective Action, Social*

Movements, and Cycles of Protest. Ithaca: Center for International Studies, Cornell University.

Thomas, Hank, and Chris Logan. 1982. *Mondragon: An Economic Analysis.* London: Allen & Unwin.

Thompson, E. P. 1963. *The Making of the English Working Class.* New York: Vintage Books.

Tilly, Charles. 1978. *From Mobilization to Revolution.* Reading: Addison-Wesley.

Tovar, Antonio. 1957. *The Basque Language.* Philadelphia: University of Pennsylvania Press.

Tovar, Antonio. 1959. *El Euskera y sus Parientes.* Madrid: Ediciones Minotauro.

Tusell Gómez, Javier. 1974. *Historia de la Democracia Cristiana en España, Tomo II: Los nacionalismos Vasco y Catalan. Los solitarios.* Madrid: Cuadernos para el Diálogo.

Ulam, Adam B. 1960. *The Unfinished Revolution.* New York: Random House.

Unzueta, José Luis. 1980. "La Va Asamblea de ETA." *Saioak* 4(4): 3–52.

Unzueta, Patxo. 1988. *Los Nietos de la IRA: Nacionalismo y violencia en el País Vasco.* Madrid: El País.

Urrutia, Víctor. 1979. "Estructura socio-económica del Bilbao. In *Comun 2: Bilbao.* Bilbao: Instituto de Arte y Humanidades de la Fundación Faustino Orbegozon.

Urrutia Abaigar, Víctor. 1985. *El Movimiento Vecinal en el Area Metropolitana de Bilbao.* Bilbao: Instituto Vasco de Administración Publica.

Urrutia, V. 1989. "Socialización Política e Iglesia Vasca." In *Sociología del Nacionalismo,* ed. Alfonso Pérez-Agote. Vitoria: Universidad del País Vasco.

Villán, Javier, and Félix Población. 1980. *Culturas en lucha, Euskadi.* Madrid: Editorial Swan.

Vingileos, Demetrio G. 1966. "Desarrollo de la industria de Guipúzcoa y ordenación de su territorio." *Información Comercial Española,* special issue, "La metalurgia del Norte," 390(February): 105–13.

Walker, Jack L. 1966. "A Critique of the Elitist Theory of Democracy." *American Political Science Review* 60(2): 285–95.

Whyte, William Foote, and Kathleen King Whyte. 1988. *Making Mondragón: The Growth and Dynamics of the Worker Cooperative Complex.* Ithaca: Industrial and Labor Relations Press, Cornell University.

Winston, Colin M. 1982. "The Proletarian Carlist Road to Fascism: Sindicalismo Libre." *Journal of Contemporary History* 17(4): 557–85.

Wirth, Louis. 1938. "Urbanism as a Way of Life." *American Journal of Sociology* 44(1): 1–24.

Wolfinger, Raymond. 1974. *The Politics of Progress.* Englewood Cliffs: Prentice-Hall.

Wynn, Martin. 1984. "Spain." In *Housing in Europe*, ed. Martin Wynn. New York: St. Martin's Press.

Zallo, Ramón. 1980. "La crisis del PNV y los intereses de clase." *Egin*, January 19: 8.

Zeitlin, Maurice. 1984. *The Civil Wars in Chile (or the bourgeois revolutions that never were)*. Princeton: Princeton University Press.

Zirakzadeh, Cyrus Ernesto. 1985. "The Political Thought of Basque Businessmen, 1976–1980." In *Basque Politics: A Case Study in Ethnic Nationalism*, ed. William A. Douglass. Millwood: Associated Faculty Press.

Zulaika, Joseba. 1981. *Terranova: The Ethos and Luck of Deep-Sea Fishermen*. Philadelphia: Institute for the Study of Human Issues.

Zulaika, Joseba. 1988. *Basque Violence: Metaphor and Sacrament*. Reno: University of Nevada Press.